GOING ORIENTAL

Thank you Japan. *Arrigatoh Gozaimas Nippon.*

MAINSTREAM *SPORT*

GOING ORIENTAL

FOOTBALL AFTER WORLD CUP 2002

EDITED BY MARK PERRYMAN

MAINSTREAM
PUBLISHING

EDINBURGH AND LONDON

First published in Great Britain in 2002 by
MAINSTREAM PUBLISHING COMPANY (EDINBURGH) LTD
7 Albany Street
Edinburgh EH1 3UG

ISBN 1 84018 677 1

A catalogue record for this book is available from the British Library

Typeset in Helvetica and Garamond
Printed and bound in Great Britain by
Cox & Wyman Ltd

Contents

Acknowledgements

Going Oriental is an effort to explore how World Cup 2002 affected both the global game and, in an unashamed parochial vein, how it feels to be English. The contributors have not been chosen because they all agree with each other. But they are all writing because they believe football matters, and have something to say about its significance. As editor I am very grateful for their ready response when asked to cancel their holiday plans for July, put other projects on hold, answer numerous queries from me and turn around their chapters in double quick time.

The idea of the book came to me on the Shinkansen express train from Niigata to Tokyo after England had just stuffed the Danes and only Brazil stood between us and World Cup glory. The glory we will now have to wait for until 2006, the hope remains. Bill Campbell of Mainstream Publishing took only a few days to be convinced that *Going Oriental* was a half-sensible proposition, though waking me up in the middle of the Kyoto night to tell me so suggests he still hasn't grasped the concept of international time differences.

I was helped in putting the book together by being able to draw on the various ideas that I had raised in the course of covering World Cup 2002 as a fan correspondent. Adam Gilchrist of British Forces Broadcasting Service, Pete Stevens of BBC Radio London Live, Brian Lindsay of BBC Radio Scotland, Barry Didcock of the *Sunday Herald* newspaper in Scotland, Mat Snow of *Four Four Two*, various producers on the radio stations Talksport and Teamtalk and the website www.football365.com were all rash enough to call me at all hours for my unscrambled thoughts from Japan. Standing in a train corridor, hurtling back to Tokyo, England just knocked out of the World Cup, mobile to ear, putting Peter Hitchens right about how we can be proud to be English without the prejudice on a BBC Radio Scotland phone-in is a particularly fond media-moment memory.

Many of my opinions that helped me conceive of this collection had been tried out via various outlets in the build-up to World Cup 2002, I am grateful to *When Saturday Comes* in particular for publishing a number of pieces I wrote concerning England fan issues. On St George's Day 2002 the think-tank, The Institute for Public Policy Research, published the report I wrote for them *Ingerland Expects: Football,*

National Identity and World Cup 2002. Writing the report helped me immensely in thinking about practical efforts towards a positive England, the support of Matthew Taylor, Rachel O'Brien and Clare Rickenson of the IPPR for this project was excellent throughout. I am also grateful to my third-year Sport, Leisure and Social Issues class at the University of Brighton for questioning, sometimes unwittingly, some of my ideas at the more barmy end of the intellectual spectrum. Colleagues in the Chelsea School at the University, particularly Alan Tomlinson, John Sugden, Ben Carrington and Ian Macdonald, were a great help in the departmental research seminar in refocusing my thinking where my fan enthusiasm had a habit of running away with my thinking self. Stephen Parrott and his unique 'Football Culture and Society' extra-mural course at Birkbeck College, London, provided one of the best evening's unpicking of my arguments.

Going Oriental does not stand alone. As a writer I am immensely aided by my involvement in a variety of fan initiatives. Since November 2001 the independent London England Fans group, of which I am an active member, has been holding monthly travel forums. Meeting together as England supporters, discussing the issues that affect us, preparing for our visit to Japan, and after July other places too, this has been a pioneering venture that shows off all the best that England can become. The support of the Japan National Tourist Organisation, especially Akemi Fujimoto and Jackie Hammond, Stuart Jack of the British Embassy in Japan, Christopher Kimber and Miranda Hudson of the Foreign Office, Doug Hopkins, Crowd Control Adviser to the Football Association, David Bohannan, head of the Home Office Football Section, Kevin Miles of the Football Supporters Federation, David Luxton of Sportspages bookshop, Barry McElwaine of the *Daily Yomiuri*, Gordon Farquhar of Radio 5 Live, Brian Oliver of the *Observer*, Tom Hall of Lonely Planet, Yuka Miura and Junko Fuse of the Institute of International Education in London, and the Melton Mowbray on Holborn, have all been vital to our success. But most of all it has been down to the committed England fans who turned out in such large numbers every month and made these evenings both effective and incredibly enjoyable, even when they were were making my life a misery while I tried to chair the discussions with a modicum of order.

The 'Raise the Flag' initiative at England home games, and occasionally away too, is one of the best practical examples of a positive England fan patriotism. Well done to, amongst others, Ken Jackson, Nicola Jackson, Sarah Everatt, Paul Jonson, Dave Chance, Imogen Tranchell, Lennie Thomas, Stephen Christopher, Phil Thorne, Jacquie Rich, Ursula Wielgosz, Matt Ball, Bill Riding, Andrew Riding, Alan Priestley, Steve Enticknap, Steve Levesen, Tim Winn, Matt Winn, Charlotte Winn, Mike Hayward, Debbie Hayward, Alan Lee, Ian

Potter, Alan Thompson, Anne Thompson, Nic Banner, Tim Ankers, Martin Groundsell, Mark Woodcraft, Lisa Adam-Smith, Steve Powell and plenty more who turn up at the crack of dawn to attach thousands of cards to seats. The snatched conversations as we turn cards and elastic bands into a St George Cross held up by supporters during the National Anthem has affected my thinking immensely, which probably explains why I'm not so fast on the layout as everybody else.

The FA gets a lot of stick for what it gets up to, some of it deserved, some of it not. Fans and governing bodies will always have their differences but a constructive dialogue between England supporters and the FA remains of vital importance for all. Thanks to Peta Dee, Susan Warrilow, Mark Sudbury, Nick Barron, Jamie Craig, James Worrall, Ian Murphy and Jonathan Arana of the FA for listening, enduring my bother and supporting fan-led initiatives.

Underpinning all my active involvement as an England fan is my business partnership with co-founder of *Philosophy Football*, Hugh Tisdale. Design guru, the artistic genius behind more than a hundred T-shirts from the self-styled 'sporting outfitters of intellectual distinction', Hugh also responds with a rare enthusiasm to crazy proposals ranging from fan goodwill cards to take to Japan, putting pieces of paper on seats to form a huge St George Cross and a cover design for a World Cup book. I owe Hugh a lot, so much I'm almost tempted to wish his Aston Villa luck in finishing higher than my Tottenham but repaying a debt can only go so far.

Going Oriental would have been impossible without an incredible four weeks spent in Japan. A warning to *Philosophy Football* customers in foreign climes, should England ever play a match in your country you might get a letter asking if you'd like me to come and stay, share some chat about the game and pay rent in T-shirts. Gary Garner, Megumi Araki, Noburo Masuda, Ray Masuda, Akiumi Masuda, Takaumi Masuda, Hiroyuki Morita, Sachiye Morita, Angus Macindoe, Trevor Ballance and Kinuko Fujii provided not only quite extraordinary hospitality which made this trip so unforgettable but also a friendship which will last too, many thanks. And all we thought we had in common was a liking for T-shirts featuring quotes from assorted philosophers.

On the home front my sister Penelope provided regular reports on the current state of World Cup fever. It was her telephone call after the Argentina match when she breathlessly told me that there was dancing in the streets of Haywards Heath that convinced me that a World Cup book was something worth putting together.

Without my partner Anne England trips would lose a considerable chunk of their enjoyment. Her excitement at not only more temples, markets and scenery than she knew what to do with, more shops than she'd ever seen in her life and the rather good football we were treated to put a smile on my face that only Anne, and the occasional defeat of Germany and Argentina, can. It probably helped also that I left the tent at home.

Finally Japan. This book is dedicated to you. You not only allowed us to enjoy being fans but let us be proud of being English too. We owe you one, big time. Of course, some silverware would have been nice to complete the trip but what's four more years of hurt when we've had to put up with thirty-six already.

Mark Perryman,
August 2002.

Notes on Contributors

ANDREW BLAKE is Professor of Cultural Studies at King Alfred's College, Winchester. He has recently written two books on the twin giants of modern fiction, *The Irresistible Rise of Harry Potter* and *JRR Tolkien: A Beginner's Guide.*

DAVID CONN is the author of *The Football Business: Fair Game in the '90s?* A frequent commentator on football's boom and bust at the expense of the supporters, he writes a Saturday column for the *Independent* newspaper.

PHILIP CORNWALL stayed in bed for World Cup 2002 to file his reports before breakfast for the website *www.football365.com.* A regular contributor to the football magazine *When Saturday Comes,* he is currently a freelance sportswriter available for hire.

PETE DAVIES wrote *All Played Out: The Full Story of Italia 90.* His full unexpurgated version of life with the England squad probably ensured the FA would allow no future writer the kind of access Pete was afforded. His latest book, *American Road: The Story of an Epic Transcontinental Journey at the Dawn of the Motor Age,* was published in the USA in 2002.

MARTIN JACQUES has travelled, lived and worked in Far East Asia. A former deputy editor of the *Independent* newspaper in the 1980s he was editor of the highly influential political magazine *Marxism Today.* Martin wrote and presented a series for BBC 2, 'The End of the Western World', on the importance to the West of understanding the 'Asian Model' of social, cultural and economic development.

SIMON KUPER covered World Cup 2002 for the *Observer* newspaper and now writes a Monday football column for *The Times.* His book *Football Against the Enemy* is a classic account of the sport's place in the world. A collection of Simon's football writing was published in a Japanese-only edition *World Cup Melancholy* to coincide with the tournament. His new book, *Ajax, The Dutch, The War: Football in Europe during the Second World War,* will be published by Orion in January 2003.

HIROYUKI MORITA is assistant managing editor of *Newsweek Japan*. He was responsible for the magazine's World Cup 2002 coverage. A translator of several football books from English into Japanese, he lives in Saitama, home of his team, the Urawa Reds.

MARK PERRYMAN is the editor of two previous collections, *The Ingerland Factor: Home Truths from Football* and *Hooligan Wars: Causes and Effects of Football Violence* and The Institute for Public Policy Research report *Ingerland Expects: Football, National Identity and World Cup 2002*. Mark helps convene the independent London England Fans group and is one of the organisers of the 'Raise the Flag' initiative at England games. Co-founder of *Philosophy Football*, self-styled 'sporting outfitters of intellectual distinction', he is also a part-time Research Fellow in sport and leisure cultures at The Chelsea School, University of Brighton.

EMMA POULTON is Lecturer in the Sociology of Sport in the Department of Health and Sport at the University of Durham. Emma contributed chapters on press, radio and TV coverage of players and supporters to both *The Ingerland Factor* and *Hooligan Wars*.

WENDY WHEELER is Reader in English Literature in the School of Languages and Arts at London Metropolitan University and the author of *A New Modernity? Change in Science, Literature and Politics*.

JIM WHITE covered World Cup 2002 for the *Guardian* newspaper. Journalist, author and broadcaster, Jim has written a number of books on Manchester United including *Are You Watching Liverpool? Manchester United and the 93/94 Double* and *Always in the Running: The Manchester United Dream Team*. The new edition of his *The Rough Guide to Manchester United*, co-authored with Andy Mitten, was published at the start of the 2002–03 season.

JOHN WILLIAMS is the Director of the Sir Norman Chester Centre for Football Research, Leicester University. John writes regularly for the football magazine *When Saturday Comes*. His latest book is *Into the Red: Liverpool FC and the Changing Face of English Football*.

DAVID WINNER is the author of *Brilliant Orange: The Neurotic Genius of Dutch Football* and co-translated into English *Ajax, Barcelona, Cruyff: The ABC of an Obstinate Maestro*. A freelance journalist who lives in Amsterdam and London, David is currently writing a history of football in England to be published by Bloomsbury in 2004.

KWON YONG-SEOK edits the 'Viewpoint Korea' column in *Newsweek Japan.* He is currently completing a PhD on Korea–Japan relations at the National Hitotsubashi University, Tokyo. Born in Seoul, he has lived in Japan for the past sixteen years. During the World Cup he returned to Korea to follow the Red Devils through to the semi-final.

HOME, AWAY AND GLAD ALL OVER: A SOFTER ST GEORGE AND NICE NIPPON

Going Oriental

Mark Perryman

'This is the first time I've felt proud to be English'
– Fatboy Slim, World Cup 2002

DJ and recording artist Fatboy Slim neatly sums up what, for many, Japan 2002 meant to them. Previously they might have shrugged awkwardly when the football nation draped itself in the Cross of St George and came over all pumped up and ready to take on the world, or more particularly Germany or Argentina. But this time was different.

There are not many experiences more miserable when following your team than to ship out to a foreign land and promptly be ashamed of the shirt you're wearing. But that was the mood of plenty of England fans at France '98. OK, the trouble only involved a fraction of those who'd made it to England versus Tunisia. And there were plenty of local Arab youths spoiling for a fight. But that hardly mattered as pictures and reports were filed all around the globe of England fans once again spoiling the World Cup party with their violent idea of fun. Pride in wearing the shirt, flying the flag, supporting the team is hard, very hard, in those circumstances. Of course most will be prepared to weather the storm of criticism, especially when armed with the inner belief that they've nothing but contempt for those who stir up trouble, and the first-hand experience that while England get the blame, there are often two sides to any story. But the weight of negative expectation is so heavy it leaves even these hardy souls pressed down with the need to explain in any way they can, 'but it wasn't us guv'.

Charleroi Euro 2000 produced the same, unwanted result. Experienced BBC Radio 5 sports news reporter Gordon Farquhar describes the trouble in the town's main square before England versus Germany as 'three out of ten' on his scoreboard for England doing their worst. But reading the papers, listening to the radio or watching the TV, it was more like the end of the world as we know it had just been visited upon the Belgians. England's awful reputation at this point seemed almost irreversible.

The fans, when asked, mostly put the self-evident argument that the majority have nothing to do with the trouble, and in fact suffer the worst from the consequences of it. Shut-up shops, closed bars and restaurants, hotels with no vacancies all of a sudden, locals spoiling for a fight with visitors they expect to be spoiling for the same, and streets full of gung-ho riot police geared up for confrontation doesn't make for England coming to town being a particularly pleasant place to be. But without any obvious way of distinguishing themselves from the fearsome few, and a national uniform of St George that has for far too long been associated almost exclusively with the racist far right, how can anyone know the difference between the good guys and the bad 'uns? With no other voice, no alternative identity and little contestation over the ownership of what it means to be an England fan, the hooligan minority have found it easy, very easy, to effectively define supporting England in their own image and outcomes. So who can blame Fatboy Slim and millions more for their reservations?

This is, of course, what Japan changed. But will we ever see the like of this again, will St George be hauled down from the car aerials in two or three years time as another episode of violence in the cause of England turns the nation off once more? That's not to say, of course, that whatever the result off the pitch many will just grit their teeth and concentrate their emotions on the players and score regardless. But it's that broader feel-good, or feel-bad, factor of what it means to be English that in some significant way frames that emotional experience. This is what helped World Cup 2002 become so very different. Even with that hapless second-half performance against Brazil, the feel-good factor vastly outscored any feel-bad.

In accounting for why Japan went so well for the fans it's also important to understand that right up to the last moment, this tournament wasn't expected to get away without at least the odd outbreak of hooliganism. After all, Japan had its part in one of those two World Wars of 'two World Wars and one World Cup' infamy. And the folklore surrounding that memory is as strong, if not stronger than *The Great Escape*. Inscrutable officers, cruel guards and a handy tune to whistle too – *Colonel Bogey*. Throw in a rather obvious race dimension – this was the first World Cup in Asia after all – and the portents for a tournament without an edge of nastiness didn't seem very positive. If not mentioning the war was one issue, another was the culture clash when West meets East. Reports would filter back that just for starters, fans taking their shirts off in public would be a national event. How would the two cultures cope after a few drinks?

Kevin Miles organises the Football Supporters Association (FSA) World Cup 'Fan Embassies'. These are fan-run mobile information and help points which turn up wherever England are playing. He went to Japan on several fact-finding trips well in advance of the tournament and in Osaka was part of a question-and-answer session with the host city's organising committee. 'We understand there are 27,000 hooligans in England,' asked one questioner. Before Kevin could answer, another chipped in, 'We also understand the British government have banned 1,000; does this mean the other 26,000 hooligans will be coming?' From the FSA, Home Office, Foreign Office, FA and other concerned bodies, the same story leaked out. The only images the Japanese had of England fans were those from Charleroi and Marseilles – they were expecting us to cause serious trouble. Kevin, self-mocking chap that he is, tried to offset the fears of his Osaka audience. 'I'm big, fat and ugly with very short hair. Most of us look like this. It doesn't mean we're all hooligans.'

These kinds of ventures, and there were many more like this, did begin to offset some of the wilder Japanese fears – helped significantly by the fact that England's last away trip before the finals, to play Holland in Amsterdam, was virtually trouble free. Less than ten arrests out of the 10,000 who travelled to what most regarded as a public order high-risk game. The many Japanese observers, media and police officials at the game were suitably impressed. When the Foreign Office took a party of Japanese journalists to Anfield for England's home game with Paraguay in mid-April, their collective response afterwards was, 'What hooliganism?' The friendly face of England's home fans and the decreasing severity of trouble on away trips was beginning to have a significant impact on how we would be received in Japan come June.

While most writers in our own press were well informed enough not to expect widespread English mayhem in Japan, nevertheless there was a fairly constant stream of news stories close to kick-off that reported on key hooligan-organisers finding fair ways or foul to make it out to the tournament. Coupled with tales of the Japanese police preparing for our arrival with everything from Spiderman-style net guns, jet-propulsion water cannons and intensive martial arts practice on all victims dressed in the flag of St George and the picture, while not super-bleak, didn't look as cheery as it might.

What made it go all right on the night? Most importantly, the Japanese were clearly fascinated rather than intimidated by the English reputation. A fascination that swiftly turned to near-adulation when Beckham was thrown into the equation. In his book *Voltaire's Coconuts*, the writer Ian Buruma wittily documents a foreign feature barely understood in English culture – that others rather like us: 'The narrow defensiveness of much anti-European rhetoric often obscures the more practical reasons why many Europeans have admired Britain in the past.' Of course Britain includes Scotland, Wales and Northern Ireland, but England is as well placed in the Euro-popularity stakes as our Celtic fringe neighbours. Interestingly, Buruma also points out that the vestiges of Englishness that seek to stand out from the continental rest, which can generate both affection from others and introspection from ourselves, has a certain coincidence with Japan where, according to Buruma, 'there, too, the matter of national uniqueness, of an essential, semi-mystical, affable "Japaneseness", to be protected from socialists and American cultural imperialism, was discussed, dissected and fretted over'. The Japanese have a hankering after authenticity, the real thing, and when it comes to football you don't get much more real than England. English claims on 'football's home' are overblown, but for fan passion and commitment, few do it better. A ready-made fan culture to adopt and adapt, the best of England, the Kop, the Stretford End, Gallowgate, North Bank and the rest of today and all our yesterdays, this is what the Japanese think of when they imagine what being a fan should be. Strip away the shoddy sponsors' logos, the commodification of our fandom and traditions, and underneath you'll find the raw energy of supporting our team. It helped that we had Beckham, too. After George Best, there have been many pretenders to the footballer-as-pop-star mantle, but Becks knocks the socks, shin pads, shorts and shirt off all rivals. Japanese fan culture was already quite feminised, partly due to its relative newness, and had its own pin-up star in the shape of one Hideotoshi Nakata, like Becks, a number seven. But Beckham was a star of a different scale; looks, clothes, the Spice Girl wife, not to mention that he plays for the biggest club in the world, all help. The fact that he has no hang-ups about pushing the implications of each factor that constructs his superstar persona to the absolute limit and only occasionally falling into the trap of becoming a self-parody is what makes him so special and attractive. The travelling English coupled with the seductive charm of Beckham proved to be a winning Far East combination of some considerable magnitude.

The latter we probably weren't so surprised about. After all, the previous summer United had played a Far Eastern tour to huge and screaming crowds. Beckham, we all knew, was a global figure but the fans' appeal remained a considerable puzzle.

Kevin Miles scoffs at the idea that the fans' success was down to what he felt others presented as 'posh fans' or 'a better class of fan' taking the place of those who'd followed England to previous tournaments. And the statistics back Kevin up; the method of allocation of World Cup tickets through the FA meant you qualified on a loyalty basis. For each away game a fan goes to a 'cap' is earned. Seventy per cent of tickets are distributed to those with the most 'caps', which meant a big proportion going to those who'd travelled to every 2002 World Cup qualifier plus the odd friendly. The remaining 30 per cent overwhelmingly went to those who'd been to at least one away game previously, some to those who'd been to none. A big chunk of these peaceful fans with lots of 'caps' would certainly have been to Euro 2000 and France '98, but they scarcely featured in any of the coverage, which concentrated almost exclusively on the trouble.

One of the most compelling commonsense arguments in shifting

England fan culture away from the violent minority is to move into the supporter mainstream a sense of football as tourism. For the most conservative of fans, this is a sell-out. The trip is all about one item only – lasting ninety minutes – but for most, a spell on the beach, tasting the local tipple, sampling something different on your plate and taking in the odd sight can all be part of the appeal of England away, and the idea that this somehow dilutes commitment to England's cause – well, it's plain daft. But a trip to Belgium, Holland or France is hardly new for fans who will have been there many times before on shopping expeditions, stag nights, family holidays and weekend breaks. Japan wasn't like this. Few fans had ever been there before, and not many expected to make the trip more than once in their lifetime. Our popular culture has been sufficiently Japanised thanks to karaoke, origami, sushi, Sony, the martial arts and so on to give us an inkling of what to expect, but the temptation to explore and engage remained overwhelming. In that frame of mind it takes a quite extraordinary level of obstinacy to take it out on the local population when you expect to spend the next few days, or weeks, enjoying the scenery.

From the moment the draw decided England would play all their games in Japan there was a real, and enduring, groundswell of fan enthusiasm about visiting Japan accompanied by a huge appetite for every conceivable piece of tourist information. The FA published a comprehensive guidebook, the Foreign Office produced foreign visitor briefings and the Japan National Tourist Organisation went out of its way to dispel the idea that Japan was the most expensive land on earth. This last factor in effect became a new way to exoticise the East. Frequently, fans would be shocked with ludicrous claims in the press that taxi rides, a pint of beer, a meal for two or a night in a hotel would set them back anything up to ten times what they'd be paying for the same back home. But finding bargain flights, booking hotels outside of the overpriced Western chains, eating where the locals eat rather than in expensive tourist-market restaurants, all this is part and parcel of making your money go further with England abroad. And it's probably an experience most expenses-paid journalists who write these pieces don't have to bother with.

Is enjoying all that a country has to offer a middle-class thing? This is a dogmatic understanding of class culture that would shame the most fundamentalist of Marxists. Some might only want to travel for the match and its outcome, others might risk the local drink, a few will explore the city where the game is played, and a few more will take in the sights, maybe a trip into the surrounding countryside. Those who venture furthest are unlikely to be easily classified as readers of the *Guardian* or the *Daily Telegraph*, though some undoubtedly will be. Instead, they are just fans looking for an all-round good time when they've travelled halfway round the world to support their team.

Of course a trip to Japan was expensive. But the most committed England fans had been confidently preparing for this trip since four, or more, years ago. It wasn't exactly news to them that after France '98 the next World Cup would be eastward bound. And of course four years on from 2002 the next tournament will be in Europe. The expense would not be matched until 2010 and a possible African host country, at the earliest. In any case, the opening up of access to cut-price flights and hotel accommodation via the Internet meant well-prepared fans were able to get to and stay out in Japan, for the duration of England's three-week campaign for a fraction of the exorbitant price many had feared. But most crucial of all was the issue of sacrifice. For these fans, a World Cup without them being there was simply unquestionable. England has more fans who think like this than most; this time round that was something the football nation could afford to be very proud of.

Most reports totalled up England's travelling support somewhere round the 10,000 mark. Far outnumbering any other away contingent, with the exception of the Irish, less than the 25,000 plus who were in Charleroi for England versus Germany Euro 2000, but a substantial enough number, and more than enough to cause trouble if the ugly side of fancy took them. The reason it didn't happen couldn't be put down simply to lacking a hooligan mass, it was about the combination of a friendly reception and that mood of expectant exploration.

There were other features that helped too. When England beat Germany 5–1 on that never-to-be-forgotten September night in Munich, Sven-Göran Eriksson set a tone in his response that only the most acute observers noticed. If his immediate predecessor, Kevin Keegan, had managed this team to that scoreline we would have had an all-guns blazing, ready to take on the world, the cup's got our name written on it kind of estimation of what the night meant. Whereas if Glenn Hoddle had still been in charge he would surely have put it down to his own tactical masterplan, with a dash of Eileen Drewery's magical powers helping some of the squad along the way to match-winning fitness too, no doubt. Sven has none of the bombast of the former or the arrogance of the latter. The result was good, there was no point in him denying that, but there were still two crucial games left that England needed to get a result from. Sven was most determined not to get carried away, his magnanimity summed up when he remarked that a match, even this one, was put into some sort of perspective when you hear that on the same night the father of the manager of the opposing team, Rudi Voller, died. How ironic; it's taken a Swede to teach us how to properly enjoy our football.

In the football magazine *When Saturday Comes*, fans swapped opinions of just how significant an impact Eriksson's management style would have on supporters. In the debate, Philip Cornwall could be counted amongst the optimists:

> Eriksson is the best chance of lancing the boil that attaches itself to England's support. Just as the increasing number of high-profile black footballers helped the game to rid itself of a good deal of overt colour-based racism, so the quiet Swede is undermining the broader anti-foreign feeling which so blights the national team.

While Tom Hall was less hopeful:

> It is something of a liberal fantasy to suppose that one urbane, sophisticated foreigner can somehow 'civilise the mob'. Meaningful change comes from below, not above, and cannot be seen in isolation from the overall climate in which England games can take place.

Tom was perhaps right to be circumspect. Lasting transformation of fan culture doesn't come out of a media-frenzy fuelled by a 5–1 score line, it comes because supporters themselves lead and affect that process. And we didn't have to wait until Japan for evidence that there was something afoot 'below'. The huge St George Cross made up of thousands of cards held up by fans has, since 1998, become a new tradition at England's home games. This flag is a fans', a people's flag, it only takes shape because the fans want to take part. When England's first friendly after qualifying for the World Cup was announced as against Sweden those behind this 'Raise the Flag' campaign looked for something with which the fans could show their gratitude to Eriksson, the Swede who'd done so much for our England. A blue and yellow extension to St George was the plan that the 'Raise the Flag' designer Hugh Tisdale came up with. A great idea, but as 50 or more fan-volunteers patiently added these cards to the layout of St George on the morning of the match none, including the FA who'd nervously backed the initiative, could know whether any would be held up that afternoon. As the first bars of 'God Save the Queen' began, St George, with its Swedish addition, filled the stands behind the two goals and it was difficult to spot anyone who'd refused to take part. What better symbol of an inclusive fandom than fans voting with their feet, or rather their hands, to merge our flag with a grateful splash of the Swedish other.

In Japan, 'Becksmania' was the order of the day. This was of a quite different style to Italia 90's 'Gazzamania', which was after all primarily a domestic concern. Kim Sengupta in the *Independent* attempted to unpick Becks' particular appeal in Japan for the Japanese:

> What makes Beckham ideal is that he is a safe rebel. He may change his hairstyle, wear a sarong or his wife's underpants but he is also a family man who has not been a regular in the tabloids in stories of drinks, drugs and casual sex.

Outlandish sartorially and tonsorially but never laddish, it is hard to find fault in this latter-day Captain Fantastic. Even when he put to flight his own personal Nemesis, Argentina, there was none of the fists in the air histrionics and Henry V 'once more unto the breach' that we'd become used to. And when the German popular press poked fun at our Becks for his pink nail varnish, what choice did we have but to leap to the defence of a man the surly Germans were calling 'girlish'. Beckham is not alone in carving out a different type of England player. Michael Owen is so wholesome it is unlikely butter even breaks into a sweat in his mouth. Paul Scholes and Emile Heskey are so quiet and unassuming they border on the reclusive while World Cup absentee Steven Gerrard has a worldly look of local boy done good that acts as a powerful barrier to wilder temptations. Rio Ferdinand had the odd rum-do at the start of his career but has learnt to put the alcopops behind him. All this makes for an innocents abroad look to our team and indications from the younger players, with Sven's disciplinary requirements impressed upon them, is that this may continue for the foreseeable future.

Mary Riddell in the *Observer* put Becks' home and away appeal down to the contradictions in his ordinariness:

> The point about Beckham is that the familiar is rare. He seems a blandly pleasant man who works hard, supports charities and avoids (Angus) Deaytonesque trysts with unsuitable women and High Court judges. The inhabitants of Beckingham Palace may be ersatz royals, but they pay their taxes. They might walk a thin line between the safe and the tacky, but no soccer star who promotes androgyny, narcissism and cross-dressing could ever quite be dull. As for the charge that Beckham is stupid, no one accused Kierkegaard of failing to make it as a full-back for West Bromwich Albion. But the real point of Beckham is his status as an idol in an age of rancour.

Rancour? Well, the Tartan Army would probably not count themselves amongst Becks' biggest fans, nor can we imagine too many Argentines being all that keen on him either. And there are plenty whose club loyalties demand they turn on him as soon as the season starts. But Beckham remains the most effective way of bringing the football nation together, home and away, whenever England are what we are caring about rather than how to halt United's forward march. In England he represented the narrative of this World Cup while in the Far East he portrayed a football culture that the Japanese fans so very much wanted to be a part of. 'Becksmania' became 'Anglomania', as England fans found themselves surrounded on all sides by people of another country, and for most of the English, another colour too, wearing their shirt, willing their team to victory, sharing the joy, feeling the disappointment. Not to be moved by this would take a stony-faced insularity that precious few could be bothered to be so miserable to bother with. Instead, for once, we threw our stiff upper-lip inhibitions away and wallowed in being liked. England, the world's second favourite team? Not such an impossible dream after the experience of Japan.

Does any of this matter? Twenty-two blokes, a ball and two upright rectangles to squeeze said ball through; when the whistle's blown, that's about all it amounts to, after all. Four factors why it might mean more than this. Jean Baudrillard, the French postmodern philosopher in an unusually lucid essay *In the Shadow of the Silent Majorities*, explains the first thus:

> Power is only too happy to make football bear a facile responsibility, even to take upon itself the diabolical responsibility for stupefying the masses.

Baudrillard was taking the old Marxist dictum that religion is the opiate of the masses and turning it on its head. When all political parties seem remarkably similar, consensus rules and the moral stature of politicians sinks to an all-time low, turnout for elections plummets. Policies change without apparent reference to the political complexion of those making the decisions, idealism and vision no longer exist, the bodies that determine outcomes are more alien, more faraway and more invisible than ever before. For the English there is no state we can call our own, no parliament, precious few institutions of much significance that belong to us. Is it any wonder then that a football shirt has become, in effect, our national dress? A football match the one time we fly our flag? None of this is to make any great claim for a cause of English nationalism, of republican or any other vintage, but the mobilisation of commitment behind the team representing the nation should not be lightly dismissed as a distracting frippery by those who fail so spectacularly to drag us to put a tick against their name every five years.

A second factor is revealed by the band, Radiohead, who have built their reputation on an angst-ridden unlocking of the modern world of emotions. Their anthem 'Bends' includes the following lines: 'I wish it was the '60s. I wish I could be happy. I wish that something would happen.' It's not so much the regret that we might be living through the end of history, it is more that anything that matters has been done and dusted, spin and spun to our delight or despite before we get the chance to experience it ourselves, make up our minds what we think, rather than have others make up our minds for us. There's the odd moment of fulfilment of course, but too often followed by the painful realisation that once more we've been had. Like the emotional commitment and mobilisation that football provides which not much else comes close to providing, the game also gives us bite-chunked bits of reality that can't be doubted, deconstructed or robbed of their meaningfulness. A goal is a goal, if we're there we witness it, if the camera catches us celebrating we're part of the spectacle. Cheque-book vandalism can't give one country an armoury of forwards to uneven the score. Michael Owen will always be ours, Ronaldo, Totti and Ballack somebody else's. Rio Ferdinand and Sol Campbell won't sell their souls to join another country, they're England through and through, forever and ever, our men. World Cup football, it's as real as it gets. And being there means being as close to history as most of us get.

Naomi Klein, author of the bestseller *No Logo*, adds a third factor why football matters so much. In demolishing the legitimacy of those she derides as 'brand bullies', Klein spotlights what happens when commercial imperatives intrude on what we most treasure:

> Branding is, at its core, a deeply competitive undertaking in which brands are up against not only their immediate rivals but all other brands in the mediascape, including the events and people they are sponsoring. This is perhaps branding's cruellest irony: most manufacturers and retailers begin by hunting out authentic scenes, important causes and cherished public events so that these things will infuse their brands with meaning. Such gestures are frequently motivated by genuine admiration and generosity. Too often, however, the expansive nature of the branding process ends up causing the event to be usurped, creating the quintessential lose-lose situation. Not only do fans begin to feel a sense of alienation from (if not outright resentment toward) once-cherished cultural events, but the sponsors lose what they need most: a feeling of authenticity with which to associate their brands.

World Cup 2002 was as much of a commercial bonanza as any recent tournament. Sponsors' logos were everywhere, product placement and closing down unofficial corporate competitors ruled. A lot of this is accepted as the necessary norm by supporters, but there is also a widespread resentment at the sponsors' receipt of much-prized match tickets, often in huge numbers, at the expense of the fans. This produces little or no obvious organised campaigning but a rumbling discontent nevertheless pervades pretty much anywhere fans gather.

Klein connects resentment of this unfocused type to a popular unease at how the big brands are colonising every conceivable public and private space. The fact that national football team shirts are one of the very few 'no logo' zones in world sport, particularly when compared to sports such as cricket and rugby union for example which might have been expected to put up more of a resistance to creeping sponsor excess, is rarely commented on. A football kit without a logo is stripped down to the bare essentials of the colours of the national flag, or in the case of the Italian blue *Azurri* and a few more, some other source. It represents a certain romantic holding out against the big business bandwagon. One of this World Cup's most abiding memories will be the tens of millions of Korean fans filling the stadiums, squares and streets of their country in their unified colour of red. Across the sea the Blue Heaven of 'Troussier Nippon' did likewise, well, until the second round anyway. This suggests that these 'no logo' romantic redoubts of the people's game have an appeal that is not over yet. Didn't stop Nike and Adidas selling lots of shirts of course, but it was the fans themselves who were very much part of the show too, in their own, positive image and on their own terms.

A fourth factor for football's overbearing significance in so many of our lives can be put down to that much overused buzzword, 'globalisation'. It's a term that is applied to the phenomenal growth in air travel, designer label clothes we wear being designed in the USA, manufactured in the Far East and worn down our local high street, chicken tikka masala being England's national dish, the World Trade Organisation determining how much tax we pay and whether the NHS stays in public hands or is privatised. The geographer Doreen Massey was one of the first to ask what all this meant for our sense of place and who we are. Her answer gives an idea why globalisation is a good way of thinking about why football matters:

> First, if places can be conceptualised in terms of the social interactions they tie together, then it is also the case that these interactions themselves are not motionless things, frozen in time. They are processes. Second, places do not have to have boundaries in the sense of divisions, which frame simple enclosures. Third, places do not have single, 'unique' identities; they are full of internal conflicts.

The World Cup is a festival of internationalism. It is a space where the globe plays as one, and nations are represented to the earth's watching population. The sharpest excesses of nationalism and difference are on show, commonalities shared and expressed in a language all fans will understand. Take the 32 finalist countries' teams represented in the English league; Denmark, France, Uruguay, Slovenia, South Africa, Costa Rica, Turkey, Poland, Portugal, USA, Cameroon, Germany, Ireland, Argentina, Nigeria, Sweden, Croatia, Ecuador, Belgium and Japan. Post-World Cup transfer activity added at least Senegal and China to the list. The tournament is transmitted to TVs all over the world but who can doubt there wasn't a gaggle of Crewe Alexandra supporters sitting somewhere sharing in a little bit of pride seeing their player Efe Sodje, complete with trademark headscarf, take the field for Nigeria at the championships. And how many England fans carrying a torch for Liverpool, Manchester United and Arsenal wouldn't have kept another eye out for how Dudek, Veron and Vieira were getting on. Even Germany has criss-crossed traditional fan antipathies with Ziege of Spurs and Hamman of Liverpool in their starting line-up. Football internationalism isn't of course an easy construct but it isn't a figment of a romantic's imagination either. The World Cup can generate conflict and tension but it's also the opportunity for local global neighbourhoods to take shape, wear their colours and get by. The big multinational sportswear companies, fast food outlets, car manufacturers and broadcasters will, of course, seek to turn all this to their commercial advantage. One world, many markets, it suits them down to the dollar, euro or pound. But they're not having the game all their own way. In their book *Empire*, the theorists Michael Hardt and Antonio Negri explain the flipside, *our* side, of globalisation:

> Globalisation, of course, is not one thing, and the multiple processes that we recognise as globalisation are not unified or univocal. Our political task, we will argue, is not simply to resist these processes but to reorganise them and redirect them towards new ends. The creative forces of the multitude that sustain Empires are also capable of autonomously constructing a counter-Empire, an alternative political organisation of global flows and exchanges.

Globalisation therefore needs to be understood as disrupting our fixed, static sense of place and affording both barriers to, and means of overcoming, a meaningful internationalism. The World Cup is second to none as a way of experiencing this. We follow our national team, in person or via TV and radio, to the other side of the world. Our club side has a handful of players turning out for other countries too. We fly the flag, a neighbour flies another's. We wear the shoes of a US sportswear label, manufactured in the same faraway part of the planet as the World

Cup is being played, advertised by one of England's finest. And so on. The World Cup is both a commercial platform for the multinational corporations and a popular platform for fan multinationalism. Globalisation meets unglobalisation.

All four factors; the decline in a public life of purpose, history passing us by, no space free of the blessed logo and its corporate hangers-on and globalisation turning anywhere into everywhere contribute to why football does matter. But the single big picture backdrop that dominated how England consumed this World Cup was Englishness.

The Conservative writer, *Mail on Sunday* columnist Peter Hitchens, normally takes righteous pride in representing the popular mood against the elite, liberal establishment. But for him, football is not a suitable vehicle for representing England:

> I hope the English football team is rapidly knocked out of the World Cup. I really do. And please don't call this group of people 'England'. They are not England and do not represent this country, at least I sincerely hope they don't.

Of course for Fatboy Slim and the many millions who shared his first-time pride in being English, it was precisely who was representing England, on and off the pitch, that swelled their emotions almost to bursting point.

But just like Hitchens, although for very different reasons, Paul McGarr, writing in the far left *Socialist Worker*, doesn't seem to think supporting England is much of an idea:

> Our rulers may cheer the national flag, and want us to do the same, but they know that class comes before nation. That is why socialists should oppose all nationalism, and follow no flag.

This argument treats all fans as idiots at best, bigots at worst. Just because we support England, it doesn't mean we remove all critical faculties the instant the whistle is blown and Michael Owen kicks off. It doesn't mean fans are left wing, right wing or anywhere thereabouts. But to deny football is a space where any ideas – except a mindless submission to my nation (right or wrong) are offered and contested – shows a singularly one-dimensional understanding of how society works.

What made this World Cup so very different was the breadth of support, and that this support was displayed overwhelmingly by the wearing, the flying and the daubing of St George. To presume that as a symbol it carries no values, no luggage, that some of us would prefer it dumped, would be foolhardy in the extreme. Likewise to surrender any attachment to the nation and its symbols just because you don't like some of its history, its representatives or because it might lull us all into a false sense of class security is to give up on shaping different ways of 'being England'.

In Japan ours was a multiracial team – once the French team went out, easily the most multiracial of the European nations left in the competition. Of course the make-up of the squad had a lot to do with all our imperial yesterdays and a lack of opportunities for some of our todays and tomorrows, but as Darcus Howe pointed out in the *New Statesman*, this moment of multicultural opportunity was largely missed: 'No journalist, no football commentator, seemed to warm to England's new community because it brought the nation so far in the World Cup.' Howe is certainly right, and he went on to recount how once that multicultural moment passed, all the power structures that produce institutionalised racism were still in place. But this shouldn't allow cynics to dismiss that moment – rather we should work away at preventing it being allowed to pass unnoticed now, and in the future. Joseph Harker would surely be counted amongst the cynics. Regretting the fact that so many of the black English were supporting England this time round, in unprecedented numbers according to many reports, he wrote:

> I know everyone's talking about how well behaved the fans have been this time, but we know it only takes an England defeat for it all to go wrong. Remember Euro 2000? England lost to Portugal; the fans rioted. They lost to Romania; they rioted again.

The above passage was in the *Guardian* the day before England played Brazil. And yes we lost. And no we didn't riot. And as a point of reference, Joseph, there *was* no riot when we lost to Portugal, or Romania, or Argentina at France '98 either. The trouble, nasty as it certainly was, occurred in Marseilles in '98 when we beat Tunisia, and when we played Germany and beat them too. Not an excuse, of course not, but it ill behoves those who do down any potential for a nice England to get their facts so badly wrong in the rush to generalise and to presume that whenever, wherever England are, trouble will soon follow.

A celebratory patriotism was being discovered by the English, black and white, in June 2002, one which hadn't broken all the links between pride and prejudice, but they weren't as automatic as had almost always been the case previously. St George was going soft. It was a process begun in Japan with the sight of the fans enjoying themselves and their

Japanese hosts adopting our team, our shirt and our flag. A process reflected in a very public celebration of 'doing Englishness' back home. Something few would feel threatened by, most could feel a part of, and many enjoyed. Not all – four weeks is too short for an English revolution – but it was an auspicious start to a movement that has been just around the corner ever since England beat the Scots at Euro '96 under a sea of St George and a year later they, and the Welsh, responded by voting for devolution.

Remaking Englishness is not, of course, just down to football – or, for that matter, vice versa. But it is for those who can be bothered to be alert to it, all around us. In their introduction to the collection of short stories, *England Calling*, the novelists Julia Bell and Jackie Gay pinpoint its significance:

> For some, being English is an embarrassment – a shame – associated with empire, imperialism, stoicism, stiff upper lip; others feel uncomfortable taking pride in being English because of the associations with nationalism, yobbishness and an inability to hold our drink. But this England, this Englishness, is changing. No one can seriously deny that. At the start of a new millennium we live in a country which is restless, uneasy, questioning and devolving. English politics is showing signs of breaking free from Westminster following the devolution of power to Scotland and Wales.

That embarrassment is beginning to subside. But a confusion still reigns. When England played in Japan each kick-off was preceded, as always, by the National Anthem, 'God Save the Queen'. But less than a month later at Manchester's magnificent Commonwealth Games each time an English athlete stood on the podium to receive their gold medal it was 'Land of Hope and Glory' that was played. Same flag, same country, different song. And no one demurred when the Scots, Welsh and Northern Irish stood to different anthems too. These things get noticed, their symbolic meanings matter.

Meanings can change too. Could today's England of hope and glory that is the mother of the free be our protector from poverty and insecurity? Possibly in some imaginations, but most certainly not in others. Though in a poll on the FA website during the Games, a third of fans voted for an alternative National Anthem to 'God Save the Queen' for England's future matches. It was the first time the supporters had been asked, and even amongst a crowd that sings their Anthem with such gutsy enthusiasm there's something stirring too.

Part of the problem is that there are so few songs that celebrate England which aren't attached to a history that, while honourable in part, has its murky side too. Two more modern songs, though, give an inkling as to how we can pay tribute to our past yet live up to the potential of our national future. In the late '70s, punk band The Jam typified a certain sort of English rebellion that lies deep inside the very best of our own post-Presley pop. Their song *English Rose* is full of open-minded national affection: 'No matter where I roam I will return to my English rose, for no bonds can ever tempt me from she.' Haunting, stark, yet sung with pride in what England meant to three mods from Woking.

A musical generation later, and deeply influenced by the varied sounds of black urban England, Mike Skinner – aka The Streets – opened his debut album *Original Pirate Material* with an extraordinary track 'Turn the Page', a tale of the sometimes violent convulsions as England grapples with another country that is its future self. The first line says it all . . . 'I'm forty-fifth generation Roman'. Or as the philosopher Hegel once put it, 'Nothing is constant but change'.

This is all part of the big picture that afforded a chance to be 'English and proud of it' in a new way in June 2002. Football has its part in that process. Take just one feature of the old England that limits the formation of a new England. An all-pervasive centralisation, London rules OK. When Wembley was shut in October 2000 England's internationals, which until then were played almost exclusively in the capital, went all over the place. The North-east, North-west, West Midlands, East Midlands and Yorkshire, the South-east too. Being 'English' at a stroke became a local as well as a national matter defined in terms of London. The fans, the players, the management, the FA and the media all celebrated this one happy outcome of the fiasco that unfolded after Wembley's closure. But this was shelved, hardly earning a single mention, as politicians and the game's top administrators fought over how and where to build Wembley's replacement. The case for rebuilding on the existing site was all about selling corporate hospitality and executive boxes to big-money investors who would never dream of stretching their long expense accounts to places apart from the capital. The pride and the joy of fans from Derby, Leeds, Newcastle, Manchester and Merseyside at an international once or twice a year being in their city or region was forgotten. And those who argued the case for Birmingham were scarcely better; one big stadium at the expense of the rest of the country is a bad deal wherever it's placed. Nobody from government, a key player in both the decision-making and funding process, has once put the case for the national interest being a wide variety of local interests. No significant public voice has proposed that wherever, whenever a national stadium is built, a decent proportion of England's internationals should continue to be played around the country. We realise the potential of a decentralised nation and then threaten to dash the opportunity that everyone has recognised as a huge success. Our England is a country for all, not just the few within easy reach of a run-down industrial estate on the north-west edge of London.

With a successful World Cup campaign, many tens of thousands of new fans will now want to be part of supporting England. There is a deep-seated defensiveness right at the core of fan culture, rejecting these new fans as in any way genuine; how can they be, they haven't been out there supporting England since the year dot. Refusing to admit that at some stage we all began that journey to sporting our country's colours, the suspicion is that no one else can share our commitment, our loyalty or our ability to weather the bad times as well as the good times. And only by seeing the team through those bad times can we earn our fan-legitimacy. Of course twelve years on from the last obvious watershed, the 1990 World Cup of Gazza, Germany in the semis and an evening or two with Gary Lineker, many who today guard England's soul against latecomers to the cause conveniently forget back then that they must have seemed new to those who'd backed England through the awkward '80s. And so this fruitless argument goes on.

The fact is though that the demand for England home match tickets might very soon easily outstrip supply. The inclination may well be to stifle the risk of disappointment by purposefully under-promoting England internationals. Not bother with the tens, hundreds of thousands who could be part of supporting England in the stands, just so long as they buy the shirt, watch the commercials and keep the broadcasters and sponsors happy with rising viewing figures. Nothing could be more conservative and short-sighted. For football to turn its back on the huge audience for England that is here, right now, would prevent the feel-good out of Japan turning into anything more long-lasting, and that would most certainly undermine the sport's commercial imperatives as well as any lingering moral ones from the final vestiges of people's game ethics.

England Under-21 games already attract crowds of 25,000 upwards dwarfing what many major European football nations would hope to attract to their senior internationals. The Under-20s filled Ipswich Town's Portman Road ground in 2002, the Under-19 matches are increasingly popular too, while the Under-17s Nationwide Tournament a fortnight after Japan packed 9,000 into Oxford United's ground for the final between England and Brazil. England's women had a recordbreaking attendance of 10,000 when they took on Germany in a World Cup 2003 qualifier at Selhurst Park. All very much to the good, and amazing, as the severe lack of publicity outside of a closed loop of those already in the know and fans from the clubs where these games are played, is startlingly obvious. Ambitiously promoted, the range of

England games would afford a vast range of opportunities to become a fan. If crowds top 25,000 then step up the capacity to 30,000 and above. And focus the scale of this ambition on bringing back the close-season Home Internationals championship at an Under-21 or Under-19s level. England, Scotland, Wales and Northern Ireland with guest countries from the rest of Europe, South America, Africa and Asia. Schedule it for the last week of the school term. Base the games at stadia around England and the home nations. Seek sponsors to bus in children and parents from the major conurbations and surrounding areas to fill the likes of the Stadium of Light, Goodison Park, Elland Road, Villa Park and St Mary's. Not a poor fans' alternative to the World Cup, but a bright, exciting way to start out as an England fan.

The same could apply to away travel. In 2002 England Under-21s played in their European Championships in Switzerland and both the Under-17s and Under-19s competed in tournaments in Scandinavia. The England supporters club run by the FA, *englandfans*, could have run trips to all three with an emphasis on families who couldn't afford the expense and time to journey out to Japan. Of course a huge administrative workload was committed to helping the fans who had gone to the Far East, but here was a great opportunity to reach out to a new generation of away fans too. The opportunity was passed up this time, but never mind, there are plenty more where those came from. The cycle of international tournaments in attractive, easy-to-reach locations, at every conceivable level, men's and women's, guarantees that. But it takes a re-imagination by both the English game's administrators, and the fans, of how supporters become fans. Valuing the vital importance of live attendance, not being afraid of providing the maximum number of opportunities to experience that thrill of your first England match, and not begrudging those who join the fans who've been there all along. England, we recruit.

In Japan a huge part of the off the pitch fans' success was down to the Japanese falling in love with our side. Unique, never to be repeated? Not necessarily so. Our principal club sides have an international following all over the world. There's barely a team in all four divisions without at least a player or two from another country. And it's not cultural imperialism that has led to our league and cup games being watched globe-wide – it's because there is a genuine affection for the way we play and follow our football. Japan was special, certainly, but a set of values that assume a will to win doesn't stand contrary with wanting to be liked, could see something of its kind happen over and over again. Throw in with the football our popular music, dance culture, film, fashion, humour, literature, theatre, the odd pint of beer and there's plenty apart from a martial and imperial history to attract a longing gaze in our national direction when the team, plus fans, go abroad. 'Love Football, Love England' sums it up neatly, a badge for players and fans alike to wear with pride and dish out to the locals too. Not to generate a fake Englishness at the expense of other national identities and loyalties, or our own, but to be grateful for what attracts so many to England, something that too often in the past we've not bothered to take much account of. When fans around the world adopt Brazil as their second favourite team, it's surely down to their spectacular World Cup success. For the present any adoption of England won't be because of that. It will be more deep-rooted, more fan-based – and that is to our good.

World Cup 2002, as so many fans who went will point out, really was the trip of a footballing lifetime. It has created the conditions for a fan travel culture around England. Not as an optional extra but an essential part of how we enjoy our football. Before heading off East, in London, a programme of fan travel forums was pioneered. Involving the FA, Foreign Office, Home Office, Japan National Tourist Organisation, Football Supporters Association and English and Japanese media, it afforded an opportunity for fans to find out more about the country they were visting, gain vital information on the basics, learn a few useful phrases, quiz the organisations responsible for fans' well-being and meet up with others also heading off abroad. The rhythm of supporting England is quite different to following a club where fans will meet up week after week, home and away, with many still living and working in the same locality too. None of this applies to England. But before a major championship a community of travel does form. Instead of keeping it at a suspicious arm's length, travel forums all over the country could begin to provide a space for a positive identity and constructive dialogue to develop further. An initiative of this sort wouldn't cost much but it sends out a powerful signal that fans who go abroad are not something England would rather be without, but a vital feature of the carnival of sporting spectacle we'd very much like our nation to go on being a part of.

Before we even travelled to the 2002 World Cup, the message was filtering back that the Japanese were mad keen on our football. A simple idea was adopted by many; take out some club pin badges or something similar that would make a nice gift for anybody who helps us out. If we can't make ourselves understood in their language the thanks will be obvious enough. A nice touch, and those who were equipped with the *Philosophy Football* postcards featuring David Beckham would often report back amazing instances of gratitude as they passed them out. One-to-one ambassadorship like this doesn't work if it is formalised, turned into some overbearing bureaucratic do-goodery venture. Putting a pack of goodwill cards, picturing the team and some of our favourite symbols of English football into the hands of anyone who wants to distribute them, would strike just the right balance between encouragement and interference.

Press, radio and TV are the fans' favourite targets to blame for the plight we found ourselves in after every tournament up to Japan and Korea. Balanced coverage, when will we ever read that? Or so the accusation goes. News values being what they are, a chair flying through the air in a Belgian town square will always outscore a group of smiling fans sitting down for a bottle of vino and *crêpes* in the neighbouring street. What changed in Japan was that in the absence of trouble, journalists and cameramen were forced off their usual stories to track down the fans who were there for anything but a fight. A new picture of what it means to follow England started to emerge, accompanied now with pictures of fancy-dress eccentricity and English arms round the Japanese wearing our shirts. Of course most fans don't go to the lengths of finding a costume of the Queen, a crusader in chain-mail or kimono plus wig to go to a match. Those who do are as small in number as the hardcore hooligans, but which would you prefer to see on the TV? Meanwhile a vast array of local media, press and especially radio, carried reports from fans in their areas out at the tournament. This network of fan correspondents should be developed, not to professionalise or police, but to encourage others to carry a similar message home. Through many media outlets, the build-up of the fan experience of the games everyone in England wishes they could be at would help form many and varied pictures of what it takes to represent England.

The fans who made it out to Japan were, of course, only a tiny fraction of those who support England. The same is true of any tournament, or indeed match, but the numbers were less this time round because even after some bargain-hunting for flights and hotels on the Net, the price was still high. For the European Championships in Portugal 2004 and the next World Cup in Germany 2006 the demand for tickets will soar once again. And this makes the need for fair ticket shares more vital than ever before. Apart from basic distribution malfunctions, there are two structural inequalities that discriminate against fair tickets. First, the allocations. At World Cup 2002 the allocation for each competing nation's fans was eight per cent of the ground's capacity. Not bad for Saitama Stadium with a capacity of 63,060, or even the Sapporo Dome with 42,122. But then read the small print . . . 'eight per cent of the saleable capacity'. When England's eight per cent for Saitama totalled just 3,533 tickets rather than the 5,044 based on eight per cent of the published capacity, it became obvious something was up; 18,898 tickets never went on public sale, with similar figures at all the other World Cup stadiums. Twenty-one per cent of tickets are already held back by FIFA for their own use, but tickets that should have gone to fans were reduced by another astonishing 29 per cent by this 'not on public sale' device. The occasional hoo-hah about empty seats is an irrelevance; there will always be some unpopular games. England's games are never unpopular. The distance reduced demand this time around but it won't in 2004 and 2006. A fair allocation would be each competing nation to receive 15 per cent, with any unclaimed to be passed, in the first instance, to the opposition's fans. Cut out this device of not putting on sale to fans close to a third of the capacity for reasons ranging from advertising hoarding to the press box; group games should be played in stadia with a minimum public sale capacity of 40,000, knock-out stages 50,000, semi-finals 60,000 and finals 70,000. The remaining percentage should then be shared 60 per cent to global or continental public sale and 10 per cent for FIFA. A fair ticket share on this basis would be in the interests of fans from all countries. FA pressure on UEFA and FIFA to deliver would help build a shared community of interest between the sports governing body and supporters.

Just increasing the number of tickets going to fans, however, won't satisfy demand. This is the second structural inequality. Good performances by the team along with rising expectations that trouble-free tournaments are a real possibility will both massively boost demand to levels that simply will never be satisfied. So how do you share out the tickets you have? Almost all clubs in the rare instance of making it to a cup final operate a loyalty scheme of one sort or another. Buying a season ticket is one way of proving loyalty, though the best proof is based not simply on the ability to purchase but on actually following the team to all the matches of a cup run. This idea is applied to who gets England World Cup and European Championship tickets. But many fans feel aggrieved that the scheme is used only partially; home games don't count, nor is there any accounting for the previous campaign, only the current one. It remains a complicated issue. Loyalty should be valued, yet not to the extent of preventing new fans joining in and getting hold of tickets. But if loyalty is undervalued we actually lose the entire rationale of fandom, keeping the faith when all around are losing theirs. In Japan, the supporters who everyone ended up being so chuffed about were, in large part, those who hadn't lost their faith in what being an England fan *could* become.

It was after France '98 that comedian and writer Rob Newman set out his theory as to why England fans would never be anybody's favourite World Cup guests:

> Foreign fans have more fun. Apart from England, the only other country not to have a hundred-foot flag or silky banner passed overhead is the USA. This is because Anglo-Saxon capitalism does not encourage collective life, nothing is owned

> collectively ('Look that's *my* hundred-foot flag, pass it back. Come on please.'). No, collective life is also why England fans are the only ones in the whole world reduced to singing the fucking National Anthem – of all things – at a game.

Before and after World Cup 2002 the collective life of fandom that Newman couldn't see happening around England has started sparking into life. Those cards, thousands of them, that form a St George Cross at home games – what could be more collective than that? Fans swapping cheap travel and accommodation tips on the FA website – isn't that sharing? Supporters meeting in World Cup travel forums, coming together to invest the positives of following England – isn't that a group identity taking shape? Oh, and from Saitama to Shizuoka we did have a bloody great big flag we passed over our heads too, Rob. As for God Save the Queen, all his pet theories of Anglo-Saxon antipathy to collectivism are probably confirmed by England's new terrace anthem, the song from the movie *The Italian Job*'s closing credits, 'The self-preservation society'. Or maybe that's just English irony for you, eh?

Twenty-one days that changed England. Hardly, but it was a start. Being loved was more fun being loathed. National pride for all, with no necessary exceptions either. John King, author of *The Football Factory*, was having none of it. 'The 2002 World Cup shows that passion has become a commodity, something to be controlled and channelled towards a profit.' Sure, Umbro sold a lot of overpriced shirts, but then the current England kit with subliminal St George red stripe down the side is the best since '66 vintage red. And if you were canny enough to get into the flag business then the tills no doubt rang all June long. But this particular big-business conspiracy theory is way off the mark. Instead, we should celebrate a pride without prejudice that is fan-led, owned by the supporters. England dreaming? Yes. But at least we are beginning to see how it might look, and rather liking it, thank you very much.

And FIFA too. Two years ago, Lennart Johansson, as President of UEFA, had been on the verge of booting England out of Euro 2000 on account of the trouble caused by some of our fans. In 2002 as Chair of FIFA's World Cup organising committee he instead singled out England fans for praise: 'We always hear quickly enough and loudly enough when fans do not behave. So let's make plenty of noise this time that their behaviour has been perfect. They showed that real football fans know how to enjoy the game, support their team, celebrate when they win and take defeat when they lose.' John King would put the earning of such plaudits down to a middle-class fan malaise taking over football. No, not class – just a way of supporting our national team that is legal, decent and honest to a positive potential too many presumed England never possessed.

When the third goal went in against Denmark in Niigata I was sitting in the stadium – well, standing on my seat actually. The England end erupted. Congas broke out everywhere, snaking up and down the aisles, kids on shoulders, English and Japanese arms round each others' waists. A murmur of a chant grew and grew, at first I couldn't make it out. It was to that 'la-la-la' conga tune of course, but what were we singing? Then it hit me full square, 'Let's Go Oriental, la-la-la'. Incredible, we were paying tribute to a faraway country that had allowed us to become fans again, the best of fans. For that, thank you Japan, *Arrigatoh Gozaimas Nippon*. You took us from 'No One Likes Us, We Don't Care' to 'Everyone Likes Us, We Do Care' on a journey to the Orient we'll never forget, if we care about England's future.

* * * * *

Postcard from Japan

Simon Kuper

I had expected members of the Japanese parliament, the Diet, to have rather plusher offices than this. Seishiro Eto, LDP MP and director general of the Japanese Parliamentarians' League for promoting the World Cup, works from a 1960s room with cheap furniture and a grey carpet of the sort you would expect to find in an Eastern European parliament.

The atmosphere, though, was more like Alice in Wonderland. Sometimes I felt I was talking to the Queen of Hearts or attending the Mad Hatter's Tea Party. Nothing quite made sense. After a month in Japan, I was again hit by the depressing realisation that I would never understand this place.

I was trying to work out the significance of the World Cup (you remember, last summer's football thing) and I wanted Eto's views. Everything he said surprised me. 'Japanese people have seen shadow hooligans this time. I would have liked to see real hooligans and hooligan acts.' He laughed, so this may have been a bit of a joke, but then he went on to say: 'I don't want people to think that the moderate version of hooligans we have seen out here are the real hooligans.' He added hastily that he was not hoping for any trouble.

Surely, after a month of peace and love at the World Cup, Eto didn't still think hooligans were a big problem in Europe? 'I believe hooligans only exist within sports at the moment. But in Europe especially, because of the immigration problems which lead to unemployment, poverty and uncertainty, if hooliganism occurs at the time of an election, it can be a big political problem. And it could become linked with terrorism.'

I am afraid I disagree. Hooliganism is a minor law and order problem in a couple of European countries. It has about as much to do with revolution and Osama Bin Laden as does Junichi Inamoto. I had hoped that the largest influx of foreigners since General MacArthur might have rid the Japanese of some of their stranger ideas about Westerners, but if Eto was anything to go by, apparently not. So much for the World Cup bringing the world together.

But then Eto proceeded to claim that it did. 'We can use football as a peacekeeping operation,' he enthused. 'For instance, even if a war is breaking out, when there is a World Cup people forget about their disputes and they play football.'

He envisaged an international organisation led by the Japanese to spread peace through football. 'In the next four years the aim is for peace in the Middle East. Most members of this League have an interest in that,' he said. Again I disagree. The World Cup has been going since 1930, and it has yet to rid the world of war. Countries fight over their perceived interests, not because there is not enough football.

A World Cup fades like a dream, leaving nothing behind. Many foreign newspapers have claimed that this Cup has 'changed' Japan, allowing young people to throw off the shackles of convention and jump in rivers or take their shirts off in public.

I know next to nothing about Japan, but I doubt the World Cup changed anything here. It is just that everything to do with the competition gets noticed. So when young Japanese people jump on taxis to celebrate a victory, some Japanese people and most foreigners realise that young Japanese people are not as they imagined them. As I wrote before the tournament: 'World Cups generally change perceptions rather than governments.'

Most World Cups at least change football itself. Often a team emerges that surprises the world: the unforgettable Brazil of 1970, the Dutch team of 'total football' in 1974, or Cameroon, the first great African team, in 1990.

There has been none of that this time. Satellite television has done its work too well. Long before the World Cup, we knew all the best players in the world. So it turns out that Oliver Kahn is a great keeper and Ronaldo a great striker – one wonders if this is news to anyone. World Cups have lost their mystery.

This competition may have only one legacy: more people in Japan and Korea will now follow football. It is often said that the World Cup was just a fad among the Japanese. I suspect it will prove more than that, simply because the game is so beautiful.

Its power dawned on me one Sunday afternoon in Central Park in New York five years ago. I was picnicking with some men and some women, and after the food we men began playing football. The women mocked us for wasting our time on a silly game, but eventually they joined in. Several hours later we finally persuaded them to stop. They were hooked. This week one of them sent me an email saying: 'You will be pleased to hear I have been watching a lot of the football and was entirely gutted when England lost.'

Her experience in Central Park was replicated in June by tens of millions of Japanese. I gather old ladies have been going around saying, 'I never realised *sakka* was so interesting.' It may be a while before a match draws two-thirds of the population to their TV sets again, as Japan–Russia did, but football will surely not return to the outhouse here.

It would help if Japan's team improved. For that to happen, more players must move to Europe, where the best football is played. In the old American phrase, 'Go West, young man'. Just don't think you'll change the world.

* * * * *

Playing the Global Game

Martin Jacques

It was widely thought that this World Cup would be the most open and unpredictable for years. And the reason was simple and well founded. Usually the host nation does extremely well, if not actually winning it (England '66, Germany '74, Argentina '78, France '98 spring immediately to mind) and this time neither of the host nations – Japan and South Korea – relatively new to football as they both were, were expected to get anywhere near the final stages, let alone win the tournament. As we all know, South Korea reached the semi-finals and Japan the second round. They were the standard-bearers of what became the motif of the World Cup 2002 – the way in which nations relatively new to football turned the tables on the established powers in the game.

Of course, it is a fact that countries like South Korea and Japan – or China, for that matter – are relatively new to football. The rise of the game in these countries dates back not much more than a decade, or, even giving ourselves a wide historical berth, two decades at the outside. Compared with Europe, where the game has been widely played for well over a century, the game is still in its nursery phase. The spread of football to these countries is one aspect of cultural globalisation – and tells us something about the nature of globalisation. We may be familiar with sumo wrestling, or martial arts emanating from East Asia, but the cultural traffic, not least in sport, while not one-way, has been overwhelmingly in one direction. Even the sports played at the Olympics are largely western in origin. That is part of the story of western hegemony over the last two centuries through the processes of colonialism and globalisation.

There is in one sense, though, that the global spread of football bucks the trend of modern globalisation. Take East Asia, for example, easily the most economically successful region of the world after the United States and Europe, and home to over one-third of the world's population. In virtually every aspect of life, from business to culture, when East Asia looks west it sees not Europe but the United States. Indeed, in my experience, and I have travelled widely in these countries, Europe is almost invisible. The popular imagination, when it is not national or influenced by Japan, is obsessed with the United States – for film, universities, entrepreneurial heroes, technology, basketball and much else besides. In a recent attitude survey of Shanghai teenagers, they described Europe as 'football, fashion and old buildings'. A sobering thought for European hubris. Nonetheless, it also demonstrates the extraordinary influence that football, a European creation, has enjoyed, at a time when the European presence more generally has been in precipitous decline in this part of the world.

But let us return to our original proposition. The belief that the 'new' football nations cannot really shine a light to the established European and Latin American nations is deeply held, and mirrors more general attitudes. Many in Europe are at least vaguely aware that most East Asian countries have enjoyed extremely rapid economic growth over the last 20 years or so, but we still see them, with the partial exception of Japan, as less developed than ourselves, as still having a long way to go, that, as latecomers to modernisation, they need to go through all the same stages as we did, that it is impossible for them to jump stages or define a novel – and accelerated – way of arriving at the same sort of level of development as we have. These attitudes are to do with western hubris, a born to rule, top of the pile mentality, insular ignorance and, it must be said, a deep racial prejudice. When these countries got into economic difficulties during the Asian crisis of 1997, western commentators were quick to describe them as victims of 'crony capitalism': the present crisis in the United States has exposed practices at least as bad if not worse, but so far, at least, the US has not been described in the same derogatory terms. If it is possible to jump economic stages and arrive at modernity in double-quick time, as countries like South Korea and Taiwan are presently demonstrating, then it is even more possible to do it in a sport like football where the same inherent historical obstacles are fewer and more surmountable.

Although England is now well used to stumbling in the face of what it regards as lesser nations – be they East European, Latin American, North African or whatever – for many years the mentality, when we were playing such nations, was to belittle the opposition and then express shock and surprise when we lost, drew or won only narrowly. This inherent sense of superiority is still barely hidden and regularly resurfaces. One might describe it as the imperial mentality – as true in football as it is in everything else. But in this World Cup, the exemplars of this insufferable superiority were not England nor even France (who seemed to take their early and ignominious exit as a reflection on their own inadequacy rather than blaming everyone else) but Italy, Spain, and Portugal. For them it was all too much; the national reaction was to blame their defeat by a football 'minnow', namely South Korea, on a conspiracy by the match officials. They just could not accept the idea that they might have been beaten fairly and squarely; instead they cried foul. In the torrent of nationalist and racist bile, it should not be overlooked that the match officials were non-white: the racism was thinly veiled. For me, one of the pleasures of the World Cup, even more than seeing players of colour adorning the game with such skill and technique, is that many of the matches were overseen by non-white officials. Rare it is in this world that whites have to defer to the authority of colour.

Given that Europe is the home of the professional foul and many other unsavoury practices, it is a bit rich for these countries to shout 'cheat' at the first opportunity. The most revealing incident of all was perhaps when the president of Perugia football club summarily sacked the scorer of the winning South Korean goal the day after the match. The reason was not that he scored (even for such a bigot this argument would have been a little preposterous) but what the player is alleged to have said – that South Korea was a better football nation than Italy. You may or may not agree, but it is certainly fair comment. In this context, hopefully one of the things that Europeans will have learnt from this World Cup is the exemplary conduct not only of the Asian players but also their fans – and the people in the streets. If football can bring out some of the best features in a culture, it can also bring out the very worst. Virtually all of the European nations are besmirched by brutish and loutish behaviour by a section of fans – a continuing and persistent feature of the game, which mirrors aspects of the wider society. In contrast, there was a total absence of this kind of behaviour by the

Korean and Japanese fans; on the contrary, they set totally different standards of mass behaviour and civility. Again this reflects wider society. The kind of male violence that scars European societies is unheard of in East Asian cities. In this respect, East Asian societies are far pleasanter and more civilised than those in Europe.

Italy, Spain and Portugal were incapable of accepting their defeats in a sporting fashion. As imperial football powers, that is just not the order of things. But of course the roots of this kind of prejudice go well beyond football. The attitudes in football mirror those in the wider society. For imperial football powers just read former imperial nations; they – we – just think we are better. And the fact that countries like South Korea and Japan are not only relatively new to football but have players with strange sounding names, who are shorter than Caucasians, speak funny languages and have different facial features only served to accentuate this sense of national outrage. The World Cup, you will recall, took place in June. Over the previous twelve months, the electorate in many European countries had been busy voting for the far and racist right in numbers not seen since the 1930s. Football, as the overwhelmingly most popular sport in these societies and with the decline of other popular modes of representation, has become a powerful conduit for national passions and racial prejudice. Indeed, the interconnection – in the broadest sense – between football and the new right is worthy of more thought and discussion. Silvio Berlusconi, the Italian prime minister and a prototype of the modern European neo-fascist leader, modelled his party, Forza Italia, on the official supporters club at AC Milan, the club that he owns.

World Cup 2002 offered a window on the world of tomorrow – not just the world of football, but the world more generally. In the nineteenth century, the world was almost exclusively European. In the twentieth century, it was American, European and for a period also Soviet. But as modernity spreads across East Asia, and to a lesser extent other continents, so the world is characterised by a new diversity. Modernity is no longer a western preserve. This World Cup offered an exhilarating insight into that new diversity: the rise of South Korea and Japan as football nations, not to mention Senegal and Turkey, three of whom reached the last eight. It is also one of the delights of football that a poor and hugely populated country, Brazil, is the game's superpower and that the United States, the global superpower in virtually everything else, is the game's minnow. In this World Cup of course both countries made it to the quarter-finals, but it was Brazil, not the otherwise almighty USA, that went through and won the tournament.

In this sense, at least, football is at the cutting edge of a new emergent world, an ambassador for a different future. More than television programmes and magazine articles could ever do, this World Cup opened the eyes of millions of people – the fans who travelled, the viewers who watched – to the culture and achievements of the host nations; the fact, for example, that millions of people could turn out on the streets of Seoul on several occasions without a whiff of violence and barely a drop of alcohol. We learnt to respect and acknowledge cultural difference, even if, in the case of all too many in Italy, Spain and Portugal, it was done grudgingly and resentfully. And even if football is one – perhaps the only – spectacle where the public display of racism can be seen and heard, and overwhelmingly tolerated, in Europe at least, it is also true that this is a game where the English and French teams give greater representation to men of colour than ever happens in the rest of society, where officials of colour enjoy an authority which is never tolerated in any non-sporting international arena, and where we all celebrate the artistry of the multi-racial Brazilian side who, decade in, decade out, play the game like no other nation seems capable of.

Football operates according to similar laws as everything else; the power of money. And so the game's grandees, or moneybags, namely the European clubs, buy up and buy off the best players around the world; once the traffic in players was mainly intra-European, now it is global – Latin Americans, Africans, Japanese, Chinese and the rest. It has left Brazilian football denuded of its greatest players, likewise Argentina, Uruguay, Cameroon, Nigeria, now Senegal and many more besides; the power of, in this case, not the dollar, but the euro (or even the pound). We Europeans are the beneficiaries of this process, able to enjoy football genius from around the globe in our own backyards. Similarly, the players who find themselves the objects of such largesse are also beneficiaries, rich beyond their dreams and enjoying a professional experience second to none. The casualties are the national leagues that find themselves bereft of their best stars. Inevitably this has resulted in a certain trend; Brazilian football is no longer a mystery, something we can only watch once every four years on the television. As in everything else, globalisation in football has led to a process of standardisation and convergence.

And yet, and this is another of football's small offerings, somehow, amidst all the pressures towards 'one game', the World Cup – this one and all the others – reminds us that there is not one game but many, that national differences have endured, even in homogenised Europe, that Brazil play the game quite differently from anyone else, with a unique combination of technique and artistry, with a wholly different set of values from those that prevail in Europe; and we can see that there is a distinctively African style of playing and now, with this World Cup, distinctive Korean and Japanese styles as well. As such the game offers hope for the future, that despite all the economic pressures, diversity will survive and prosper, that just as there are many footballs so there can, and will be, not one way of being modern, the western way, but that the world will be characterised by many modernities.

THE WORLD CUP TURNED UPSIDE DOWN:
NEW AND OLD FOOTBALL ORDERS

Chaos

David Winner

Some 30 years ago, the computer giant IBM hired an oddball mathematician to work in the company's research division. Benoit Mandelbrot was known to be bright, but he looked like an old hippy, he was a loner, and his methods were weird. He would disappear for months at a time and was rarely in the office. After a while his colleagues became worried.

Concern changed to alarm when it became clear Mandelbrot was spending thousands of dollars endlessly flying back and forth to Las Vegas. He was summoned to head office to explain what the hell he thought he was up to. His answer seemed preposterous. Mandelbrot said the plane journeys were useful because they allowed him to look out of the window at the shapes of passing clouds. It was no scam.

Benoit Mandelbrot was in the process of making one of the key intellectual breakthroughs of the late twentieth century. He was discovering Chaos Theory. He had noticed that a simple-seeming phenomenon – a fluffy little cumulo-nimbus, for example – was actually staggeringly complex. On his journeys Mandelbrot stared at the clouds. Each one, he reasoned, must consist of trillions upon trillions of water molecules, all dancing in unique patterns around each other. He contemplated. He observed. What factors governed the behaviour of the cloud? The wind? The density of the air? If one could solve the riddle of the clouds, might one also begin to make sense of other illogical-seeming shapes and patterns?

For Mandelbrot had begun to see similar 'chaotic' patterns everywhere: the surges of the stock market, the unpredictable dripping of a tap, the ever-changing rhythm of the beating human heart. Chaotic systems seemed to be a basic organising element of the universe. He became obsessed with discovering the mathematical laws which might explain the way they worked. Since no existing mathematical model could help him, Mandelbrot began to imagine a new form of mathematics.

His landmark book, *The Fractal Geometry of Nature*, opened the way for an intellectual revolution. In the depths of apparently random chaos, Mandelbrot found deeper, subtle rhythms, a new kind of logic – fluid, 'fuzzy'. Instead of two-dimensional mathematical diagrams, he saw fractal infinities existing in several dimensions simultaneously. The universe may seem random and illogical but it must be mathematically comprehensible.

Mandelbrot's work was merely a starting point and Chaos Theory is still in its infancy. If a complete theory is ever discovered, as Stephen Hawking puts it, it will allow us 'to take part in the discussion of the question of why it is that we and the universe exist'.

Back on earth, the World Cup in Japan and Korea has left in its wake a general sense of both wonder and unease. We thought we understood football, knew its general principles, could predict its outcomes. Football seemed fairly stable. Then it went haywire. France, Argentina, Italy, Spain and Portugal collapsed. Senegal, South Korea, Turkey, Japan and the USA advanced. The game seemed plunged into a state of chaos.

At the end of the tournament John Carlin, writing in the *Observer*, exulted in it all:

> There is no science to the game whatsoever. Football is not susceptible to reason. Because, as the mad and magnificent events of this last month in the Far East have demonstrated beyond doubt, football is baffling, enigmatic, unfathomable. Those who should know the most, who think they know the most, know, if anything, the least. Socrates – the Greek, not the Brazilian – said all he knew was that he did not know. And that goes for everybody. From your Sven-Göran Erikssons and your Tord Grips, to the planetary Babel of pundits and football writers, all the way through to you, dear reader, and the hundreds of millions who share your lust for the greatest game of all. Everybody should bow their heads before the football gods and, while offering thanks for the joy they bring us, humbly acknowledge that we are in the face of a mystery that surpasses human understanding.

The World Cup as a chaotic pagan mystery? Or is it a Mandelbrotian puzzle that will yield its deeper patterns and harmonies only if looked at in the correct way, using fuzzy logic?

Picture this: January 2002. A 55-year-old Dutchman who loves to ride motorbikes is on board a Korea Airlines jet several miles above Siberia. He travels first class, of course, and has a window seat. Far below him, sparse clouds, an infinity of ice. The Dutchman stares down at the clouds. What does he see? What is Guus Hiddink thinking?

'Act normal: that's crazy enough.' The Dutch tell each other this all the time. Until June, I never really understood what it meant. I had taken it to be a warning against outlandish behaviour. Now I realise it is (and always has been) a reference to World Cup history. For history teaches us that many World Cup matches go against form, especially in the early rounds. In many ways, the 2002 World Cup followed patterns from the past. Senegal's victory over France was a carbon copy of Cameroon–Argentina in 1990. Portugal's defeat by the USA was no more bizarre than Germany's defeat by Algeria in 1982 or Scotland's failures against Peru and Iran in 1978. Lumbering Russia lost to nimble Japan, a well-supported, highly motivated home nation (what's surprising about that?). Turkish clubs and the national side have been steadily advancing for more than a decade, so Turkey's surge to the semi-final was less surprising than Bulgaria or Sweden in 1994 and Croatia in 1998. The Irish performed at about the same level as 1990 and 1994. Belgium and Mexico punched their normal weight. Cameroon and Nigeria were disappointing, as is now their way. China and Saudi Arabia were awful, as anyone who knew could have told you they would be. Sweden, England, Denmark and Uruguay are all decent middle-weights, so for Argentina and France to fail against them was unexpected but hardly astounding. England got to the quarter-final and no further, as was widely predicted.There was nothing unusual about Brazil's success. Germany did much better than anyone expected (as usual).

Ah . . . but I left out the Koreans. All perceptions of the World Cup as a freakish event depend on South Korea's sequence of victories over European opponents Poland, Portugal, Italy and Spain en route to the semi-final. Poland were simply poor, and the Portuguese imploded (Luis Figo unfit and the 'golden generation', complacent against USA in their first match, had two men sent off). It was the next match, when Korea came from a goal behind to beat the new favourites, Italy, which was the defining moment of the World Cup.

Soon after Ahn Jung-hwan headed South Korea's lethal golden goal, I called my friend, Maddalena, on her mobile phone in Rome to commiserate. The city sounded like no place to ponder the intricacies of Chaos Theory. Instead, Isaac Newton's third law of motion applied: 'For every action, there is an equal and opposite reaction.' South Korea was erupting in previously unimagined scenes of mass joy, but Italy was stunned. A couple of years earlier, on the back of her Vespa on my first day in Rome, Maddalena took me to the Piazza del Popolo and proudly showed me the square's perfect dimensions, its sublime twin churches and the Obelisk of Rameses. Now, according to the BBC, there was a large, appalled Roman crowd in the square which had watched the match from Daejeon on big screens and greeted Korea's winning goal with chants of 'death to the referee'. Across the city, Maddalena, like everyone else in Italy, was shocked and angry. 'We were robbed,' she said firmly. 'Robbed?' 'Absolutely robbed.'

Madda looks a bit like Nancy Dell'Olio but is more intellectual. Raven-haired, sad-eyed, mischievous, she once wrote an existentialist novel about architecture, sex and death, with herself as the central male character. She speaks at least four languages and is a noted criminal defence lawyer. She lives near the Vatican but worships Francesco Totti. Whatever was going on at the cutting edge of mathematical theory, she pointed out that the old laws of football had just been mangled by the Ecuadorean referee. 'Why was Totti sent off?' she asked. 'For nothing. Why was Tommasi's golden goal disallowed? For no reason. He was completely onside. We won the game and it was stolen away from us.'

Four days later, it was Spain's turn to experience that sickening feeling, succumbing to the Koreans on penalties after Spain had two goals wrongly disallowed by a linesman from the Maldives and a ref from Egypt.

Chaos Theory teaches that systems depending on a huge number of variables (the weather, snowflake formation, football, etc) are unpredictable. And such systems, which involve lots of delicately balanced interacting elements, can be disturbed by relatively small changes. Chaos mathematicians point to the humble waterwheel as an example. Generally, the wheel turns faster the more water flows onto it, but when water pressure reaches a critical point, the wheel appears to go haywire, spinning backwards, lurching forward, becoming, in a word, 'chaotic'. The movement of the wheel obviously cannot be explained by a simple equation (more water = faster spinning). But all becomes clear when it is seen in a wider, more complex, Chaos Theory way. A man called Lorenzo did the mathematics and found the explanatory equation was the shape of an exquisite butterfly. What might a Chaos Theory representation of Italy–South Korea look like? A demented squid is my guess. But whoever does the research will need to consider the effect of the dynamic variable known as Guus Hiddink.

When the former Holland and Real Madrid coach took charge four months before the World Cup, South Korea had never won a match in the World Cup. It was easy to see why. Their technique and tactical knowledge was low compared to the best of Europe or South America and cultural traditions worked against team spirit (at meal times junior players had to wait for their respected older colleagues to finish before they could eat). Hiddink made lots of changes. He brought in a Dutch assistant coach and technical coordinator and an American computer analyst. He persuaded the Korean federation to cancel its domestic season and give him four clear months to work with his players. He broke down the stifling old hierarchies, scoured the college teams for new talent, and introduced a Dutch style of permanent attack. He fused Korean toughness with as much Dutch finesse as could be transmitted in four months (which turned out to be rather a lot). All jolly impressive, but, seeing as not one of Hiddink's team would have got into the squads of Spain, Italy or Portugal, hardly enough to frighten

Europe's football superpowers. But there was something else. Working with his 'high-tension physiologist' Raymond Verheyen, Hiddink had also turned fit players into super-fit ones.

Pressing is an old European concept. Dutch total footballers did it best in the 1970s; AC Milan perfected it in the late '80s; Manchester United and Arsenal do it now. Dutch coaching orthodoxy used to have it that high-intensity pressing was only possible for about 60 minutes per game. But Hiddink and Verheyen developed the Korean athletic capacity to extraordinary levels, closer to the honed perfection of Olympic athletes than normal footballers. The Koreans' ability to chase and harry opponents became astonishing. Whipped to ever greater efforts by the relentless intensity of their supporters, the Koreans were able to press for 120 minutes at a time. Nothing quite like it had been seen before. The Koreans swarmed over more technically gifted opponents like enraged wasps. Under this pressure, world-class technicians, already jaded by the excessive physical demands of their European club seasons, simply wilted: Luis Figo, Rui Costa, Francesco Totti, Alessandro Del Piero, Morientes and others were blitzed into irrelevance. The Europeans had no answer to the Koreans' energy. The Portuguese were hustled out of their rhythm, Italian defenders hounded into uncharacteristic blunders, Spain forced onto the back foot against players they would normally have expected to dominate. In military terms, Hiddink's hyper-running tactic was decisive. It was the equivalent of introducing a surprising and superior new weapon onto the battlefield.

Exhilarating as it was for neutrals to watch, the long-term impact of the Korean approach may prove worrying. It will probably strengthen the trend towards athleticism over artistry. (The other surprise teams all showed strength and energy, though none took it as far as the Koreans.) On the other hand, Hiddink was operating under conditions so unusual and unrepeatable (home advantage, domestic season cancelled, no demands from clubs, etc) that his triumphs may prove to have little application elsewhere. Whereas top European players are obliged to play a never-ending cycle of big matches (60 a season is normal) everything Hiddink did with his Koreans was aimed at bringing them to a peak for what was expected to be a run of just three or four games. (Korea's pre-tournament objective was merely to reach the second round.) As it turned out, their super-fitness held out for five matches.

By the time they faced Germany in the semi-final, just two days after extra time and penalties against Spain, the Koreans were plainly knackered. Now they played like Superman under the influence of Kryptonite. The Korean system began to break down, as the laws of physiology dictated it must do eventually, and their technical and tactical limitations were exposed. Germany, outplayed by Ireland in the group, outrun by America in the quarter-final, and soon to be outclassed by Brazil in the final, disassembled Hiddink's tired team with minimum fuss. Intriguingly, refereeing decisions now went against Korea, as they would again in the third place match against Turkey. The magic and the energy were gone: the Red Devils could no longer make their own luck.

In Korea, Hiddink is now revered. His leadership style has been adopted as a model by Korean business. And tens of thousands of grateful Korean citizens have signed up for Hiddink pilgrimage tours to Holland. (Highlights include visits to Varsseveld, the village where Hiddink grew up, De Graafschap, the club where he spent most of his playing days, and PSV Eindhoven, where he is now the boss.) But will South Korea do as well in the 2006 World Cup? No chance.

And what of the USA? The nation of IBM and Cobi Jones was one of the other surprise packages of 2002. Unlike Senegal or, for the moment, South Korea, the Americans have the potential to become footballing heavy hitters. In 1960, President Kennedy announced America's intention to land a man on the moon and return him safely to earth 'before this decade is out'. Sure enough, bang on time, Neil Armstrong was home after his 'one small step for man'. Just before the 1998 World Cup, the leaders of American 'soccer' called a portentous news conference at RFK Stadium, named after President Kennedy's murdered brother, to announce a scarcely less ambitious venture. It cost $50 million. It was called Project 2010. And it laid out the route to American global domination of football. The plan predicted that by 2002, USA would reach the quarter-final of the World Cup. (They did.) By 2006, USA would make the semis. In 2010, America would win the World Cup. 'Americans, when they set out to do something, they set out to do it right,' said the then national coach Steve Sampson.

Soccer has become a mass participation sport in the USA. Once the preserve of big city immigrants, it has spread to the kids of the affluent middle-class suburbs and the country is awash with how-to soccer books with titles like *Coaching Youth Soccer: A Baffled Parent's Guide* and *High-Performance Soccer: Techniques & Tactics for Advanced Play*. America's cultural attitudes to soccer are also changing. On the day of the 1986 World Cup final, Henry Kissinger wrote a famous article – 'The World Cup According to Character' – for the *Los Angeles Times*. 'Soccer evokes extraordinary passions, especially during the quadrennial World Cup competition,' he explained for readers who hadn't the faintest idea about the game. 'Soccer has never taken hold in the United States,' wrote Kissinger. Yet now that taking hold has begun. During this year's tournament the same newspaper ran an intriguing piece about the way attempts to sell US sports to the rest of the world had backfired. 'A funny thing happened on the way to global domination,' wrote Steven

Zeitchik. 'While we were busy making the international sports community a little more like us, the members of the international sports community made us a little more like them.' While Europeans now wear NBA jerseys and New York Yankees hats, he noted, 'the person walking down Fifth Avenue wearing the Adidas sneakers and the British soccer jersey is probably an East Village hipster, not an immigrant from Leeds'.

All this has been making officials at the State Department nervous. They feared that an American triumph in the World Cup might inflame anti-US feeling in some parts of the world, and were relieved when America lost to Germany. Manus J. Donahue III, on the other hand, is here to tell us we have nothing to worry about.

Manus, a soccer-mad student from Duke University in North Carolina, is one of America's leading popularisers of Chaos Theory. He may be only a philosophy and mathematics undergraduate, but his lucid website on Chaos (amazingly, written when he was just 14) has had hundreds of thousands of hits and been quoted by the *New York Times.* Meanwhile, his homepage (Nietzschean motto: 'Every day I count wasted in which there has been no time spent dancing') reveals a lively mind and a gentle, self-deprecating wit. There are poems by Wordsworth and John Donne, cartoons by Calvin and Hobbes and a photograph of himself ('that's more or less what I look like, although I'm a little less "pixely" in real life').

Manus adores football and plainly understands the game, partly the result of spending several months in Scotland and having a good friend from Argentina. 'There are a lot of problems in US soccer right now,' he explains.'I think it's the greatest game on earth and it's huge among kids under the age of 14 or 15. But when you get to high school level, the really good athletes don't go into soccer.' Baseball, American football and basketball still dominate, and look set to do so for decades to come. Outside the big cities, TV coverage of world football is poor and, he says, the English language commentaries still reveal deep ignorance. 'Also, the level of coaching is really poor. Most coaches just don't understand the game as the British or Italians or Brazilians understand it.' Despite apparent US progress, he reckons Project 2010 has little bearing on reality. 'Look at the Germany game. We were the better team, but we didn't have the culture of the Germans. The Germans go out and expect to win, but the Americans don't have that expectation and it hurts us. I think it will take a couple of generations before you get coaches and veteran players in there who will have been on the world stage and really know what it takes to win.'

As a good Chaotician he also urges us to view the World Cup in a much longer, wider perspective, to look at its underlying deep historical pattern rather than its occasional surprises . . . 'The more you zoom out, the more the system is going to show the same kind of patterns. When you zoom in on details and particular matches, you're going to see specific ups and downs of a certain team or a certain component of the system. Those are always going to be really hard to predict because there are so many variables. But I don't think we're seeing a huge shift in the overall structure of soccer. I think it's always going to be more or less the same. There's always going to be the surprise teams who get to the semi-final. But in 50 years time you're not going to see a World Cup final between Senegal and South Korea. It's still going to be the usual big teams, Brazil or Germany or Italy or Argentina or England.'

* * * * *

The Dysfunctional Family FIFA

David Conn

It didn't take long for the glitter of the 2002 World Cup to banish from the world media's headlines the previous six months worth of stories of scandal, intrigue and internal warfare which had left blood on the Swiss carpet of football's world governing body, FIFA. Dark rumours have swirled for years around the running of FIFA by its current President Sepp Blatter and his predecessor and mentor, the Brazilian transport magnate Joao Havelange, but in May, FIFA's own Secretary-General, Michel Zen-Ruffinen, openly made allegations against Blatter – his boss – of corruption, graft, favours, profiteering and bribery. The guts of FIFA were laid bare at its Zurich lakeside home, and the drip of allegations and political manoeuvrings continued across the world's press before Blatter faced re-election for the FIFA presidency on the eve of World Cup 2002.

He was resoundingly re-elected, rejected by most of Europe but supported by the bulk of the smaller, more impoverished national delegations. Zen-Ruffinen's chop was swiftly organised, his P45 gleefully minted. But the allegations stayed on file with a Zurich prosecutor, which has a duty to investigate. Our own FA weighed in after their favoured candidate, Issa Hayatou of Cameroon, was defeated; Adam Crozier, the Football Association's chief executive, condemned Blatter's re-election as 'disgraceful', saying trust in FIFA had been 'fundamentally broken', and scoffing that Blatter should 'look up the word "transparency" in a dictionary'. Sports Minister Richard Caborn added his critical voice too, saying:

> We want to see a full inquiry into the serious allegations of corruption and financial cover-up which have been made against Mr Blatter and FIFA. If football's world governing body wants to be respectable, then they have to be more open and transparent.

Days later, the tournament itself started. Mighty France lost to the skills and adventure of the team from their former colony, Senegal. We woke up, bleary-eyed in the mornings, to read with near-disbelief the three-games-a-day feast the TV schedules were rolling out for us. It had finally come round, The World Cup, the football fan's fantasy month, which connects us not only to the greatest football on earth, but also to our own pasts, back on four-yearly stepping stones to tournaments of memory, and what we were doing when we watched them.

Blatter, Zen-Ruffinen, presidential votes, alleged corruption? Forgotten. If it was important before – and it was deemed to be by front pages and news schedulers across the world – once the football kicked off, even though this was FIFA's own tournament, there was nothing. Barry Davies, the BBC commentator with some pretension to a cultural hinterland did make an attempt in an early match to summarise the organisers' malaise, then gave up.

John Motson, the anorak in a sheepskin, didn't try, introducing his commentary on the England v Argentina match with: 'There may be more important things than this going on in the world, but just at the moment I can't think of them.' At the time, India and Pakistan were engaged in a nuclear standoff, the Middle East was ripping apart and millions, as ever, were going hungry or needlessly dying.

But let's not be self-righteous: 'Motty' hit the mood, even if the scale of the event, the absoluteness with which it dominated media, conversation and everybody's lives, was unprecedented and surprising. Record numbers watched games starting at 7.30 a.m., millions of people draped their homes in flags of St George, stamped with the logos JJB and Umbro – a symbol for England today whose meaning we might take a few years to fully understand. Football's conquest of every other form of sport, entertainment, TV and occasions for national unity was finally driven home to me when I overheard an old woman musing about England's midfield against Nigeria, while having her hair crimped in the hairdressers. Our newspapers began, with a very English insularity, to really believe that Beckham, Ferdinand, even Danny Mills, were true world greats who would inevitably end up lifting the trophy, and would crush Brazil, a team of second-rate poseurs privileged to be allowed to shake hands with them. When a new generation of schoolkids were taught, on big screens in assembly, by masters Rivaldo and Ronaldinho, that there is, for all the jingoism, a world outside our shores, they were lent a shoulder to cry on by no less than the Prime Minister, who said we were all 'devastated', before returning, like the rest of us, to boring old work – in his case, planning a war with Iraq.

Around the world, more than a billion people were similarly consumed. The TV distributor, KirchSport, published the territories which had bought World Cup rights and it effectively constituted a list of every country in the world, from Slovakia to Somalia, China to Chad: 215 nations. The UN has only 189. Football and this, its greatest tournament, have captured the imagination since their inception, but the World Cup now is a phenomenon of the modern world, probably the largest collective experience humanity now has, or has ever had. The World Cup is the global village fete. Its unique, near-universal appeal explains why, while it was on, nothing else seemed important to so many, least of all the back-knifings and grandstanding among the suits in FIFA's committee rooms. But football's central role in modern human experience – and that's no exaggeration of the game's current status – is in itself the reason why it is vital for it to be run well; positively, with a generosity of heart and purpose.

There is a duty to serve it cleanly, too. The amount of money TV companies are now paying for the rights to broadcast matches, and multinationals for the right to sponsor and be associated with football, make it imperative that the game is honest, accountable, and spends its vast wealth wisely.

Kirch are estimated to have sold the rights to the 2002 and 2006 World Cups for at least £1.5bn. The long list of 15 multinationals, 'marketing partners' as FIFA mellifluously calls them, paid around £140m for the right to burn their brands into world consciousness while we all thought we were just enjoying ourselves. The day after England's defeat by Brazil, many papers carried an excellent three-picture spread of the progress of Ronaldinho's free kick over Seaman's head and into the topmost corner of the net. The largest image in the photographs was the bright red billboard behind the goal: McDonald's.

Stories that all was not well and above board at FIFA go back almost 30 years, to Havelange's election in 1974 over Sir Stanley Rous, the very picture of a British referee and sports administrator, who had considered it undignified to actively campaign for re-election. Accompanied by his secretary and pet dogs lolling about the office, Sir Stanley had run FIFA in the style he had learned at the English FA, with its amateur tradition and royal patrons. Conservative, a stickler, seeing himself as benign, with a sense of fair play and old-fashioned sportsmanship, Rous had become resented by what Havelange would call football's 'family', seen as a colonial bureaucrat in a changing world. He was devastated when Havelange, a millionaire from an altogether different culture, beat him. FIFA changed instantly; it grew and reached out to more countries, expanded the World Cup to include more African and Asian countries. And it became commercial, starting to seriously exploit football's potential to make money.

In at the beginning was Horst Dassler, founder of Adidas, who provided Havelange with office space in Zurich while new palatial offices were built for the governing body. English marketing man Patrick Nally courted Coca-Cola, and that company, always in the vanguard of westernisation, became the first multinational to ride into new territories on the back of FIFA's missionary football programmes.

Dassler talent-spotted a bright young man then working in marketing for the Swiss timing company Longines, and picked him to run, as technical director from 1975–81, the Futuro football development plan sponsored by Coke and Adidas. His name? Sepp Blatter. He demonstrated skill in doing deals and smoothing local difficulties in often awkward countries, and Havelange promoted him to become his right-hand man and bag carrier, as FIFA General Secretary.

Dassler founded the marketing company ISL – International Sport and Leisure – in 1982. Havelange immediately granted the company the exclusive right to sell FIFA's properties, mainly the World Cup; ISL pioneered the marketing of sports tournaments as exclusive sponsorship packages, sold to a few multinationals. When Havelange retired in 1998, he boasted that mainly due to him, football had become a $250bn industry, and FIFA a $4bn operation. He was succeeded by Blatter, beating off the rival candidate Lennart Johansson, of European football's governing body UEFA, who had stood on a ticket of cleaning up FIFA.

For many years before ISL went spectacularly bust in 2001, questions were asked about its closeness with FIFA and about the relationship between Dassler and Havelange. Brazilian football, which Havelange had run previously and was now administered by his son-in-law Ricardo Texeira, almost imploded under the saga of endemic corruption, which would lead to federal inquiries in Brazil. FIFA's accounts were opaque and it was never clear enough how much money was coming in or where it was being spent. But the smaller nations were being awarded money for development programmes, wrapped in corporate brand names, and they were, mostly, happier than ever, their votes guaranteed.

Unhappiness with FIFA's slavering commercialisation and lack of accountability only tracked its amazing growth while football played its way into becoming the globalised world's sport of choice. Havelange, as FIFA President, had a gift to bestow for which Kings and Prime Ministers were happy to abase themselves. He had the power to swing their country's way the hosting of the World Cup, that greatest of parties, morale-raisers, revenue earners – and vote-winners.

Our own FA and Government, so righteous in their disgust at Blatter in May 2002, fawned over him as recently as 1996 to 2000, in the vain, doomed bid to attract the 2006 World Cup to England. Given short memories at Soho Square and Westminster, it is worth a brief refresher about the circumstances of England's bid. It followed the success of Euro '96. The FA, then embarking on its own rebranding, and John Major's government, saw the tournament as a great cheer-up and advert for the country, and decided to mount a follow-up bid for the greatest prize of all. They might have been provided with an ounce of depth and advice had they consulted the FA's outgoing chairman, Sir Bert Millichip. He'd have reminded them that Euro '96, and English clubs' return to European competition, had been granted by UEFA so soon after the disgrace of the Heysel disaster in 1985, only because of the steadfast support and encouragement of the major European countries. English football's rehabilitiation was due to some generosity and vision from other national football federations, Germany prominent among them, but Millichip's successors and the Government were too self-absorbed to acknowledge or realise it. In UEFA meetings, it had been proposed that a single European country should mount a World Cup bid, supported by the others, so as not to split the vote. As England had just hosted Euro '96, it was understood that no country would bid against Germany for the 2006 tournament.

When the English FA suddenly announced their bid for the World Cup, Germany, understandably, pointed to this 'gentleman's agreement'. Livid, they accused the English FA of, amongst other things, ingratitude, betrayal, double dealing. Unmoved, the English pressed on, assembling a campaign costing £10m, paid equally by the FA, Sport England – a strange use of Lottery money – and the Premier League, although the cunning old operators running the Premiership provided it mostly in 'kind', on advertising hoardings, rather than parting with any cash.

The details of the bid, the lavish hospitality, the courting of FIFA delegates, are the stuff of embarrassing legend. The BBC tend to replay Geoff Hurst and John Barnes doing some kind of boogie at an awful looking outdoor cocktail party, and you don't need to know much more about the classy style of the lobbying. Tony Blair had Blatter to Number 10 Downing Street twice, for tea and smiles, and appointed the former Sports Minister Tony Banks as his own personal envoy to the World Cup bid. You'd struggle to make this up.

Banks admitted to me in an interview in June 2002 that once he was on the FIFA circuit, the stories about possible wrongdoing at the highest level in the organisation were everywhere. FIFA was also even less transparent than they are now: in 2002 they issued a very long, detailed financial statement. Some, like David Will, chairman of the audit committee, claim the statement massages the figures and that FIFA is technically bust, but nevertheless the document surpasses anything available about the running of the governing body when England was spending public money trying in vain to woo it.

England lost. Germany won, after all. Banks claimed that had we known then what we know now about FIFA, England would not have mounted its bid. We have to take his word for that. What we know now has arisen mostly because of the dramatic decision taken by Michel Zen-Ruffinen to present to FIFA's executive committee meeting of 3 May 2002 a detailed dossier about alleged wrongdoing he laid at the door of Sepp Blatter, FIFA's president and effectively his boss.

This great act of corporate theatre was revealed to the world press by a Swiss Sunday newspaper, *Die Sonntags Zeitung*, which published the document in full. It's an extraordinary read, finally giving shape to the whispers around Blatter, with whom, he said, he had fruitlessly tried to discuss his concerns. 'FIFA is flawed by general mismanagement,' it said, 'dysfunctions in the structures and financial irregularities.' He went on, using one of Blatter's warm FIFA slogans against him: 'I therefore decided to stand up for the good of the game.'

Blatter's other most favoured jingle for FIFA, 'the football family', was also blasted apart by Zen-Ruffinen, whose document exposed the family as creepily dysfunctional. He accused Blatter of running FIFA 'like a dictatorship', with a handful of chosen trusties, removing any who threaten him. The performance was carefully staged; executive committee members were handed documentary evidence and affidavits in binders, which Zen-Ruffinen claimed supported the allegations. These were grouped into four broad counts of major mismanagement and four of financial or legal irregularities, which were: 'misleading accounting practices, conflicts of interest, actions or omissions damaging FIFA, and corruption'. Zen-Ruffinen said the details, supported by the evidence in the binders, 'touches the tip of the iceberg only'.

The document seethed not only with the weight of detail, some of it dealing with its internal structures and workings, which are arcane and difficult to understand. There was also, between the formal wording and awkward English – it was written by a Swiss lawyer, after all – a raw fury, in which Zen-Ruffinen, constantly referring to himself in the initialised third person, as 'GS' – the General-Secretary – fumed about how he was sidelined, ignored, his authority undermined, by Blatter.

The heart of it constituted straightforward accusations, some of which Zen-Ruffinen stated might constitute criminal offences under the Swiss Penal Code. Regarding the finances and the relationship with ISL, Zen-Ruffinen alleged that ISL were favoured for contracts, for example that they were, with Kirch, granted the US broadcasting rights for the World Cup when another company, AIM, had offered $100m more. 'For political reasons,' the document said, 'FIFA (President) decided to accept the second best offer of Kirch/ISL.' Zen-Ruffinen alleged, as FIFA Vice-President David Will did subsequently, that FIFA has massaged its accounts by including as income, payments in advance – for not only the 2002 but the 2006 World Cup. He said that the losses from ISL's collapse were uncertain and had been under-estimated. 'The President only pretends that the ISL issues are under control. They are not: the whole ISL issue is not properly reviewed in detail and risks are not satisfactorily discussed.'

On the politics, Zen-Ruffinen alleged what many others have also done, that Blatter did irregular or even corrupt things to sweeten sufficient FIFA delegates round the world to ensure he was re-elected. Particularly serious was the allegation that he 'used and abused' FIFA's 'GOAL' project, the key football development scheme whose good work is always cited by those who defend FIFA. Zen-Ruffinen said Blatter gave out artificial contracts and jobs to his allies, and also scheduled visits to participating countries to suit his own election campaign.

The document went on to say that Blatter had handed out contracts and money to friends and relatives, including the consultants McKinsey and Co, who had become 'integral' to FIFA, invoicing roughly 12 million Swiss francs (£5.36m) between June 2000 and March 2002. Zen-Ruffinen noted that Blatter's nephew was a principal in McKinsey's Zurich office, which, while not putting that principal's integrity in question, 'makes the conduct of the President unacceptable.'

Zen-Ruffinen also alleged that Jack Warner, president of the CONCACAF football regional federation, and his family, were favoured with contracts 'contrary to the financial interests of FIFA', and that Warner was granted the TV rights for the World Cups of 1990, '94 and '98 for one dollar, although this was done before Blatter's time.

Blatter, according to Zen-Ruffinen, had always refused to disclose his own remuneration, despite 'numerous requests from the executive body to do so'.

Finally, under the broad heading 'Corruption', Zen-Ruffinen alleged that Blatter had paid a member of the executive committee back pay from July 1998 to 2000, even though he had only started in August 2000. Exclamation marks dotted this section of the document. Secondly, he alleged that Blatter paid, in front of witnesses, $25,000 to a former referee, Lucien Bouchardeau, for information which would damage one of Blatter's enemies, Farah Addo, 'mentioning that Bouchardeau would receive an additional $25,000 if the information he provided would suit the purposes of the President'. Addo, the vice-president of the African Football Confederation (CAF), had previously gone public with a claim that he was offered $100,000 to vote for Blatter in the 1998 election.

These among others, according to Zen-Ruffinen, could amount to criminal offences in Switzerland. One further point, mentioned by Zen-Ruffinen and stressed by David Will, was that when FIFA's audit committee began to investigate some of these most troubling aspects of FIFA's finances, Blatter suspended it. It is very difficult indeed to find any positive light with which to look at that act.

Blatter, for his part, mounted a persistent, adamant defence, denying all wrongdoing. He has always denied all the allegations which have surfaced in connection with his 1998 election. This time, yet again, he marshalled his bonhomie and smile at press conferences for a global media, saying the stories were merely a vicious campaign to unsettle and destablise him before the election. But five FIFA vice-presidents and six other members of the executive committee filed, on the strength of Zen-Ruffinen's allegations, a formal complaint against the FIFA President with the First Prosecutor in Zurich.

UEFA and its president, Johansson, gathered behind Blatter's election challenger, CAF president Issa Hayatou, in politicking that turns the administration of football, a simple, great game, into a snake-pit. Our own FA firmly opposed Blatter, the man with whose diary they had so recently been dancing for an opportunity to schmooze him into Downing Street.

On 29 May 2002, Blatter emerged from an eight-hour FIFA congress in Seoul with a victory whose scale crushed those who had worked so hard to remove him. Of 195 valid votes, Blatter won 139, well clear of the two-thirds majority required for victory in round one. He took the rostrum with a classic Blatterism: 'I register your deep trust, your deep trust in FIFA and in me. I have to install peace in this family here and I will do it.'

The patriarch moved swiftly: a new executive committee was installed and instantly announced that Zen-Ruffinen, 'by mutual consent', was leaving FIFA on 4 July, immediately the World Cup was over. The executive committee also announced they would seek to withdraw the Zurich Prosecutor proceedings against Blatter. But under Swiss law, the prosecutor has a duty to investigate serious charges filed with it and the investigation is currently continuing.

What this all left, in a nutshell, were allegations that the governing body running the most popular, beloved and lucrative game on earth was effectively insolvent but covering that fact up, suppressing its own audit committee's investigation; it was corrupt at the highest level, undemocratic and run like a feudal barony, doling out favours for friends, raising the drawbridge for rivals. And that, officially, it had decided not to investigate or clear up these allegations.

Then France kicked off against Senegal. The football started, dancing across the stadia of Japan and South Korea and the TVs of the globe. The world painted its face and struggled to think about anything else, certainly not the games played by dimly recognised bureaucrats in the back stairs of Zurich. When Brazil, magnificently, romantically, won the Cup, their monumental captain Cafu standing on the plinth with the trophy, who was there, hugging the players, handing out the medals alongside Pelé? Sepp Blatter. Smiling as brightly as the floodlights. Survivor supreme. Truly a suit among suits.

But if the World Cup wiped the FIFA stories from the press and the short-term memory, this does not mean they can be forgotten. Nor that FIFA can be allowed to ignore the need to provide answers and reform. Why is it important, if the game is still there, as engaging, as magical as ever? Well, football's great spectacle and its miraculous popularity, which put the board games into so dull a shadow, are the very reason why FIFA's honesty matters. It is the power of football now, its wealth, its central role as the sport of choice in a globalising world, which require that the serious allegations about its running are investigated.

It's necessary because we need to know the game is clean, but there is a more positive vision here too. Decent people would want a governing body genuinely intent on harnessing football's remarkable power as a force for good, around the world, not merely as a vehicle for multinationals' marketing budgets and a four-year licence to print money. One which would carry the game with some values, dearly held and stubbornly adhered to, which mean the sport can really benefit the nations and populations being turned on and tuned into in globe-conquering numbers.

Will it happen? Will we get answers, reform? Don't hold your breath. Expect more revelations, as journalists dig and officials sing. Expect Sepp to ride them all. And then, in 2006, expect the next World Cup to be even bigger than this last one, even higher profile, yet more dominant of the whole world's attention. Expect Blatter to be there, basking in its glory, handing out the prizes with a smile. Germany, who did, after all, win the right to host the tournament, clearly believe that's the safe bet. In Seoul, they voted for Blatter.

Note: Background to FIFA in the 1970s used with reference to *Great Balls of Fire*, by John Sugden and Alan Tomlinson (Mainstream 1999)

* * * * *

Football's Leaving Home

John Williams

At last, football goes truly global.
– *Observer*, 9 June 2002

The 2002 World Cup finals were being beamed, through the night, to the soccer-aspirant melting pot that is the modern USA. According to the *Observer*, the Café All'Angelo in New York in early June could offer only worn-out waitresses, sleepless for 28 hours, because televised World Cup games in the bar kicked off for all-comers at an unforgiving sequence of 2.30 a.m., 5.30 a.m. and 7.30 a.m., local time. Italian, Antonio Pasini, the *Gazzetta Dello Sport* correspondent in the USA and an All'Angelo patron, was having trouble staying on track: 'I have not slept since last weekend and I am living in three time zones,' he told reporters. 'Japan time for football; Italy time for deadlines; and New York time – where I think I live.' A man lifted out of his normal experience of time and space, for sure. Welcome to late-modern global football.

Fans of the USA team, predictably, were still outnumbered at such gatherings by the kind of 'hyphenated' Americans, whose footballing loyalties clearly lay elsewhere; by Portuguese-Americans, Mexican-Americans and Italian-Americans, to name but a few. Indeed, polls in the US press suggested that, even after Luis Figo and his fancied Portugal pals had sensationally lost 3–2 to the USA in Suwon, only 9 per cent of all Americans claimed to be 'very interested' in the finals and 53 per cent were 'not at all interested'. The possible boost to the stuttering professional game in America following group qualification in Korea and the gallant USA quarter-final defeat by Germany remains, of course, still to be assessed.

Elsewhere in the summer of 2002 things were very different. Up to 5 billion people worldwide were estimated to have watched the 2002 World Cup finals (compared to 3.8 billion for France 1998). FIFA suggested – fancifully, surely – that eight out of ten of the world's entire population would 'connect' at some point with the event. In England alone, a stunning 19 million people watched a 10.30 a.m. kick-off group phase meeting with, frankly, boring Sweden – including five million who watched collectively in specially opened pubs to rival even those in New York. In Dakar and Dortmund, from Kilkenny to

Kinshasa the story of street crowds gorging from large screens and packed football bars was largely the same.

The global game, then – but with the free world's school bully virtually standing on the touchline? Could be. 'Make no mistake,' wrote Jonathan Freedland in *The Guardian*, fairly frothing at the international football bonhomie on offer in the Far East in June:

> There is a global community at work here. This tournament has surely overtaken the Olympic games as the pre-eminent global sporting event, followed with passion throughout Africa and increasingly Asia too. But here's the twist. This is one form of globalisation in which America is not the driving force. The US is a bit player, albeit a competent one in the current context. No, this is one area in which Europe and Latin America lead, recruiting the world to their own obsession.

There is some hyperbole here, but it is also hard to disagree with some of the core fundamentals. Notwithstanding the convincing accusations of corruption and financial mismanagement against the re-elected FIFA President, Sepp Blatter, the recent FIFA leadership cabal has succeeded, nevertheless, in making the World Cup finals an extraordinary worldwide cultural success, and one which now comfortably supersedes, by between 50–70 per cent according to analysts' estimates, competing 'mega events', such as the Olympic Games, both in terms of its cultural reach and especially the size of its global TV audience.

The still expanding FIFA membership (210 World Cup entrants in 2002 compared, for example, to 189 members of the United Nations); FIFA's recent funding of football development initiatives in some of its smaller member countries (against the wishes of some of its stronger, more influential stalwarts); its 1998 increase in the number of World Cup finalists, from 24 countries to a near-impossible to manage 32 (against more opposition, not least from the established European leagues); and FIFA's recent siting of the finals in profoundly 'non-traditional' football locales – in 1994 in the USA and in 2002 in Japan and Korea, in order, of course, to open up new markets for the sport, its sponsors and its teeming products – have all contributed to the extraordinary recent World Cup boom.

UEFA, the largest of all the FIFA confederations, keenest sceptics of Blatter, and housing the strongest and richest clubs and national leagues in the world with 80 per cent of the football's global economic power, have been the least impressed of all of FIFA's worldwide 'family' by recent developments. Hosting the World Cup finals anywhere outside Europe – and troubled South American venues are simply not currently viable candidates to host 32 countries and the massive media circus which follows – is regarded as lost revenue from the UEFA strong-room. The early timing of the 2002 finals (to avoid the monsoons in the Far East), coupled with the growth of Champions League football, and the intensity of the top club action in Europe, also produced alleged 'tiredness' and injury crises for some of the European powers, who also felt faced with worryingly alien climatic conditions in World Cup 2002. A host of Europe's stars succumbed to body failure before or during the event. Consequently, it was argued, the challenge of the European elite in Japan and Korea crumbled into just so much exhausted sand.

The G14 European clubs are the powerful new city states in world football, of course, now demanding fewer international matches from FIFA, grimacing as their costly players move to national duty, and even seeking wages from national associations to cover for their absent stars. Significantly, the wily South Korean coach, the Dutchman Guus Hiddink, had convinced the powers that be in Seoul actually to close down the popular Korean League in March 2002, thus offering months of vital World Cup preparation for the co-hosts – and no injury worries.

As a result, his team played with a passion and togetherness during the finals matched only by Brazil and the USA and perhaps the embattled Germans. Do the very top players in Europe, these multi-millionaires at clubs whose commercial domains are now truly global, really care that much these days about national team glory in the World Cup? The post-elimination tears of some of these wealthy professionals certainly suggest that this is still more than just another tournament. Remember, too, that the victorious Brazilians – substantially European-based, unconvincing winners in 1994 and without even a goal in a World Cup final since 1970 – had also played fully 18 qualifying matches for the finals. The cash incentive for struggling national associations in South America is obviously strongly in play in this context; and it produced hours of long-haul flying time for the top Brazilian players leading up to World Cup 2002. Tiredness hardly seemed the key issue here.

If globalisation involves, as new Labour Third Way guru Anthony Giddens argues, 'the intensification of world-wide social relations which link distinct localities in such a way that local happenings are shaped by events occurring miles and miles away and vice versa', we can already see that the processes of the 'televisualisation' of sport and the 'sportification' of TV show the contemporary World Cup finals to be manifestly both a product and an example of these new global dynamics. From here, however, it becomes a little more complicated.

The arguments for reading these developments as the simple, dystopian spread of a global cultural imperialism, an homogenising and usually Americanising spread of global corporate ideologies, initially seem hard to sustain in relation to football. Europe – and especially the top football clubs of Europe – remains the symbolic and economic power base in the sport these days, and one which is currently set against FIFA's developmental policies in, say, Africa and Asia. Here, as the sociologists Alan Tomlinson and John Sugden argue, FIFA emerges as both a transnational body that promotes globalisation and an unlikely resister of imperialist domination. There is no doubt, however, that the tendency towards the increasing commodification – the buying and selling – of cultural experiences, including sport, in modern societies is accelerating. But is this, in itself, a signal for the emergence of some sort of European-driven, homogenised global culture for football?

We can come at this in a number of ways in relation to the World Cup. If, to use the language of social theorist Manuel Castells, the global 'hub' – the network centre – in this particular case study of globalising trends is Europe, and not the USA, then the signs of 'sameness' in the preparation and playing styles in international football – in the homogenising 'Europeanisation' of the sport – seem pretty clear. The commercial power and range of the top European leagues is an obvious factor here, of course. The cash-rich FA Premier League, for example, boasted representatives in all but six of the 32 World Cup squads in 2002 – though only one English-based player actually kicked off in the semi-finals. Senegal soon joined this list of 'included' nationalities as English clubs quickly flashed their cheque-books following the success of the West Africans in Japan and Korea.

One hundred and fifty countries worldwide now take TV coverage of FA Premier League football for a global audience of 1.3 billion. One hundred and forty countries take Italy's Serie A, and coverage of Spanish football on a global scale is also catching up fast. Seeing them in the flesh was a thrill, but watching the tricks of Ronaldo and Rivaldo was no novelty to football fans in Japan and Korea who tune in weekly to the European club game. Many of the top Brazilians play in Europe – mainly in Spain and Italy. It also became a famous debating point of the complex new global economies for player transfers that the Senegal team – which effectively eliminated world champions France in the competition's first match – was made up of players who all play, for reasons of finance, history and language ties, in the 'mid-range' (for Europe) French league, while all the French players – excepting the labouring and ageing Leboeuf – were based elsewhere, in the wealthier European elite leagues. A delicious, if confusing, example, then, of a French Football League squad defeating the French national team in the World Cup finals.

So this is no simple case of the mutually enriching 'global flows' of players across national boundaries, though who could doubt that the Senegalese players had brought experience and savvy to the Far East accrued, in part, from playing much of their competitive football in Europe? Who would dispute, either, that winning in the finals for the

African nations is not just about sport? Two-thirds of the Senegalese people are poor and illiterate in a country that is 171st in the world in terms of GDP. Beating the French in Seoul was experienced in Dakar – at least in part – as a symbolic payback for pre-1960s colonialism and exploitation, as well as for the inequalities and struggles of today.

But for Senegalese journalist, Mamadou Kasse, it was also about:

> Showing the world that when we work hard in Senegal we can succeed in the same way as the people of Europe. A successful football team is the expression of a confident nation, one in which there is democracy and stability and human rights.

Idealistic? Sure. But the triumphant multi-cultural French team of 1998 – including, of course, the Senegalese-born Patrick Vieira – was supposed to reflect and reinforce the new vibrancy and modernity of a successful and integrated France. By 2002, economic downturn, loss of confidence and the rising spectre of Le Pen had drained such optimism. Should we be completely surprised that the French football team flopped so badly in 2002?

You might also believe, like former PFA official Brendan Batson, that World Cup 2002 proved, conclusively, that the global movement of African players to European clubs is 'working' for the African nations and also 'bodes well for international football'. The performance of Senegal, and even of Cameroon in Japan and Korea, seems to say as much. Nigeria was more disappointing. Rather than the structures of 'dependent underdevelopment' of classic Marxist approaches defining global sporting relations, we may have here a kind of 'dependent development' at work, which offers an uneven but progressive shift in North/South sporting connections, especially to the extent that young domestic football prospects in Africa are inspired by the international successes of their heroes. But things are rather more complex even than this.

Arriving (and suitably expensive) Africans certainly add to the attractive cosmopolitanism and the glamour of European leagues – and they can also, helpfully for the elite, reduce spiralling domestic wage bills in Europe. But not all new arrivals on the big stage survive free from the effects of cultural exclusion and racism. There is also plenty of recent evidence about the unscrupulous work of agents in trafficking young Africans to top European clubs – and then simply discarding their unwanted stock. Even FIFA spoke recently about the dangers of this 'new slave trade' in young black professional players.

Nor is there perfect free trade in the new global football arena, of course, far from it. Players from outside the EU are still restricted in their travelling and playing in Europe. Players imported to England, for example, have to be internationals who have played three-quarters of their country's games in the previous two years. The players' unions in Europe are also deeply protectionist in their concerns about the arrival of cheap(er) foreign talent from outside the EU – which produces pressures on Africans and others to 'naturalise' themselves in their new countries, thus possibly losing their potentially strong representative functions back 'home'.

All this means that in the hybridised 2002 World Cup, characterised by what the writer John Lanchester dubbed as merely limp 'homeopathic nationalism', the French, Polish and German squads all contained players of African origin, and the Japanese a Brazilian, Alex. It is largely the same story, these days, of course, concerning post-national fandoms. Even in provincial Leicester, for example, it was possible for a news reporter from *The Leicester Mercury* to find and speak to locally based fans who were drawn from – and were following – almost every nation represented at the World Cup finals. Many of these interviewees, as it turned out, were also supporting their 'new' country, England. In prosperous Fulham in the South of England, a local pub offered the Turkey v China match complete with commentaries in both Turkish and Mandarin for local residents, while previously sleepy New Malden became dubbed in British news reports as 'the Seoul of Surrey' because it is home to 8,000 of Britain's 25,000 Koreans. Most of these people were depicted, of course, as being positively glued to the TV progress of the new Red Devils.

Precious few top European players today, of course, do much to reciprocate in this 'global flow' of sporting talents and cultures by travelling in the opposite direction on the football escalator, to Africa or to Asia or to South America to play, even as their own careers and salary demands wind down. Which means that footballers from developing countries are also part of the wider professional 'brain drain' to developed countries, joining doctors, teachers and engineers – and often leaving behind disintegrating domestic sports league structures which no stronger sporting nations have any real interest in helping to sustain.

In Brazil, according to Alex Bellos in his book *Futebol: The Brazilian Way of Life,* the discovery of the global market for players means the sport has become an export monoculture, breeding cheap players for sale abroad, like coffee or cotton in the days of slavery. A number of Brazilian players have recently even settled in the Faeroe Islands to escape the problems of sports business at home. Corruption rules in the domestic Brazilian game, and this commodification of the global trade of footballers abroad – and the national restraints on such flows – is also liable to encourage bending the rules in order to oil the easier passage of these valuable products across national boundaries. In Italy, where a little rule bending is not exactly unknown, non-EU player passport 'irregularities' are currently under criminal investigation.

Despite the obvious barriers involved, this uneven and largely unidirectional global movement of footballers to Europe contrasts sharply with the wider technological and economic advances made in the Pacific Rim area, and the barrage of restraints which face Africans and inappropriate 'others' in different forms of travel and trade with European and other nations. At the same time as the Asian Tiger economies have been increasingly integrated on an equal level with their OECD equivalents – including at the level of worker exchange – problems faced by asylum seekers and other non-EU migrant workers in Europe are becoming increasingly severe. These issues were filling the news pages of the northern European press throughout the summer of 2002 and continued to do so during the celebrations in the sports pages of the rather more harmonious global event that was taking place in distant Japan and South Korea. Despite the constraints placed upon them and the maltreatment they sometimes face, migrant young footballers, rather than other labourers and dissidents, still tend to have more chances than most of a real future in the 'new' Europe.

Legislation, like the recent protectionist US farm bill which offers some $180 billion worth of subsidies to domestic farmers, also means that African equivalents to the US farm lobby simply cannot compete in this trading forum. So much for a global free market. According to Oxfam's Kevin Watkins: 'If Europe had the same approach to market access in areas like agriculture and garments as it has for footballers it would go a long way to improving economic prospects for the region and the lot of ordinary people.' Yes, if only.

European football coaches, the new migrant technocrats of the world game, are certainly central to the kind of gently homogenising tendencies which are at the core of 'global football' playing cultures today. China, Japan and South Korea all imported experienced European coaches for the 2002 finals and Cameroon and Senegal each relied on white Europeans in order to help add the sort of organisation and discipline that Africans are popularly supposed to lack, to the raw speed, flair and power which narrow stereotypes suggest are rather more 'typical' African qualities.

But all of this dispensing of globalised European supposed know-how and rigour also occurs within strongly shaping localising contexts. The social theorist Anthony Smith is sceptical about the existence of a 'global culture' in sport or anything else. Instead, he argues that although national cultures are themselves constructs – 'imagined communities' – they remain obstinately 'particular, time-bound and expressive'. Constructed nationalisms are parasitic upon deeper senses of collective identity shared by people in specific locations and involving 'feelings and values in respect of a sense of continuity, shared memories, and a sense of common destiny'. The South Korean coach, Guus Hiddink, for example, knew very well about the nature of the deep 'ethno-identity' of the South Koreans – the subjective core upon which the construction of modern national identity builds and elaborates. He described early on in his new job in Seoul the selfless devotion to the team ethic, the power of 'shame culture' and the pain of loss of public face in a country such as South Korea, which meant that his footballers played with both real passion and togetherness – and extreme caution: they were too afraid to make errors, to gamble to win.

It was Hiddink and his staff who injected more controlled risk-taking into the coaching of the squad, but without compromising on the excellent South Korean fitness, teamwork, technique and enthusiasm. This intense preparation and the local/global mix of influences involved – what the media analyst John Tomlinson calls the effects of processes of 'cultural disembedding' – eventually helped the Red Devils outstay the Portuguese, the Italians and the Spaniards in World Cup 2002. The studied 'simulations' – diving – now common in European and South American football culture, had also not yet colonised the Koreans, who were favoured instead in 2002 by incompetent and inexperienced officiating. Perhaps, as some commentators argued, rather than mere incompetence it was simply that these erring referees and their assistants now just assumed that the game's more 'advanced' nations would probably try to cheat, and at every possible juncture?

Hiddink later promised his team would approach the semi-final match with Germany, 'like a bunch of young dogs', a description which pressed the Korean Minister of Commerce, Shin Kook-hwan, to call for Samsung, Daewoo and other flagging companies in Korea to, 'adopt the Hiddink style' and go out in a more determined and inventive fashion to get more foreign investment. Increasingly in these global times, the language and techniques of sport – and the heroic imagery it promotes – seem eminently transferable to the realm of commerce and marketing.

In these and in other senses, global capitalism is not exactly innocent in the shaping of a global sports culture, even if such a culture has pronounced and telling local inflections. Nor, despite the European domination of football at the moment, was the influence of corporate USA entirely absent from the 2002 World Cup finals, far from it. Some theorists of globalisation in sport – notably the British academic Joseph Maguire in his book *Global Sport* – seem to favour a relatively benign model of competing 'isations' in the modern global sports arena. This approach envisages a neo-evolutionist model of the regionalisation of sport into integrated circuits of influences of Africanisation, Americanisation, Europeanisation, Orientalisation and Hispanicisation, which produce particular styles, images and local meanings. This is a world, in fact, of near universal, and increasingly complex, sporting hybridity. But it is also one that seems to lack anything approaching a sophisticated or convincing political economy of professional sports development in the age of dominant transnational sports sponsorship and the ambitions of the new global media giants of satellite TV.

More convincing is the recent work of Toby Miller and his Australian sports sociology colleagues from the universities of Queensland and Newcastle, who argue instead in their recent book *Globalisation and Sport* for the more central influence of other 'isations' in reconfiguring international sport: corporatisation, commercialisation, rationalisation and, of course, globalisation. In the global age, culture is produced and sold to an international market in a way that renders the nation-state of decreasing direct relevance. This is in part because of sport's ambiguous place in the para-state, para-corporate societies of the global era, but it is also because of the capacity of satellite and cable TV viewers throughout the world to receive, watch – and interpret – a wide variety of sports programming that would otherwise be unavailable locally.

Again, this is not simply a picture of a dominant global sports culture flowing in a single direction to uncritical sports consumers. It is one, instead, in which sporting tastes, attitudes and values are regularly destabilised and reconfigured as key media interests, and corporate actors remake relationships through sport at local, national and global levels. These multiple 'imagined worlds' of sporting engagement are often shaped, too, by a 'repatriation of difference' in terms of the specific local meanings which emerge out of sporting events in specific locales, and out of the sports goods sold and the sporting signs and symbols which are used and consumed in local contexts.

In this regard, the writer Mike Marqusee noted during the 2002 World Cup finals the ways that international sport typically was formally utilised in the era of modernity as a means of promoting national identities, and also international harmony among nations. But in the era of globalisation – when the commercial value and cultural presence of sport has become ever more hyper-inflated – the old sporting mission has now been cast in a new light. Global TV sport has now become a TV spectacular of competing national identities, which is often underwritten by multi-national corporations. Marqusee wrote:

> When Yahoo! joined FIFA's exclusive club of 'official partners' it was hailed as a natural one – because both football and the Internet cross national boundaries with ease. But the same companies that solemnly preach the virtues of a borderless global market have been investing substantial sums in egging on a wide variety of national standard-bearers.

After September 11, domestic US sports events, for example, became soaked in patriotic symbolism, with sponsors quite happy to pump up the patriotic volume when it suited them in order to make good their investment. In such cases, sports sponsorship crosses national borders, but it also exploits them. In the global era, as Marqusee pointed out, sports patriotism itself is also less tribalistic, less rooted, and is more malleable and hollow. It is more amenable to clever marketing – and it can also more easily be turned against enemies within and without.

The Japanese, especially, seemed keen to be ironic and 'playful' in their approach to national identity during the World Cup finals. As the journalist Richard Williams put it, whereas the Koreans were friendly, if regimented, and supported their own team with a 'visceral passion', the Japanese were usually more reserved and more concerned about hooliganism and responded, especially to England and Brazil, with 'the kind of innocent and slightly synthetic enthusiasm that they might have once reserved for the simultaneous arrival of the Beatles and the Rolling Stones'.

Just before the 2002 finals, the appalling Laureus Sports Awards in Monte Carlo – which 'starred' Vinnie, as well as Catherine Zeta Jones – displayed the powerful new nexus of blue chip sponsors, show business 'stars', sports celebrities and global television. The media-orchestrated celebrity industry which now also promotes the David Beckham and Michael Owen 'brands' in the Far East and elsewhere, when added to the TV promotion abroad of the English game and the traditionally uneasy outsider status of England fans during World Cups, were together, probably behind the determination of so many young Japanese apparently to appropriate 'English' identities during the finals. The costs and distance involved in travel, and the cultural closure offered by the Far East, also meant that this was largely a football tourists' World Cup; it was one which was unlikely ever to be destabilised by real European hooliganism.

This sort of ersatz cross-border national 'fandom' of the Japanese – which fits well, incidentally, with the FA's professed new determination to make England not the object of the globe's fiercest hooligans but, instead, 'everybody's second favourite team' – is also likely to be irksome, of course, to some committed supporters. It might be expected, nevertheless, to figure increasingly at TV global sports spectaculars of the future, in which the performance and size of crowds – and here FIFA was widely caned by the media for failing to fill expensive, empty seats, especially in Korea – becomes a more legitimate focus for public interest and consumption.

It was actually nice, nevertheless, for the English to be generally liked in Japan, and commentators in England argued that this reflected back to domestic shores a rather different, and possibly more inclusive, way of 'doing' Englishness during the finals. This new direction drew upon novel dimensions of the resources of gender – women's stores were full of 'football' and 'Japan' clothing, and the influence and popularity of the androgynous David Beckham was everywhere – but especially on new idioms about 'race'. In *New Nation*, a paper aimed largely at the black British market, for example, it was widely noted that, for the first time, more readers favoured supporting England in the World Cup than either Nigeria or Brazil.

But it was not all playful pastiche and globalised identity blending and blurring during the finals. Despite one prominent English commentator, Mark Lawson, describing the 2002 World Cup as, 'the most good-natured and least nationalistic ever staged', examples of the intrusion of 'real' politics, and associated demonstrations of more intense national patriotisms, were not entirely absent. Both Brazil and Argentina, for example, competed in 2002 against the background of rapidly disintegrating domestic economies. The Argentinean writer Alfredo Disalvo argued that Eduardo Duhalde, the fifth Argentinean president since the street riots in that country of December 2001, hoped for 'two months of oxygen' from the performance of the national team in June: 'One month if the team does well and another of euphoria if they actually win.'

Protesters at the G8 summit in Calgary in June 2002 turned up in large head masks depicting the errant leaders – and in appropriate football kit. In Japan, favoured right-wing Tokyo governor Shintaro Ishihara wanted a first phase Japan victory over Russia because he thought it might help the country regain the four Kuril islands still under historical territorial dispute with its Eastern bloc adversary. Meanwhile, in South Korea troops blared the commentaries of World Cup matches across the demilitarised zone, according to Major Yoon Won-shik, 'as part of our psychological warfare against the North'.

But the real battles for hearts and minds at the tournament, as Mike Marqusee suggests, were going on among the new post-national global elites, the competition's sponsors. While in Scotland the brewers Tennents gamely and provocatively produced their 'lager' flags in the supportive colours of England's World Cup group opponents – 'C'mon the Tartan Argie', and memorably for the England meeting with Nigeria, 'Och Aye Kanu' – elsewhere the stakes were rather higher. The involvement of Yahoo! for the first time, as one of the 15 global brands sponsoring the finals – FIFA insisted on complete control of all signage at the World Cup this time in order to maximise unpolluted global media coverage for its 'family' of major brands – was confirmation that this was the first real Internet World Cup. Although Europe's biggest Internet sports site www.sports.com tellingly went into administration on the very day the finals began, the official FIFA website, designed and run by Yahoo!, reported 500 million hits in the first week of June alone.

Supporters at the finals also shaped their own tournament sites and used the Internet extensively for information about venues, tickets and to send fan updates home from Japan and Korea. Discussing the outcome of games and getting information on the Internet about matches and ticket availability certainly proved rather easier, however, than actually purchasing tickets for the finals. Excessive concerns about security – each ticket was individually stamped with the details of the purchaser – were blamed for perhaps the biggest technical failure of the entire event, a damaging blockage in the Internet ticketing and selling systems. Blocks of seats, even at some prestige matches, remained embarrassingly unsold.

Bookmakers, it turned out, were rather happier than many fans: they were perhaps the real 2002 World Cup Internet winners. A global betting market involving, for the first time in earnest, punters from China, Japan, Korea and the USA swelled legal Internet betting across the world. In Britain – with spread bets on the number of injuries, fouls and corners, as well as on match results – over £200 million was wagered. Estimates, including illegal bets, put the total global spend at over £2 billion. Here, it seemed, was a truly lucrative borderless and timeless world to satisfy any globaliser. According to the excited Christopher Bell, chief executive of Ladbrokes: 'This is the first World Cup where the Internet plays a part. It makes the event time zoneless. You can bet in any language, any currency.' And on anything. The odds on David Beckham wearing two hairstyles during the World Cup? A cool 4–7, and the great man did eventually fly out his own hairdresser. There were, sadly, few takers.

An estimated £300 million was shelled out by official sponsors in support of World Cup 2002. A further £560 million came in from the sale of TV rights. The usual exploitative global division of labour for World Cup sports goods was highlighted by the Global March Against Child Labour in May when they discovered children in Pakistan on wages of 14p to 28p per ball, churning out footballs which 'had the appearance of officially licensed merchandise'. FIFA blamed sub-contracting for masking illegal child labour practices. The vivid presence of many of the usual global event transnational corporation sponsors in Japan and Korea also implied that the 'McWorld of homogenising globalisation', in Roland Robertson's phrase, was strongly in attendance in these particular media sign wars. Multiple images of David Seaman's fatal goalkeeping misjudgement for England against Brazil in Shizuoka, for example, were framed for the world's press and TV, by the grindingly familiar yellow-and-red boards, behind, of burger giants McDonald's. The latter, incongruously, now also have their very own UK 'Head of Football', the former England World Cup hero Sir Geoff Hurst. With even the current England international novice Joe Cole already establishing three companies to deal with his own nascent promotional activities, we are increasingly tempted to ask: where exactly does the sport stop and the product development and placement begin?

But more 'local' companies also did serious World Cup spending: Korea's own global giant Samsung was estimated to have spent £140 million on finals-related advertising for mobile phones, DVDs and computers. LG, the Korean-based electronics group, reported booming World Cup TV sales, while 60 companies in the UK alone were reported to have had World Cup advertising campaigns.

On the pitch, there were commercial failures as well as successes. Renault acquired big name Thierry Henry for a major European TV campaign, but the Arsenal man soon departed the world's stage, his reputation – and Renault's pride – severely dented. 7-Up's key figure, the irascible Roy Keane, never even made the main event, a costly marketing mistake. But these are small beer, merely transient, regional icons compared to the commercial longevity and the global reach of the great Brazilian Pelé, now a 61-year old grandfather and, so far, paid some £14 million for 11 years World Cup-related promotional work for the US-based financial powerhouse Mastercard. Even today's football multi-millionaires might get out of bed for these kinds of sums.

With 17 'strategic markets' across the globe, 76 per cent of which have football as their major sport, Mastercard are very clear about the extent to which the World Cup itself, and the image of Pelé on two million credit cards, offers guaranteed global market penetration. The man also works a punitive transcontinental schedule for his cash: he made some 150 jet-lagged appearances worldwide for Mastercard in just the 12 months preceding the 2002 finals. John Stuart, Senior VP for global sponsorship at Mastercard, said of the Brazilian:

> He is a unique individual who transcends borders as well as the affinities people have for their local teams. You buy the World Cup for the global reach that it gives us. It doesn't matter that it is in Tokyo, because you know Latin America will watch.

It doesn't matter either that no World Cup matches were actually scheduled for Tokyo in 2002: you sort of know what the Senior VP means. That most young consumers today are more likely to associate the world's greatest ever footballer first with borderless plastic cash, than with his heart-stopping step-over against Uruguay in the 'Brazil' finals of 1970 in Mexico. Business, after all, is business.

Meanwhile, sports equipment manufacturer and long-time FIFA commercial partner Adidas collared sponsorship of ten of the competing countries in the 2002 finals, while Puma practised some neat horizontal integration by transferring the styling and colours of its banned, sleeveless Cameroon football kit to US tennis star Serena Williams at the French Open, with major publicity effect. Umbro, meanwhile, chose its own, very different, marketing niche by combining football exclusivity with masculine closure – and a side-swipe at more consciously 'gender sensitive' rivals such as both Puma and Nike: 'Your sister definitely hasn't got a dress with this logo on . . .' boasted one World Cup Umbro advert. As BAT, the cigarette manufacturers, nudged commercial lawyers in Britain into threatened action by launching guerrilla ads in Malaysia featuring top English players, advertising industry 'insiders' in the UK bemoaned the lack of real imagination and brio in the major World Cup campaigns. Nike effectively reran a less inventive version of its 1996 TV 'Good v Evil' pastiche under veteran ringmaster Eric Cantona, while Adidas offered a tiresome spoof about famous football stars contracting 'footballitis' and being studied by painfully nerdish boffins. Each of these giants traded hard, of course, on being able to exhibit a global TV roster of playing talent. The ubiquitous David Beckham, meanwhile, played around with, wait for it, sumo wrestlers, for Pepsi. In fact, it seemed widely agreed by advertising analysts in 2002 that Ikea's ironic and mildly subversive billboard poster from way back in 1994, featuring the later banished Maradona triumphantly holding up a svelte Swedish lamp rather than the World Cup, and promising that the Ikea sale of that year was certain to be 'the biggest event of this summer', seemed like pure genius in comparison with the very best from 2002.

Of course, for all their global effects and associations, sporting mega events also happen in specific places at specific moments and have specific local consequences. According to Maurice Roche, an academic writer, mega sporting events can promote the localisation of international and global events, by promulgating the sense of the world as a knowable spatial planet of event-identifiable cities and by identifying host cities as unique places, which are transformed from 'mundane' places into special host city sites. Osaka and Kobe, Busan and Suwon, for example, entered – if perhaps only briefly – into the international consciousness in the summer of 2002 as 'special' places, as did, of course, the extraordinary new sports stadia in Japan and Korea.

Drawing on Japanese and Korean history and cultural icons, 'They look like swans, moons, eyes – anything but football stadia,' said British architecture critic, Jonathan Glancey, approvingly. Jeonju's 42,000 seater will be popular, he argued, because, 'sited on a pretty island off the south coast, it is near to the beach'. The battle-helmet-shaped Miyagi stadium, carefully landscaped into a hill, offered a design 'with many centres', according to its architect Hitoshi Abe. 'It offers a gentle sense of enclosure.' The Sapporo Dome looked, from the air, for all the world, like a gigantic high-tech computer mouse, with its gently curving roof and nearby retractable pitch.

Maurice Roche also points out that mega events often reanimate the importance of 'embodiment and place', especially in relation to 'being there' – to sharing the live experience of an event with other fans. The 'being there' quotient was certainly very high in the exotic locations of World Cup 2002, but some European fans might also have preferred something rather more intense – more 'traditional' – in terms of a stronger sense of enclosure, active participation and simple proximity to the pitch in some arenas – and also a slightly more appropriate stadium context. The new venue at Saitama, an hour from Tokyo, was described in one press account, perhaps unkindly, as sitting 'like a newly landed UFO in an empty area of paddy fields and vegetable patches'.

And this is also the enduring local problem. A total capital spend by Japan and South Korea on 20 stadia and on infrastructure of an estimated $7.5 billion, but no long-term prospects of a reasonable return on this investment, because stadia were purpose-built, but in relative isolation, without local users or clusters of leisure, hotel or retail facilities to encourage long-term profitability. Furthermore, 83 municipalities in Japan and more than a dozen in South Korea also invested in training facilities to try to attract teams to establish World Cup training camps, thus boosting local economies and identities. According to press reports, some countries were asking to be paid up to £1 million for locating at a desired training base; Brazil, the eventual winners, were reportedly asking for – and probably got– £3 million.

In these crazy market conditions, profit estimates for the finals also seemed to be wildly unrealistic. The governments of Japan and Korea had apparently predicted 800,000 visitors to the finals, each spending £1,200. This works out at some 25,000 for each visiting country – way out of line, of course. Nevertheless, the South Korean Development Institute (SKDI) estimated some $8.8 billion (£5.9 billion) direct and indirect financial benefit from hosting the finals – equal to 2.2 per cent of that country's GDP – and the expected creation of 350,000 jobs, as a powerful response to the negative effects of the 1997 financial crisis. *The Financial Times* reported that South Korea's Ministry of Commerce had invited 50 'business leaders' to the World Cup opening ceremony. 'They might have intentions other than watching the World Cup,' said the Director-General for international trade Jung Joon-suuk, mysteriously. The bullish Roh Kee-sung of the SKDI commented: 'This event has a tremendous media value, so the intangible effect will be far larger. It will increase Korea's public image; Korea will get global recognition and that will be very helpful for business and marketing in the future.' He has hopes. We shall see.

In June 2002 there were actually very many different 2002 World

Cup finals. They may have accentuated processes of football global flows from the weak to the powerful, but they also tweaked the noses of the elite. They were simultaneously both local and global; they took place in unique locations in Japan and Korea and also in many English school assembly halls, in my local pub and in thousands like it around Europe and elsewhere. They 'happened' in the streets of Istanbul, as surely as they did in Lagos homes, in the squares of Rio and in the bars and markets of Madrid. They were both an embodied and a highly mediated experience, and also a sign-driven commercial proposition riding on an international sporting celebration. They trashed the international football past and also reasserted aspects of its older roots and traditions, subverting as well as confirming the established order. And, finally, as Mike Marqusee points out, quoting the words of the Uruguayan football writer, Eduardo Galeano, in the end even these hugely choreographed events of capital and national interests also continue to throw up an aesthetic and a vital sporting uncertainty. The lowly are always likely, on their day, to bring down the high and mighty because: 'The more the technocrats programme it down to the smallest detail, the more the powerful manipulate it, soccer continues to be the art of the unpredictable.' Amen, at least, to that.

DO TRY THIS AT HOME: WAKING UP TO KOREA AND JAPAN 2002

7. All Laid Out with Football for Breakfast

Pete Davies

The best World Cup is the one that you go to. If you've been to more than one, you are (please select any or all of the following) admirably determined / absurdly profligate / one of the Lord's chosen people / a journalist. For the rest of us, it's a once-in-a-lifetime excursion, and every other tournament has to come our way through the telly. For me, therefore, the best World Cup was Italia '90. I saw a dozen games in six different cities in 27 days, I wrote *All Played Out*, and if I'd had the foresight to slap a copyright on the phrase 'Planet Football', I'd have been made for life.

So I have a hefty bias towards that Italian festival – but it seemed to me then and still seems now to have been a defining competition. England's intensely dramatic progress through it, culminating with Gascoigne's tears in Turin, was a watershed story that changed the nature of our game forever, in more ways than we could possibly have guessed at the time. For many fans over thirty years old, Turin was an unforgettable, life-enhancing event – a moment when English football, after all its woes and travails, rediscovered self-respect.

In the 1970s, we weren't at the party. In Spain in '82, we fizzled limply out of that cackhandedly cumbersome second group phase because we couldn't score against the hosts – and what sort of a way to go home is 0–0? That was the game when Ron Greenwood sent out Keegan and Brooking in the dying stages, neither of them fit, and they failed to break the deadlock. It was a game only memorable to me now because, on the living-room floor in front of the screen as our hopes faded out, I made love for the last time to a girlfriend who was leaving me. It was apposite, perhaps, to finish a relationship and a World Cup at the same time – but both were duds anyway.

Then we went to Mexico and got famously robbed. That was a better story by far, albeit a brutally unjust one, but '86 was all about Maradona – it wasn't about us, not the way Italy was.

Italy was electric. It didn't matter that much of the football was crude and cynical. What mattered was the context of the place, that sense of an entire nation ground to a halt, glued to the competition in an otherworldly fever. What mattered for those four weeks was the game, the whole game, and only the game. It was an operatic epic, with a ripe and vivid cast of heroes and villains – so if I say there'll not be another one like it, it's not just because I was there. It's because there hasn't been, and there won't be, and the 2002 World Cup in Japan and South Korea only proves it.

After Italy, FIFA's marketing imperatives have come to dominate the thing completely. First they went to America – and a very good tournament it looked to be as well. It just wasn't at home any more. It was showing off, like a hyperactive kid trying to grab the attention of a bunch of people who aren't really interested. Then France, and the gargantuan obesity of 32 teams. It's too much. I go wall-eyed thinking about it, never mind watching it. The first ten days I was in Louisiana anyway, and finding a channel that was showing the thing at all wasn't easy. At least I got home in time for the Argentina game – another classic, another robbery – but I'd missed the build-up, and then I had to go to Hong Kong. I watched the semi-finals jet-lagged, in the small hours, in an Asian hotel room. It was hardly ideal – so I don't know if France was a good World Cup or not. Work and travel left me out of synch with it, dislocated, unable to get involved – which, as it turns out, was a pretty apt preparation for the game's own journey to Asia.

So how was it for you? How did you get on with this unwieldy but intriguing merger of Japan and Korea? In a nutshell, what word or phrase might we agree to settle on to define our impression here at home of 'Japorea '02'? I don't mean our impression of the football, which was largely unremarkable, if sporadically dramatic. I mean our feelings in general about this New Millennium World Cup. What was it like? Nice? Polite? Curiously cerebral? Sober? Very far away? Semi-detached, or just detached altogether? So detached, in fact, and so entirely at the wrong time of day, that it was a bit hard to get worked up about it at all?

At least the flags of St George were a help. I took to counting them any time I drove someplace to see how many more had sprouted. Every shop, every business, every car, every home, every bedroom window that wore one – you knew there was a stranger there sharing the same hopes that you had. It was sweet. The flags carried with them from out of nowhere an unaccustomed sense that supporting England this time was non-confrontational, communal, just plain celebratory – and how radical a change was that?

A short while before the tournament, a friend of a friend had a night out in Burnley. By chance, her jacket was white with a red cross on it. The associations of our national emblem in that particular town, with its unhappy recent electoral history, were so uncomfortable and the looks she drew so forbidding, that early in the evening she took the jacket off and stowed it. Yet just a few weeks later, football – itself for so long associated with the worst nationalist and racist excess – suddenly converted that emblem into something that English people of all creeds and colours could drape about themselves and their streets, without shame. It felt like the team, at last, belonged to all of us. It felt like being a normal country. It felt like we wouldn't smash things up if we lost. Maybe it felt as well, once we beat Argentina, as if anything else was a bonus – and after we lost to Brazil, I read in *The Guardian* about a bloke stumbling red-eyed out of a pub in London. He said he just wanted to find a Brazilian, so he could shake his hand and tell him well done. He said if he could do that, it'd make him feel better – and that seemed to me to sum it all up. This World Cup, for once, we were decent people. It was a strange feeling, and a good one too. But this lack of intensity, this bizarre pleasantness about the whole thing – where did it spring from?

Was it Sven? The weird experience of being led by a calm, rational foreigner rather than some home-grown, media-frazzled, over-excitable, language-mangling chump with a dodgy haircut – did that chill us out? I'd like to think that was part of it. I'd like to think if we've learned one thing, it's that football matches are not, after all, reruns of past wars. Or was it Becks? The weird experience of being led by a mildly spoken male model rather than some clench-fisted, vein-bursting yeoman – did that nudge us towards realising that we didn't, after all, have to get quite so passionately deranged over a sporting event? Consider the difference between Stuart 'Psycho' Pearce's celebration of his penalty against the Spanish at Euro '96, and Becks' sprint to the corner flag after he scored from the spot against Argentina. In both cases, the sense of vindication and absolution must have been extreme – but Psycho, bless him, punching the air with roaring gob and wild eyes, was the very essence of Battling Yeoman. Becks, by contrast, was an 'Ode To Joy' in an England shirt – and the costly coiffure somehow diminished the manic aspect of the moment, did it not? You cannot, after all, be a yeoman when you're a style icon and you call your sons Brooklyn and Romeo. With Becks, you don't just get inch-perfect crosses and magic curlers past the wall – you get a fashion-mag sheen of insouciance as well. I know some people don't care for this, so let's be clear that I'm not belittling the man's talent or attitude for a minute. Against Greece, after all, he dragged us to qualification pretty much single-handed. I'm just saying instead that Celebrity Football, by its very nature, doesn't froth at the mouth.

At World Cup 2002, therefore, our whole image was changed – not least because we know that image rights in the modern game are part of the contract. This odd sense that the current England football team has been transformed into a kind of collective New Man. The well-mannered boy Owen, Danny Mills actually behaving himself, the dashing Ashley, the manly tears of Big Dave – I'm sure this must have helped us all calm down. Still, I don't think anything calmed us down as much as the plain fact that we had to watch the thing at breakfast time. Sure, you can have your guts in a knot all week ahead of the Brazil game – but the last six or eight hours before it actually kicks off, you're asleep. And unless you've got a serious problem, you can't get worked up when you're unconscious. So then you go into the big game with a cup of tea and the sleepy dust still in your eyes, and let's face it – it's not much of a build-up, is it?

For the Nigeria game, my mate Sarah was eating her cornflakes on the sofa in her dressing gown and her lucky jester's cap with the tinkly bells on. She believes England tend to win when she remembers that cap. Then her partner came in and he asked her, 'What do you look like?' She thought, 'right . . . who watches football at half past seven in the morning?'. So she took the cap off, and then the game was a humid, heat-addled dud. She should have known better, shouldn't she? Where Sarah works they cut deals to put in extra time on other days, so come the England games they'd be free to watch. For the Brazil game, her cousin Zena picked her up at five past seven and they drove to The Royal in Kirkburton. She kept the lucky cap on this time but her head inside it wasn't feeling too great, because she'd had a few the night before. So there she was, staring at a flat half of lager and a bacon sandwich thinking, 'this is not what I want at this hour of the day'. Her mate told her she had to have a lager if she was watching England, didn't she? She demurred. She went onto Cokes, and everyone else got bladdered – and that's why she skinned them all at cards after the match fizzled out and the boys were done crying. So at least the cap brought her a little bit of luck.

Myself, for the Brazil game I made a really big effort. It was my first big effort of the tournament, in fact. I got smoked salmon, and whipped up a fresh dill and mustard mayo. I got apple-glazed ham, and some tasty Dutch breakfast cheese with one of those names that sounds like you're gargling molasses. I got crusty rolls warming in the oven, and sunblushed tomatoes to garnish. I got fresh orange juice and steaming coffee, and I set a modest half-bottle of champagne to chill in the fridge for the 'Great Moment When We Won'. I actually find the idea of drinking at breakfast time pretty ghastly, but hey – World Cup quarter-final, Brazil, Saint Sven at the tiller, for that I can make an exception. I really believed we could win, too. So the four of us hunkered down – me, my wife Rebecca, and our two kids aged twelve and nine. We had the proper telly on BBC in the living room with the breakfast, and in the dining room the portable was on ITV to keep me posted when I made forays to the kitchen. And I *wanted* to be excited, I really did.

But I wasn't. The kids were trying to watch, but they had to get their school stuff together as well. Rebecca and Joe had to leave at half-time, to catch the second half on the big screen in the assembly hall at school, because she works there and he had to be ready for class when it was over. So Brazil equalised just before they went, and I could feel yet another tournament going phut on us all over again, and it just made it hard to get excited. Second half, there was only me and Meg, our youngest. Ronaldinho mugged Seaman, England played like the heat had boiled their brains, half of me was watching the game wither away, and the other half was getting Meg's lunchbox ready. On two screens in two rooms the World Cup – for us – died out with a faint whimper. It wasn't a proper English ending, all blood and thunder, was it? It was just an exhausted fade to black. I sent Meg out the door to school, put the champagne away for another day, then watched the Beeb play their summary medley with the Oasis soundtrack. I felt sad, of course, because you have to look at it and wonder if we'll ever win anything anywhere, but I can't say I was cut raw the way I was in Turin. Then the phone rang. It was an American friend in Miami. He'd got up at half past two in the morning to watch England–Brazil, and he was calling to console me. The funny thing was, I got the impression after a while that he cared more than I did.

Like pretty much everything to do with the whole event, it really wasn't normal. England are supposed to be heroic failures, not modest successes. We're supposed to provide Big Games With Screaming Injustices And Terrible Endings. We're supposed to be admired for our courage on the pitch, and loathed for our disgraces off it – but this time, what were we? Not much, really. Just another Quite Good Football Team among 31 others, doing more or less OK, then coming home. End of story. A nice, polite, faraway story. Perhaps it was the first World Cup in history that we could sum up by saying it was, all right.

The word Amy Raphael settled on in *The Observer* to define it was 'illogical'. This is Spockish but perversely apt. Japorea '02 was actually the logical conclusion to the journey football's made since the early '90s. Seen from afar it looked polished, airbrushed, altogether cute and harmless. It was Theme Park Football, a glossy vehicle for gobsmackingly vast amounts of promotional blather in which the game itself got reduced to a cheesy kinship with Hollywood – never mind the sport, spot the product placement. In this environment, the crowd aren't fans any more. They're extras – except the producer takes their money, instead of the other way around. Now I'm sure if you were there it wasn't like that at all – I'm sure if you were there you had a wonderful time, and good luck to you – but that's what it looked like on TV. On TV, it just looked like FIFA tilting for new markets, the same way they did in the States eight years ago. This is the logic of where they've been going all these years – getting into bed with their fat-wallet sponsors, bloating the competition up to 32 teams, nuzzling up to nations with less tradition of playing football than the planet Mars, making the whole shiny thing just another arm of the global entertainment industry. Shiny on the outside, anyhow. But inside, corrupt to the core, riding the global airwaves on ripe thermals of cooked votes and fishy deals. Which is logical enough to them, maybe – but it's illogical to me. It's not the game that won my heart when I was young. It's not the game that consumed a nation, and a world, the way it did in Italy. It's not got the passion in the bone any more.There are too many ads in the way.

From the money churn of the Champions League to a World Cup in Asia, that's New Football – and I've got nothing particularly against it, either. Sending the game off to these new frontiers is fine and dandy, and why not? Besides, trying to stop what's happened, trying to turn back the clock – you could no more do it than Canute could halt the tide. All I'm saying is, it's just not the game I grew up with. I'll readily admit that in many ways, you could actually say it's a better game. The stadiums aren't crumbling urinals any more, it's safe to take my kids to them, and assorted rule changes have definitely speeded the thing up – but it doesn't have that old edge any more. It's not visceral. It's a circus, with executive boxes and sponsors' logos all over the interview zone. Still, I'm not mourning for my lost youth when I used to stand in the Shed at Stamford Bridge. The Shed was grotty and it was full of nutters – but at least you could jump up and down and shout in it. Whereas if you jump up and down and shout at New Football, you get thrown out in case some rich bloke in a suit chokes on his canapés. And fair enough, I don't mind sitting down, watching the game pass along in this mannerly comfort. It's just harder to care about it.

By now, some of you will doubtless be wondering if I got out the wrong side of bed this morning. Can't I just enjoy it? I did enjoy it. In our house, we definitely bust the odd spring in the sofa as we hung on for those last 15 minutes against Argentina. England aside, Senegal were nifty, the Roy Keane-less Irish were wonderful, and the French were satisfactorily invisible. It was a good laugh watching more and more people find out that it's impossible to score against South Korea at home no matter how many times you put the ball in the net. The Mexicans were Janus-faced, scaring the Italians to death, then losing the plot in hilarious fashion against the Americans. Did you count how many of them tried to foul Cobi Jones? When he'd only been on the pitch for ten seconds? The Americans themselves were disarmingly good (in parts) and seemed almost without exception to be peculiarly small, which was another reason for supporting them – although the best thing about the Americans, of course, is when you look at the FIFA world rankings. Where do they stand now? About 13th? This is, almost certainly, the only time when you can look at those three letters U, S, A, and think with a brief flare of delirium that they're just another country like the rest of us.

My mate Sarah liked the Italians, of course. It's always fine entertainment watching them fall prey to their dark neuroses and, as ever, they definitely had the best shirts. Figure-hugging, Sarah sagely notes – and while we're on the shirt issue, she goes on to wonder if the shirt-tugging bane could not be eliminated by the simple expedient of dressing all the players in Lycra – so when you grab your opponent's apparel, he slips from your grasp like a bar of soap!

Next along at the bar, Mike chips in with the questionable contention that in American football, they wear shirts pre-designed to disintegrate when you grab them. Thus, when grabbed, the victim is free in one bound, while the offending grabber is left clutching a swatch of fabric in flagrante delicto. Sarah and I have no idea whether this is true or not. It does lead her to suggest, however, that never mind shirts – it would be a tremendously good idea if the Italians were to wear shorts made of such readily fissile material.

Which is the kind of thing we talk about these days, when the subject of New Football comes around at the bar – and it wasn't like this at Italia '90, I'll tell you. Back then you talked about whether you could get to the stadium without the riot police and/or the yobs giving you a clout along the way. Back then you talked about 4–4–2 and the sweeper system, and the madness of King Maradona. That was proper football, eh? When no one made crazy money, and no one had image rights, and you could still tackle people from behind. Whereas New Football – it's cleaner, it's quicker, it's sanitised, it takes place in all kinds of peculiar countries, and it's fun. On balance, I view this is an advance. It's not life and death any more – but you know what? It never should have been.

So the difference between Italy and now is that, in Italy, you could never have said it was only a game – and now you can. This leads you to watch it with a disembodied rationalism – and in my case, it led to me supporting the Germans in the final. I know that for many people this is still unpardonable heresy, and psychologically quite impossible. But hey, guys, the war ended 57 years ago, you know? Whereas with Brazil, I'm sorry, but all that tosh about beach footy romance masks some serious issues. As Alex Bellos noted in *The Guardian*, the Brazilian parliament held investigations into the state of their game after that humbling collapse against France in the '98 final. They found that squillions of Nike's sponsorship dosh had mysteriously disappeared, and they recommended prosecuting over 30 people. Bellos went on to say that Ricardo Texeira, president of the Brazilian Football Confederation, was 'accused of 13 crimes, including tax evasion, withholding information, giving misleading information, lying on his tax return and using CBF money for his private needs'.

So has Texeira resigned? Not a bit of it. On the contrary, he fancies taking over Sepp Blatter's job as the next boss of FIFA. Now I suppose, the way things are at the minute, you could probably say he's the perfect man for the job – but anyhow, that's why I supported the Germans.

Seeing as Sarah couldn't bring herself to do that, maybe I should have borrowed her lucky hat. But I didn't, and we know how it turned out – and it doesn't really matter anyway. FIFA don't care what you or I think, and they'll go on doing what they do regardless. I mean, this has to be the only organisation in the world so dodgy that the bloke who campaigns for election on a clean-up ticket comes from Cameroon. And how illogical is that?

* * * * *

An Other and Another World Cup

Andrew Blake

Whether watching in stadia, at the local pub, or even from the privacy of our own front rooms, we all watch football as in some way partisan, acting out and buying into football identities and usually national, ethnic and gender identities as well. We can choose who we are through choosing a team to support. But because of our increasing exposure to football from all over the world, the allocation, consumption and performance of these identities are not obviously and directly connected to nationality any more. With each World Cup the boundaries of nation and identity seem weaker, and this is as true of television coverage as of any other aspect of the game. Consuming the 2002 World Cup in the UK could (and often did) involve a reinforcing of a particular national identity: but there were many other ways of navigating through the mass of broadcast material.

There is a school of thought in cultural studies, prominent since the 1980s, which claims that we define ourselves by reference to what we are – whether a shared or individual identity – but equally by what we're not. These presumed differences aren't harmless – they accentuate already existing power differences. The argument goes something like this. Western men, with their history of Imperial control, think of themselves as still controlling the way the world works – only they are fully rational, and fully masculine. But people from other cultures and places, and especially women, are a constant threat to this assumed authority. Here's a taste of the way this kind of argument is worked through, in an essay by Jopi Nyman on *Obasan*, a novel by Japanese-Canadian writer Joy Kogawa:

> Western discourse relies on objectivity and rationality, both of which are masculine in the Enlightenment tradition . . . Since the body of the Other cannot be known and governed, a whole mythology of sexuality and erotica is connected with Asian women's bodies . . . this body of the Other is at the same time both one of desire and fear.

We recognise some of what we are not but want, or want to be, in other people and groups of people, and we are afraid of these desires. 'The Other' – whether he or she is a member of an Other ethnic group, or religious group, or gender, or has a different sexual identity – is therefore an object of fear and loathing.

We expected to meet this particular Other as the world's media (and fans) travelled to the Far East for the 2002 World Cup. This Other commonly feared throughout the West is Asian or 'oriental'. 'Orientalism' is the useful word reminted by the literary critic Edward Said for a collection of negative stereotypes about people from the Middle and Far East – such as the cunning, evil and cruel Chinese, a stereotype exemplified by Sax Rohmer's fictional character Fu Manchu. Westerners fear the supposed cunning and cruelty, but they also desire Asiatic societies with their apparently very different moral codes and sexual practices (thus all the salacious stories about the harem, or the geisha). This ambivalent Western desire for the East (and vice versa) was explored in Puccini's 1904 opera *Madam Butterfly*, and there have been various reworkings of this theme since, such as David Kronenburg's film *M Butterfly* and the hit musical *Miss Saigon*. Meanwhile the cumulative experiences of the Second World War, Korean War and Vietnam War reinforced the Western sense that the East could be the site of great cruelty and inscrutable, impenetrable difference. Whether feared or desired, the Other was, it seemed, over There – and 'we' were going to meet it.

The trouble with this school of thought is that – war experiences apart – finding 'the Other' in a pure (and therefore fearsome, or desirable) form is no longer so easy. Perhaps in the nineteenth century, when journeys overseas took weeks or months and McDonald's had yet to open its first branches in Singapore or Tokyo, there was a There to go to. Not any more – Antarctica, northern Siberia and a few similar trackless wastes apart. Today, hopping on to a plane takes us elsewhere quickly and easily, and the same ease of transport brings 'others' in our direction. Meanwhile food, clothing, language and music have flowed in each direction. The world has become a multicultural swap shop.

Football has been affected by this tendency along with everything else. The game is no longer easily mapped on to national identity, in England or elsewhere. A generation ago, even the most successful First

Division teams contained only English, Scots, Welsh and Irish players. The teams which now play in the Premiership – like those in the Italian Serie A or Spanish La Liga – are multinational and multicultural assemblies of expensive mercenaries – the best a particular team can buy, from anywhere in the world where they kick a ball. The coaches likewise. These people are not born into the representation of nation or locality, and neither are many big-city fans. Big European cities such as London, Paris, Berlin and Vienna are inhabited by people from all over the world, people who mix experience of and commitment to various nation-states and ideas of community (including football communities). There's no particular reason why Arsenal fans, for example, shouldn't also support the 'national' team their best players play for – France. Many north Londoners don't identify as English, let alone British. And anyway there's no reason why you should be a north Londoner in order to follow Arsenal. Fans can, and do, express their loyalty and commitment through the remote consumption of teams from any part of the globe, and Western Europeans have television access to football from almost anywhere. We experience the World Cup through that grid of knowledge and experience, in which it is no longer unusual to view players from the Americas or Africa alongside Europeans. In fact it is unusual not to.

Football, in other words, is subject to all the manifold and contradictory forces which have been labelled 'globalisation' – which in the case of the World Cup is about contemporary capitalism, but also about the worldwide movement of people who can afford it (whether fans or tourists), and about those people's identities and performed identities.

Global capitalism is structured around several kinds of trade – in capital itself, in commodities (or objects for sale) and in rights to use or broadcast intangibles such as music, movies or sport. The World Cup as we see it on television, whether we watch the BBC or the various commercial channels, has been sold to the television company as a 'right to broadcast'. The commercial companies have then sold advertising time on the basis of the rights – the individual matches – they have acquired; but some of the time is always taken up by advertising from the sponsors of the competition, who also have rights to broadcast their expensively acquired association with the beautiful game's most globally successful product.

However, the World Cup is also structured within television's developing sense of the ways it can best present the game, its stars, its history and sociology. Before the World Cup there is always some sort of a Phoney War through which the media try to whet our appetite – in 2002, as usual, there were programmes on soccer history (generally concentrating on England, or from an English angle), and on great players such as Bobby Moore. Again, as usual, these were interspersed with programmes on hooliganism. We saw Japanese and Korean police limbering up menacingly for the expected onslaught, and we saw a lot of stock pictures of English hooligans in action at home and away, presented with the assumption that somewhere they, too, were getting into beer-bellied shape for the forthcoming competition. One of these hooligan programmes, interestingly and unusually, abandoned the usual coverage of the phenomenon as a dark side of English laddism, showing instead the fans of Boca Juniors (Buenos Aires) and Lazio (Rome). The latter – and viewing this was painful indeed for fans of English teams – may be a bunch of thuggish near-fascists, but they have a closeness to the players and management of their team of which we (whether season ticket holders or members of sanitised travel clubs) can only dream. However, there was comparatively little in the build-up about the current politics of FIFA, which in the weeks leading up to the competition was embroiled in a bitter succession dispute, complete with predictable allegations of corruption and cronyism.

What coverage there was appeared on news programmes such as *Panorama*, rather than on dedicated sports programmes or channels. Presumably, those who buy rights from FIFA sell their silence in return.

As the competition itself got under way, the phoney war turned real, not only on the pitch but also on the small screen, as the channels were locked in competition for ratings. The coverage by the rival teams of match commentators and studio pundits was enthusiastically assessed by the print media and (on radio phone-ins and on the web as well as in the office) by the rest of us. And as we watched and listened to the commentators' and pundits' banalities, the globalisation of the global game became clear.

There was more of an ethnic balance than in any previous coverage, and it was largely provided by footballers playing in England; Peter Schmeichel, for example, was on hand to discuss Denmark's performances, while Efan Ekoku discussed the various African teams. Added to this new and welcome balance was an atmosphere of political correctness among commentators. We had more of a sense of competing teams, less of competing stereotypes. The days of referring glibly to all Africans as naïve defenders had, it seems, vanished (though to an extent – and there was some residual Orientalism here – it was transferred to the Japanese and Koreans). When commentators did speak of 'typical' German efficiency or Brazilian ball-skills they did so with conscious, and often readily acknowledged, irony as well as admiration.

Meanwhile, for most of the time and for most of the games, the commentators themselves were naïvely enthusiastic. Their enthusiasm for the spectators was as great as for the teams, and there was little criticism of anything except the ticketing arrangements, some aspects of stadium design (too many of the stadia had atmosphere-strangling running tracks), and the occasional poor game or questionable refereeing decision. But towards the end of the competition, comment on the refereeing of the finals did allow the politics of the game to appear (if in their silliest form), as the possibility of a conspiracy to keep South Korea in the competition was raised, in echoes of similar concerns at the 1988 Seoul Olympics. (These debates raged far less fiercely in England than in Spain and Italy, whose national teams had been eliminated at the expense of South Korea after surprising decisions by officials.)

What then of the Orientalism – the mix of stereotypical fear and desire of the Other – which we might have expected from the media? The presentation of this first World Cup outside Europe and the Americas did include moments of Orientalism, but in small doses, and usually with very conscious irony. The phoney war included a few obligatory mentions of the Korean appetite for dog meat, references which disappeared as soon as the tournament began, but – although there was an amusing and very silly Pepsi ad featuring Sumo wrestlers defeating a number of global football stars (at football), for the prize of a few fizzy drinks – little was said to the detriment of Japan. No one mentioned the war; something impossible to imagine when the contest is next held, in Germany. ITV featured an appropriate 'Japanese word of the day' spoken with aplomb by the television presenter of *Banzai*, a British-made spoof Japanese TV game show. And that was about it, as far as anything which could be seen as stereotypical was concerned.

The BBC offered manga-style cartoon adverts and programme openings, which echoed the increasingly general presence of this style in the West – Madonna's 2001 *Drowned* world tour, for example, included a five-song sequence which included a manga cartoon, alongside martial arts and geisha imagery. This is part of a more general Japanisation of global popular culture, which has seen, among other things, the adoption of sushi cuisine, the rise to cult status of films such as *The Audition* and the three-movie *Ring* sequence, and the fetishising of fast Japanese motorbikes and cars (for example, in the Hollywood movie *The Fast and the Furious*, one of the surprise hits of 2001). This is Orientalism in an older sense than Edward Said's use of the word. It signals rather than fear or contempt, a consuming Western interest and respect for the Other – an Orientalism with a globalised and mutually respectful face. And it uses images of an oriental culture which is no longer There, but here, there and everywhere. We can, and do, buy sushi, Sony and Subaru. And we like them.

The incorporation of a few aspects of Japanese culture offers a benign vision of a commodified globalisation, which the agents of global capital were all too happy to reflect and promote. In advertising and sponsorship, those wishing to cash in on the global game's success accentuated the positive. Ford, for example, marketed some if its larger passenger vehicles through a series of images emphasising the universality of a happy (and very uncombative) fandom; mainly young fans with happy, enthusiastic and expectant faces, travelling towards the match in Ford people carriers.

Fiat marketed a car through another universal image, showing the Italian international Francesco Totti kicking a ball round his back garden, the voice-over suggesting that he was dreaming of success on the field in the way we all do, don't we? Nike, meanwhile, in a way typical of their recent campaigns – but still interestingly at a time of national competition – showed us the 'secret tournament'. Rather than opposing national sides who wear its shirts (such as Brazil, Portugal or South Korea), this represented some of the top-level mercenaries who choose to accept its sponsorship deals – including the Brazilian Ronaldo, the Portuguese Luis Figo and the Japanese Hideotoshi Nakata – in a silly parody of the game, compered by former footballer Eric Cantona. This ad was also available on the World Wide Web, along with a lot of other would-be-cool cash-in material. No global advertiser gave any hint of the game as a national war-substitute, or otherwise hateful, dirty or even spitefully competitive. Instead football as advertised was a game subject to universally positive values, and universally desired: the globalisation of football, indeed. And therefore rather different to the matches we actually saw during the World Cup, in which diving, shirt-pulling and petulant and/or cynical fouls had their usual place – such as the game in which the Nike-shirted Brazilian forward Rivaldo feigned injury in order to get a Turkish opponent sent off (and was, after a derisory fine, allowed to continue playing in the competition).

If ads continued to remind us of the influence of global capital on the people's game, in one sense the television coverage has also become more democratic. The studio audience, and in a wider sense the fan in general, is now a much more important part of any channel's presentation of the game than in, say, the early 1980s. Thanks to satellite television – whose sports channels needed cheap programming – fan-based shows have become routine. In this World Cup fans were included beyond the token chat shows and routine radio phone-ins, through the 'reverse view'. Here the camera takes the place of the television, watching fans watching, taking in the emotional responses to the game. Hardly an England goal was scored without studio replays of responses by fans gathered in London bars, a Manchester cinema, and more exotic locations such as Afghanistan (where the watchers were 'our boys', British soldiers, not the locals, which might have been more interesting).

These locations had been set up by the television companies, and in them fans were expected to perform as fans, displaying the requisite moments of tension and release.

Some of the presenters also performed as fans. ITV pundits included Paul Gascoigne, who was sent out to do vox pops with laddish passers-by, and who was several times seen celebrating along with the rest of the fans in Trafalgar Square, while over in the BBC studio, Ian Wright also regularly crossed the line between pundit and partisan.

Many of us saw one or more games at the pub. The pub has been an increasingly important arena for the watching of football since the arrival of satellite television and the subsequent increases in ticket prices at the Premiership grounds changed the economy of spectatorship. The pub experience has also changed our sense of the public and private viewing of televised sport, offering a collective, remote fandom that has moved beyond the sofa.

Because of the time difference, this World Cup saw pubs opening as early as 7 a.m., often providing breakfast as well as beer. There was occasional mayhem thereafter as people kept drinking all day when England did well, though most public disturbances were reserved for the aftermath of the England victory over Argentina, which was a midday match. After this surprising England win, Christchurch Road (a major town-centre thoroughfare) in Bournemouth was closed on police advice because – not of riots, exactly, but of the large numbers of very happy and very drunken fans rolling around the street, kindly informing each other of the score ('1–0 to the Ingerland').

All of which meant problems for employers. In many offices, work was suspended for the duration of the England and Ireland games. In others, televisions appeared in offices and workers were encouraged to turn up early to watch the 7.30 a.m. matches, and only afterwards start the working day. Several of the games became the occasion for de facto bank holidays as many people, faced with less understanding bosses, restructured their leave arrangements in order to stay at home (or go to the pub) and watch. A pattern has now been established which will apply to future competitions. This is a global festival, and like other carnivals, the world of work is increasingly going to have to stop for it.

The 2002 World Cup was also consumed at home, work, school and college via the Internet. Most of this interactive contact was not actually with the broadcasting of games – which is still a technological impossibility thanks to poor server capacity and limited broadband connection – but there was talk and news in plenty, along with much more advertising and a generally pervasive sense of the competition's virtual presence. Everywhere you looked on the net, it seemed, some aspect of the World Cup was being discussed, speculated and/or gambled on (through office sweeps alongside the activities of commercial betting companies). The portal first seen by many users of

Microsoft's Internet Explorer software, www.msn.co.uk, as they switch on their machines, was temporarily redesigned to show the St George Cross flag as background – when it was clear that England were doing comparatively well. The flag quietly disappeared after England's inglorious defeat by ten-man Brazil, though the site continued to carry a great deal of news, speculation and advertising from the competition until its end.

The St George's Cross was at the heart of the public display of fandom, as people not only symbolised but performed their allegiance. Replacing the Union flags which had been omnipresent during the Jubilee, the St George flag appeared in house windows and waved from innumerable television aerials and car aerials. The best England shirt design for a generation, with its sidestripe redolent of the national flag, was matched by designs from a number of stores which sold their own World Cup ranges, many of them echoing the England team design and/or incorporating the newly rediscovered national symbol. Paul Smith, FCUK, Ted Baker, Marks & Spencer, and Philosophy Football all launched their own World Cup wear, and people responded, dressing up their national allegiance as part of the performance of fandom. They also displayed their allegiance through sound, with a range of patriotic downloadable ring tones for mobile telephones meaning that public space was sonically as well as visibly part of the World Cup.

And along with the telephone sounds, T-shirts and baseball caps people bought music. The pre-tournament phoney war saw the release of the usual set of singles, fronted by 'We're on the Ball', an unspeakable (and unsingalongable) effort by Ant and Dec, who really should have kept to kids' Saturday morning TV rather than try to hit primetime stardom either as presenters or singers. CDs of 'footie anthems' graced the dump-bins of the nation's record stores – including a 'FIFA Collection' of music from the competing nations, released by the Sony label, which was topped with both an 'official (pop) song', and an 'official anthem' by Vangelis, which FIFA's website described as: 'A sensuous classical piece composed to reflect the international significance of the first FIFA World Cup to be held in Asia. The anthem takes classical drums and percussion elements from Korean and Japanese music and fuses them with a hypnotic oriental melody.'

Vangelis was not alone. Even in the unregrettable absence of the Three Tenors (who launched themselves at the World Cup finals in Italy in 1990), in these days of commodified high-culture it was not only pop which proclaimed its allegiance, and then put the results on sale. Budget classical music label, Naxos, got into the act with the 3-CD album 'Sven-Göran Eriksson's Classical Collection', a predictable sequence of mainly English and Scandinavian pieces. This mixed the whimsical (e.g. Swedish composer Alfvén's String Serenade) with the bombastic (such as

Elgar's Pomp and Circumstance March No.1 – 'Land of Hope and Glory'). Sven had been asked by the FA, apparently, not to include the Dambusters March, a piece of pseudo-Elgarian war movie theme music which had featured in a number of silly anti-German lager commercials in the 1990s, and was adopted as a terrace tune (accompanied by arm-waving in imitation of Lancaster bombers) thereafter.

The phoney war also included film. Television, predictably, rolled out the great 1960s movie, *The Italian Job*, whose end-credit song 'Self-Preservation Society' (part of a score written by the African-American composer and arranger Quincy Jones) has also become a terrace anthem. Perhaps more interestingly, the cinemas were showing *Bend it like Beckham*, in which a young British South Asian woman confounded family, schoolfriends and all and sundry with her footballing ability.

As the tournament began, the arrival of tens of thousands of fans in Japan and Korea was presented as a great success – and as surprisingly peaceful. Television showed us fans who came, saw, and went, performing their allegiances in reasonably good humour the while. England fans visiting Japan were seen waving to the camera, singing a lot, and wearing team shirts and/or the St George's flag. They did not all, always, give the impression of being entirely sober. But apparently they did not then threaten rival fans or the locals, thus provoking police responses. This is the chain reaction which at previous contests since the mid-1970s journalists have written up as adjacent to the end of the world as we know it. The pitched battles which the media expect were not there in 2002 to be reported on. The hooligan programmes from the phoney war seemed, this time, to have missed the prophetic mark. Fandom was changed from the sublime to the picturesque. That Ford ad came to life. This was, it seemed, the friendly finals.

This was shown to us as being due to the welcome the visitors received. The hosts were characterised not as 'polite but withdrawn', nor – of course – as cunning or cruel, or hostile to visiting foreigners, but as welcoming and eager to meet the incoming fans. It was clear that they, too, were committed and enthusiastic supporters of their national sides, but there was an interesting variation. Many Japanese and Koreans appeared to have adopted an incoming team and were performing portable identities, wearing the shirts and face paint, and standing within the section of the ground reserved for their adopted team, where they joined in the chanting. Doubtless there were some travelling Asian England fans, but what we noticed was that there were as many Japanese-looking people wearing England colours as there were short-haired white men.

The host nations were also well supported. The Japanese 'Blue Heaven' and South Korean 'Red Devils' filled the stadia with colour and noise; streets outside were just as full. 'We are copying you', was how some Japanese fans explained their support to the English. The Koreans, wearing red T-shirts with slogans in English – they claimed to have sold around five million of them – were all too obviously copying that leading football brand, red-shirted Manchester United (aka 'Red Devils'), whose David Beckham was the recipient of a screaming, Beatlemaniac reception whenever he appeared.

'Copying you' to the letter, Japanese and Korean fans had adopted a wide repertoire of off-the-shelf Anglo-European songs and chants. One intriguing Japanese choice was the 'grand march' from Verdi's opera *Aida* – which was commissioned by the King of Egypt for an important occasion in the evolution of globalisation, the opening of the Suez Canal – and first performed at the new Cairo Opera House in 1871. An equally intriguing choice by the Korean fans included the last-movement theme from another piece of music with global pretensions, Beethoven's 9th Symphony, which was commissioned by the London Philharmonic Society and first performed in 1823. The last movement sets Schiller's poem the 'Ode to Freedom' (which in the nineteenth century was referred to for censor-defeating purposes as the 'Ode to Joy'), and the long melody associated with the poem has subsequently become the European Anthem (it was also used by the BBC as the theme tune for its coverage of Euro '96). In singing 'our' tune, the Koreans were signalling their wholehearted acceptance of the globalised people's game.

OK then, as far as television coverage was concerned the global language of football has rung up another success story. 'They' became part of 'us'; the best team won; and apparently the fans – including the England fans – behaved themselves. The emergent national flag was not, this time, besmirched, and this particular symbol of Englishness will continue to make its way as a benign answer to the vexed question of national identity in a UK which has Scots and Welsh devolution, the Northern Irish peace process, but, so far, no English parliament or anything similar.

Yes – but this is a revival of Englishness in the context of globalisation, and though the English coverage of this world event was more balanced and inclusive, in some ways the broadcast media failed to see the implications of globalisation for national identity – though their coverage actually illustrated it. It's worth commenting on one or two paradoxes, which the television viewer could decode, even if the programme makers couldn't.

All British television and radio broadcasts were presented in the context of an assumed shared support for England and Ireland, complemented with an assumed polite interest in the supposedly better sides such as France (oops) and Brazil. But – however pervasive the national flag seemed to be – were 'we' all rooting for the local sides, even in their hour of need?

Probably not. BBC's reverse-view coverage of England–Brazil showed several Brazil supporters at Rio Ferdinand's old junior school in East London. These were 9–11-year-olds who – despite their Ronaldo shirts didn't appear to be in any obvious way ethnically Brazilian – the cameras showed jumping for joy when David Seaman neglected to catch the ball from Ronaldhino's free kick.

Most of David Seaman's long and in various ways distinguished career has been with Arsenal. Therefore Spurs fans don't like him. After England's exit from the competition the various Spurs fan websites discussed aspects of the Arsenal/England problem. Should they be pleased that the first Brazil goal was down to a schoolboy dummy on Ashley Cole, after which the treacherous Sol Campbell had been naïvely drawn away from marking Rivaldo, who scored past the then-groggy David Seaman? Should they be even more pleased that Seaman had gone on to repeat his excellent non-save against Nayim, who lobbed him from the halfway line in the last minute of the 1995 European Cup-Winners' Cup final? On the whole, they agreed, yes they should – and though there was a minority which insisted that they should forget these parochial differences and support whoever was playing for England, others variously said that they were English but did not support England, that they were not English, or there was no necessary connection between following a Premiership team and following a national side, whatever your nationality. Spurs fans on one web-thread discussing this issue identified themselves as followers of Ireland, Scotland, Slovenia, Denmark and Argentina as well as England, and all were agreed that Brazil were the best side in the competition and had deservedly beaten England.

There were more clues that 'England' is not simply a geographical location which attracts an automatic loyalty from its residents. Throughout the competition team shirts were on sale from the www.msn.co.uk website – Cameroon, Nigeria, China, Mexico and Turkey were among the finalists whose shirts sold out. England's didn't. London fan-gatherings visited by the television included, alongside the heavily Anglophile Trafalgar Square, bars attended mainly by followers of France, Turkey, and Brazil. (French television, similarly, had many moments featuring Paris-based Senegalese, and they increased after the French side's ignominious exit.) It's easy to comment that London is no longer simply a part of England or Britain, but of the world. But beyond London this representation of the country's mixed population was also happening – my local paper, the *Winchester Evening Echo*, carried a story and 'reverse view' photo featuring Japanese students of King Alfred's College watching Japan play, and in a post-match interview graciously responding to Japan's defeat by Turkey by promising to support England from now on, and of course saying nice things about David Beckham.

After the competition there was talk of the better South Korean and Japanese players being bought by Premiership or other European league clubs. This means we will see more of them in the Champions League. FIFA's plan to turn the Beautiful Game into one of the primary modes of communication and trade, it seems, has worked well. Onwards to the first African World Cup finals in eight years time. We know many of the players now, and through the very welcome television coverage of the African Cup of Nations we know how the national teams play. It is worth speculating that even so, there will be another Other there, an Arabic-speaking, Islamic North African Other less amenable to globalisation, present in any Africa sited competition – and that this Islamic Other will be less easy to draw into the dialogue of globalisation which was so successfully registered this time around.

Meanwhile there remains one particular, peculiar and paradoxical Other in this globalised gameshow world. As far as the big corporations are concerned, football is part of the project of globalisation. Many of these multinational companies bought into the game and advertised their investment on television during the contest. Of these big spenders Ford, McDonald's, Yahoo! Coca-Cola, Pepsi, Nike, Budweiser – are all US companies. US singer Anastacia recorded 'Boom', the 'official' FIFA tournament song. However, and for all the commercial success of the 1994 World Cup and their 2002 achievement in reaching the quarter-finals, those curious people in the United States of America remain very much football's Other. Even the word 'football' means something very different there, where there is enormous resistance to the cultural uniformity of the feared 'new world order', and strong belief in American 'exceptionalism'. The US 'soccer' team did far better than expected in World Cup 2002, but still the folks back home didn't seem to care. Or know, in most cases. This is a huge cultural paradox. After World Cup 2002 the Far East is, it seems, just like us, speaking the international language of football. Football's unknown, its Other, is located not in the exotica of orientalism but in the USA, right in the Western heart of globalisation. Is the US like us? Not as much as we presume, it seems. While with our more traditional eastern Other we've more in common than we thought.

* * * * *

On the Press Pack Stereotype Hunt

Emma Poulton

'Sayonara to the Neanderthal Fan' was the none-too-fond farewell to England's hooligan reputation from Mick Dennis, sports columnist for the *Daily Mirror*, on returning from his World Cup 2002 posting. Reviewing his time out in the Far East, he told readers how 'most of the best memories involve the camaraderie between supporters from different countries'. Among his recollections were giving a little Argentine lad an England pin badge and the boy instinctively offering him his hat in his country's colours, and explaining what 'nil' meant to a group of Japanese fans wearing England shirts so that they could joyfully join in singing 'One–nil to the Ingerland' on the way out of the ground after the Argentina match. Then, after the same game, listening in wonder as England fans broke into a chant of '*Nippon! Nippon!*', a spontaneous tribute to their ever-smiling, ever helpful hosts. Dennis then asked, 'Wait a minute. What's that? England supporters characterised all over the world as bigots, showing appreciation of foreigners? Yes, and it confirmed my own prejudices.' He explained:

> You see, I've always refused to believe English football folk are all Neanderthal nutters. Of course, some get lagered up and some enjoy a ruck and, if pushed around by police in riot gear, some will shove back and might eventually gear up for a riot. And certainly supporting a football team is a tribal pursuit which encourages antagonism towards people from a different tribe. So it was inevitable that, before this World Cup kicked off, the Japanese media, like so much of our own, chose to portray the old brutal stereotype of England fans. But like all stereotypes, it is a generalisation and this time it proved inaccurate.
>
> England supporters have proved that most of them are fundamentally decent people, and if you treat them decently, they'll behave decently. And that could be this country's most significant result.

In part this is surely an admission of guilt on the part of Dennis' and other papers' coverage of England fans. During Euro 2000, for example, the *Sunday Mirror* dismissed all of the national team's supporters in Belgium and Holland for the European Championships as 'drunken, tattooed, crop-headed oafs', while the *Daily Mirror* wrote the fans off as 'drunken, violent, mindless creeps', with the message: 'GRUNT GRUNT GRUNT. That's Neanderthal for: just behave, you mindless, pathetic excuses for Englishmen.' Other writers shared Dennis' observations of what it meant to be an England fan in Japan. The *Independent on Sunday* described 'a remarkable metamorphosis from hooligans to heroes', while in the *Daily Mail*, Jeff Powell wrote of how:

> The conversion of the fans on the road to Japan has been one of Damascene proportions. From the vile, brawling, drunken and shaming rabble of so many football championships, they appear to have been transformed into human beings, exchanging polite bows in accordance with Japanese custom rather than beating the locals over the head with beer bottles.

What remained unclear in these pieces was the process of change. Had an entire body of fans changed overnight into friendly ambassadors for team and country, or had these people been there all along, and it was just that the journalists had never had the good sense, or perhaps grace, to notice them? *The Sunday Times* reflected the former school of thought:

> As well as a reborn team, a new type of fan seems to have emerged. Gone is the beer-sozzled 'foolian' (as the Japanese say); in has come a new sophistication. The Japanese have watched in curiosity as many English supporters have queued politely to check their emails at airport Internet cafes and produced laptop computers to while away the time. At 1 a.m. yesterday, two England fans, daubed with paint, astonished staff in one Sapporo restaurant by ordering fried squid and beer in fluent Japanese. The good behaviour has come as a shock.

Of course this 'new England fan' hasn't just miraculously appeared out of nowhere. They have always been there. However, there has been a frequent failure by the media to distinguish between the various sections of England's support. This has commonly resulted in the misrepresentation of the vast majority. As soon as trouble breaks out, almost all distinctions between the violent, xenophobic minority and non-violent majority is lost in the media coverage that emphasises the behaviour of the hooligans, which of course makes for much better copy. Consequently, the majority loses all sense of identity, voice and presence.

The media continually put all England fans in the frame for the hooligan element's misdemeanours. While not all fans are innocent (nor indeed all foreign police forces and host communities), there is a need for balance in the media coverage. Those forming the middle ground of England's support have been made invisible. These are passionate patriots who follow the national team with no inclination towards aggression, racism or violence. We have seldom heard in the past about the exemplary behaviour of this vast majority of fans. Instead, the violent minority has been allowed to tarnish the image of all England supporters.

The English media regularly boost feelings of shame and disgust by affirming that the English are synonymous with hooliganism and that the 'English Disease' is our most infamous export, overlooking the fact that football-related violence blights countless other countries. Indeed, football violence occurs – in varying degrees and different forms – in almost every country in which the game is played. Evidence of this was finally acknowledged during this World Cup. *The Guardian* reported unrest in Moscow by saying . . . 'Up to 8,000 people, mainly young men and teenage boys, many of them drunk, rampaged as Russia lost 1–0 to Japan, setting cars on fire, smashing windows, and fighting police and each other'. The riot left two dead. Meanwhile the *Daily Mail* covered 'running battles in African townships between surrogate supporters of Argentina and Brazil'.

Yet there was none of the widely predicted trouble involving England fans. Just as before Euro '96, France '98 and Euro 2000, the domestic media's agenda was dominated by an almost ghoulish interest in the host police's preparation for the tournament, focusing on measures for preventing, but particularly dealing with, outbreaks of unrest. This was manifest in numerous stories in both the press and on television news bulletins forecasting widespread public disorder in Japan. The *Daily Mail* documented how the Japanese had 'beefed up its military preparations in trepidation'. There was particular interest in how the Japanese police were extensively trained in numerous martial arts and how, according to the *Daily Mirror*, they would be 'armed with water cannons which they carry on their backs and Spiderman net-guns'. For those in any doubt of the likely consequences of 10,000 or more England fans arriving in Japan, we had the ill-timed BBC 2 documentary series *Hooligans*, while Channel 4 screened *Football's Fight Club*.

This same theme continued in the early days of the tournament, as if to keep the potential threat of trouble ever present in the public's minds. The *Daily Mirror* told how 'former soccer hooligan Chris "Combat" Henderson was stopped trying to enter Japan. He was held at Tokyo airport after flying from Bangkok and faces deportation to Thailand where he runs a bar for Chelsea fans with Steve "The General" Hickmott, fellow ex-member of the Chelsea Headhunters.' Meanwhile an article in the *Independent on Sunday* informed its readership of the preventative measures that had been taken to minimise the risk of disorder, explaining: 'Manchester has won the "police premiership" for the force that prevented the most hooligans travelling to the World Cup. They obtained 151 banning orders on local yobs, pipping Staffordshire who managed 150. West Yorkshire was third on 89, with the Met trailing in fourth with 82.'

Similar stories were as commonplace for the first week or so of the tournament as they had been in the period of the build-up. On the day of England's final group match against Nigeria, and following peaceful match-days in Saitama and Sapporo, *The Times* was still reporting on a make-believe Japan 'bracing themselves for months for an invasion of the so-called Igirisuno furigans – the English hooligans'. In the absence of any trouble, correspondents were left to report on what might have been. According to the *Independent on Sunday* reviewing the Argentina game:

> Expectations had become so abysmally low in the run-up to Friday's match (versus Argentina) that it would have been almost impossible not to surpass them. Hooligan hysteria took many forms. A local councillor in one town warned that given 'the exceptional mood of the event', Japan faced 'the possibility of unwanted babies conceived by foreigners who rape our women'. Inn-keepers refused to take bookings from foreigners at the time of sensitive matches. And nowhere was the fear greater than in Sapporo on the island of Hokkaido. It was the Hokkaido police who prepared for the arrival of football fans not only with new riot shields, but with special web guns firing entangling nets. Fears about a lack of detention cells led them to charter a passenger ferry that they planned to use as an improvised prison ship. Everything movable and throwable was removed from the streets of Sapporo. And on Friday night they mounted what seems to have been the largest football policing operation of all time.

Yet the disorder failed to happen, to the surprise of most journalists and commentators. With England about to successfully secure its way out of their qualifying group, *The Times* grudgingly reported: 'With the tournament already 12 days old, only 12 of the estimated 8,000 English fans in the country have been arrested and only one of those was for an act of violence. The others are all alleged thieves, fraudsters or ticket touts. The country's police and sporting officials say that they are delighted by the impeccable behaviour of the visiting English who, at least so far, have remained largely sober and well mannered.'

This total of 12 arrests was still correct over a week later. Clare Allbless, Press Attaché to the British Embassy in Japan, was quoted in *The Guardian* as saying that this was 'hardly different from an ordinary month's (number of arrests)' and how they had received 'letters and people calling in to praise the behaviour of English supporters'.

There were numerous articles speculating on the reasons for the absence of any of the expected trouble involving England fans. A writer for the *Independent on Sunday* offered the following reflections on 'How Our Fans Went on a Rampage of Politeness and Conquered Japan'. He wrote:

> Yesterday was the pivot on which the reputation of England football supporters in Japan turned – from amok berserkers intent only on destruction to the unexpected heroes of the 2002 World Cup. 'There were so many reports in the newspapers about the English hooligans and what they were going to be like,' said a 64-year-old man named Mitsuharu Sakaki. 'The image we had was of violent attacks, and that kind of thing. And yet when they came here, they were quite gentlemanly.' All over the city, people were feeling the same way.

Asking, 'Why have the visitors behaved so impeccably? And why did Japan get them so wrong?' the reporter suggested that part of the reason for the 'atmosphere of apprehension' had originated within the Japanese police. He cited Ron Hogg, Assistant Chief Constable of Durham Constabulary, who had been consulting for months with his Japanese counterparts before the tournament. Mr Hogg explained, 'There's been disbelief in what we've been telling them. As it's unfolded and been seen to be true, there's been massive relief. They found it difficult to believe there was anything other than English hooligans.' As a reporter for the *Daily Telegraph* observed: 'What were the Japanese presented with when the England supporters stepped off the plane? Not a terrifying gang of shaven-headed Millwall fans, chanting "No one likes us – we don't care", but a lot of fair-minded, humorous people in bowler hats and "Richard the Lionheart" costumes.' Journalists sought for answers to explain how 'the England team escaped the curse of hooliganism and sociopathic behaviour', as Paul Hayward, chief sportswriter for the *Daily Telegraph*, put it. Previously it has been rare for the media to offer any informed analysis on the actual causes of football-related violence, preferring instead to indulge themselves in vitriol, roundly condemning the behaviour without a thought for contributing factors behind it. The apparent source of the hooligans' anti-social, problematic behaviour is commonly viewed by the press to be the hooligans themselves and their 'natural' mindlessness and savagery. Blame the 'lunatic', 'moronic', 'sub-human' football hooligan, and the deeper social roots and more enduring causal factors behind the phenomenon can be overlooked.

But at this World Cup, with the lack of trouble, for once writers appeared to at least try to give their take on the reasons for its absence. Paul Hayward, again, suggested that: 'Exclusion orders, the high cost of travel and accommodation and the civilising effect of Japanese hospitality all staunched the malevolence that turned Marseilles into a battleground four years ago.' His counterpart in the *Daily Mail*, Jeff Powell, proposed:

> The culture of change is being accelerated by the location of this World Cup. The time difference between Japan and England has shifted much of the focus back home from the boozer at night to the coffee shop in the morning. The long and costly journey to such an expensive venue has made this predominantly a migration of Middle England and the nouveau riche. Perhaps the very foreign land in which they find themselves has wrought no more than a temporary adjustment to English mob mentality. Maybe apprehension as to how severely they might be treated by so puritan a regime is restraining violent impulses just for the moment.

Powell and Hayward offer a variety of reasons for the lack of trouble. But its very lack forced news values to shift. World Cup 2002 witnessed a sea change in the media agenda, from one that is looking to castigate all England fans for the trouble caused by some of their number, to one that is willing to embrace the other side of the story.

Instead of their customary stories about the stereotyped shaven-headed, beer-bellied, drunk and disorderly 'yobs' terrorising town centres, *The Guardian* reported how England fans were 'sight-seeing and taking in the local culture'. Instead of the zoom lenses desperately seeking out flare-ups, the photographers settled for snapping England fans carrying local children on their shoulders or doing the conga with Brazilian fans, even after defeat. *The Guardian* front page the day before the Brazil game was dominated by a large colour photograph of two Englishmen dressed as Japanese women in traditional local costume, with the caption 'Kimono You Whites!'.

Many other commentators offered further reflections on the tournament after England's rather dismal defeat to Brazil as they tried to look to the future. Some of these were more positive about the reasons for England fans' good behaviour, without some of the scepticism that characterised the views of Hayward and Powell. Elsewhere in Hayward's *Daily Telegraph*, Mark Palmer mused:

> It may well be a coincidence that the England supporters have behaved themselves so well. Perhaps the travel bans and liaison with the Japanese police really did the trick. Perhaps the lack of ticket sales on the black market kept the trouble miles away. But that doesn't quite explain why at every England match, the Japanese rallied behind our team and why the English rooted for Japan with equal vigour. It is as if the Japanese found something of themselves in the English and vice-versa.

Another *Daily Telegraph* piece was headlined 'English Rediscover Pride in the Flag of St George', with writer Colin Randall arguing, 'After years of association with football hooligans and the racist Far Right, the simple red cross of England's patron saint has been recaptured by ordinary Englishmen and women'. Articles like this were almost as common as the flag itself.

On the day of England's vital group match with Nigeria the front page of *The Times* was dominated by a photo of a giant St George's Cross painted across a pair of semi-detached houses in Brighton. The paper reported how, 'The 30 million flags sold so far are an eight-fold increase on the last World Cup and the European Championships two years ago and the 12 flag companies that existed at the time of the 1966 World Cup have swelled to 551 businesses with an expected turnover of £100 million this year.' The day of England's second-round match with Denmark, *The Guardian* featured a front-page montage of photos, with the caption 'Discerning Drivers Flying the Flag with the Latest Must-Have Accessory'.

Newspapers also provided flags within their pages for readers to display. *The Sun*, the day before England's quarter-final, for example, used its front and back pages as a pull-out poster of the Cross of St George with the message 'You Can Do It Lads!'. Such stunts were not confined to the tabloids. With a detectable hint of irony on the same day as *The Sun* was doing its bit for England, the front page of *The Guardian*'s G2 supplement featured a full-page 'cut-out-and-keep new improved flag of St George with no ugly connotations'. The newspaper's Jonathan Glancey discussed the rehabilitation of the flag, noting:

> Every country has its crosses to bear and England's is St George's. Never in the field of English history, or at least not since the Crusades or Agincourt, have so many red-crossed flags been waved by so many for so many. The revival of the

> English Cross of St George might have something to do with devolution, the English taking a leaf from the book of patriotism as practised by an increasingly proud and defiant Celtic fringe. It might simply be a striking and memorable pattern or logo that, unlike the Union flag, even an idiot can paint across their face. It does look good. Which hugely paid advertising agency or design consultancy could come up with a more powerful logo? This red-cross flag of In-ger-land has, by happy accident, been saved from being tarred with a blunt nationalist brush this summer because, almost unimaginably, it has become an emblem that embraces fans of every class, creed and colour.

Glancey's conclusion raises another common theme found in the media coverage of the tournament: the apparent development of a new, perhaps softer and more inclusive, Englishness. He summed up by saying:

> Although many of us were brought up to believe that the English had no need to shout about their identity, and that patriotism was the last refuge of a scoundrel, and many more of us, whatever we feel about England (or In-ger-land), have never waved a red-cross flag (nor even Union flag) in our lives, the fact that so many people from so many different backgrounds can wrap themselves in this antique emblem shows that there might – might – just be a little chivalry behind the effing, blinding, beery bravado after all.

The editor of the *Sunday Telegraph* offered similar thoughts following England's defeat of Argentina:

> George Orwell's famous observation that serious sport is 'war minus the shooting' may be an exaggeration, but the passions which have been spawned by the England team's triumph over the old enemy show that he was not far from the truth. Indeed, the last week has provided an extraordinarily colourful, vital snapshot of national identity in this country. From the moment that the crowds started gathering in the gardens of Buckingham Place for the Golden Jubilee Prom eight days ago, to the blowing of the final whistle at the Sapporo Dome, we have seen a nation not only at ease with itself, but pleasantly taken aback by its reserves of pride, creativity and self-respect.

Martin Phillips in *The Sun* went as far as contemplating the 'Rebirth of England' as he looked back on the tournament. Trying to cheer up disheartened readers, Phillips offered these consoling words:

> If it feels like the end of the world, that's because it is – the end of the world as we knew it. We may have lost a football match yesterday, but this was the World Cup that saw us grow up as a nation. Where before there has been jingoism and contempt for all opposition, the new mature England only sent its heroes off with hope they would do their best. The Japanese saw a different England too. They had been warned to expect drunken hooligans – previously our best soccer export. Instead they saw England fans at their best – full of fun and a passion for football. Before, we had been universally loathed and detested. Now we are marvelled at from afar as the Japanese took us to their hearts and England became the most popular team among neutrals. The flags that have fluttered from homes, offices and cars should not be lowered to half mast or removed just because the adventure is over. They should be raised even higher – with pride.

It is widely recognised that sport is a key arena in contemporary society in which national identity can be displayed and asserted. Football, in particular, is a rich source of collective identification and an important site for affirmation and expression of identity, at both a local and national level. The media play a crucial role here in the construction and representation of national identity through their coverage. This helps to make the nation more real through rhetoric and images about us, with an emphasis on unity and cohesion, so helping to mobilise national feeling. A central part of the process of constructing one's own national identity is to do so in contrast to the representation of the opposition. The portrayal of opposing nations, their teams, players, supporters, homelands and cultures, is central to the championing of our own national team and, by implication, England and Englishness. The emphasis is put on 'them' being different, and perhaps in some way inferior, to 'us'. This sense of 'them' against 'us' is commonly achieved through the use of personal pronouns and the perpetuation of stereotypes that are usually complimentary about 'us' and disparaging about 'them', so reinforcing myths of national character that are deeply rooted in the national culture. However, sometimes these literary devices, coupled with the deployment of militaristic images and war terminology, can invoke overtly negative images of opponents that are xenophobic, racist and deeply offensive.

While some lessons appear to have been learnt from Euro '96 when the tabloid press received widespread criticism for their coverage of the tournament (the Spain and Germany matches in particular), such discourse was in evidence on occasions during the World Cup. This was most notable when England played Argentina, dubbed of course by *The Sun* and others as the 'old foe'. This kind of coverage has an impact externally as well as internally. The *Sunday Telegraph* reported how there was 'anti-English feeling on the streets of Buenos Aires' after England's victory, but that this was 'mainly reserved for the British tabloid newspapers, which were accused of tastelessly alluding to the Falkland's War'. The article told how the Argentine newspaper, *Olé*, had reproduced the front page of the *Daily Star*, which used the notorious headline 'Gotcha' from *The Sun* (following the sinking of the Argentine warship, the *Belgrano*), beneath a triumphant David Beckham, as well as *The Sun* headline 'Up Yours Señors!'. The *Olé* article had complained . . .'It was sad to see the English press bring up the Malvinas conflict of 1982 and compare Friday's match to the sinking of the *General Belgrano*', concluding that 'The English were hard in victory, very hard'.

Reflecting on the anti-Argentine sentiments in the English press, Argentine journalist, Marcela Mora y Araujo, writing in the *Sunday Telegraph* noted:

> Argentina has spent much of the week at the receiving end of the worst kind of xenophobic abuse the English media are capable of. This has ranged from the better-known Sunday tabloids who have set the standard for this kind of journalism right down to BBC 2's midweek drama slot. *The Falkland's Play*, so staunchly pro-Thatcher that it was originally pulled, was found a slot on the airwaves two days before England and Argentina were to meet for this much-hyped football encounter.
>
> Argentinean players who had gone out of their way to say, 'This has nothing to do with the Falklands', were consistently misquoted as saying, 'This is all about the Falklands'. The words 'cheat' and 'dirty' crept up over and over again. Argentines living in London have been telephoning each other at the sight of a new headline saying 'They're really having a go at us'. Yes, we noticed.

Certainly, references to the Falklands were in evidence prior to and especially after the match, as the English press celebrated victory and, later, Argentina's elimination from the group stage. *The Sun* carried an article describing how 'Our Boys go Wild as Old Foe Crashes Out', featuring interviews with Royal Marines posted in Afghanistan. Among those quoted was one, who said, 'It's great given the history between us.

It's especially good in the week of the 20th anniversary of the end of the Falklands War.' According to *The Sun*, 'the Marines' joy was echoed back home by Falklands veterans', with one ex-Para they quoted commenting, 'they deserved to go out. It was justice for them wanting revenge for the Falklands.' This theme was not confined to the tabloids. For example, a cartoon in the *Independent on Sunday* depicted penguins on the Falklands celebrating as they watched England's defeat of Argentina.

The game was framed as a revenge match, mixing the 1986 and 1998 World Cup games with the 1982 Falkland's War, by the tabloids and broadsheets alike. Sometimes the quest for vengeance was clearly for controversial incidents during previous footballing encounters. *The Sun* crowed: 'Diego Maradona cheated us with his "Hand of God" goal in 1986 and Diego Simeone's dive got Becks sent off in '98.' Indeed, the labelling of Argentine players as 'cheats' or 'dirty' was particularly prevalent, as Mora y Araujo highlighted. On the day of what the *Daily Mirror* dubbed 'Showdown at High Noon', the newspaper asked, 'How Foul Can They Get?', providing readers with a 'Filthy Form Guide' and an 'Argy-Bargy Sweepstake', claiming, 'It's a question of when, rather than if, an Argentinian player commits the first foul'. When Argentina was later knocked-out, *The Sun*, inspired by the musical *Evita*, jeered 'Don't Cry for Them Argentinians! The truth is they are cocky cheats, especially Batistuta'. Meanwhile, the *Daily Mirror* mocked: 'Don't forget to pack your handbags, dears', with a full front-page colour photograph of the Argentine players in a defensive wall, flinching from a free kick, carrying superimposed bags.

Following England's elimination, there were also numerous jibes at the expense of Germany, some light-hearted, others perhaps more noxious. *The Daily Telegraph* – in rather tabloidesque style – tried to provide solace for readers by providing them with '15 Reasons for Us to be Cheerful', including, 'At least we didn't go out to Germany' and 'We did beat Argentina!'. However, this seemed to be of little comfort to the *Daily Mirror*, which moaned: 'How can the team we beat 5–1 be in the semi-finals?' and then answered its own question: 'Because the Germans are bloody lucky and they cheat, that's why!' The back page was dominated by a close-up image showing the controversial goal-line 'handball' by a German defender during their game against the USA, for which no penalty was awarded. The caption, 'Hans of God'! The lament in *The Sun* was more sardonic, signing off its back page the day after Brazil's victory over England with the message: 'It's over. We're out and the Germans are through to the semi-finals. Have a good weekend.' Inclusivism, it seems, only goes so far.

Although newspaper editors have been much more cautious since the watershed of Euro '96, sometimes the reporting of particular grudge matches still appears to be misjudged. The press has often been guilty in the past of flagrant xenophobia and jingoism in their gung-ho, nationalistic rhetoric prior to games – especially against Germany – and this sometimes still surfaces. Similarly, the lampooning of the customs, traits and symbols of opposing nations can on occasion also go well beyond what might be tolerated as acceptable banter. Instead, it can be insensitive and offensive. While the English media appear to be mending their ways, there is still room for improvement. This involves playing down ideas about avenging the opposition and settling scores from on, and especially off, the pitch.

The reporting of England matches should undoubtedly involve patriotism and the promotion of pride, but we need to lose the prejudice. We can assert our own national identity, but it needn't be at the expense of others. Journalists need to acknowledge a distinction between what is wind-up humour and the unacceptable when representing nations. This also requires a shift of emphasis away from excessively high levels of expectation and recourse to martial history lessons. Evoking memories of past military conflicts is not helpful. The intention here is not to be a killjoy or to advocate taking the rich humour, rivalry and partisan passion out of football. This is all part of the game, and a valuable one at that. But media personnel must demonstrate greater sensitivity to ensure portrayals of the opposition do not offend.

Some of this was achieved during World Cup 2002, with the media generally being much more realistic about England's chances and therefore more tempered in their reporting, at least before the tournament and during the group stage. But a greater consistency of more considered, more measured and, at times, more sensitive reporting, is needed. This involves the respectful treatment both of opposing nations, their players and their fans, as well as, of course, our own.

The most significant shift in reporting of this World Cup remains the widespread, and positive, profile of ordinary England supporters. The fact they weren't all hooligans seemed to surprise many correspondents as they filed their reports, but at least gave a more accurate insight into England fan culture. Newspapers featured and embraced storylines about these supporters, who in truth had been there before at Euro 2000, France '98 and long before that too – they've just not been noticed by the journalists and photographers in the headlong rush to focus on the trouble. And so at this tournament the media provided a much more comprehensive range of representations of what it means to be an England fan today. The *Daily Mirror* suggested that 'our supporters showed that the violent mindless thugs who abuse international soccer are not the true face of English fans'. Maybe, just maybe then, the 2002 World Cup has seen the non-violent majority, supported this time by the media, begin to reverse the England fans image that has been tarnished for so many years by the hooligans.

As the press lamented England's exit from the World Cup, the assessment of the fans at least remained positive. The *Independent* commented: 'For once, English participation in a major football tournament has not been a matter of fear, disappointment and recrimination, but of fun, hope and realism.' Yet despite this optimism, there are plenty of journalists who believe that England fans, and therefore 'Ingerland', have done no more than enjoy a Far Eastern honeymoon. They seek to presume that these days of a trouble-free football competition will be short-lived.

Provocative and scaremongering coverage of football-related violence can often escalate the issue, and the expectant atmosphere, before a ball has been kicked, let alone something actually kicks off – as it may, or may not, do at forthcoming tournaments. If violence does occur, the media's forecasts are then 'proven' to be true and consequently become self-fulfilling prophecies, with incidents often reported in a 'told-you-so' tone.

The media clearly has a responsibility to inform the public about newsworthy events when they occur. As such, football-related violence is likely to be featured should it break out. However, there is a pressing need for a balanced approach to the media's treatment of football supporters, rather than framing them all as 'hooligans'. This is not to disregard or cosmetically disguise the indisputable fact that a hooligan element follows England, especially away, and that there are outbreaks of football-related violence. But until the 2002 World Cup, we were exposed to a very one-sided picture of England fans through the media frame.

This is evidently due to prevailing news values that reflect the media's specific agenda to inform, but also entertain. Indeed, the media plays a vital role in providing this information and entertainment service, none more so than when the greatest sports event in the world is played on the other side of the globe. As such, selective editorial processes constantly seek out the dramatic story. This ensures that the spectacle of trouble will always dominate. It makes for much better copy to concentrate on an exchange of patio furniture between drunken rival fans, than a group of supporter-sightseers taking in the local scenery and cuisine. Given these prevailing news values, the media often excites the issue of 'football hooliganism' by fanning public and political indignation through graphic headlines, exaggerated reports and vivid images implicating all England fans.

While the public has a right to be informed about incidents of disorder, this needs to be done in a considered and reflective manner, which does not amplify the situation or ignore the good behaviour of the vast majority. Otherwise, a media-generated frenzy can develop whereby the impact of a relatively minor incident is framed in such a way to appear much more than it actually was.

Media portrayals of football hooliganism tend to vary over time. Sometimes – for example during the domestic season – these portrayals appear to downplay the violence and scale of the issue. But at other times, especially at times of international competitions, it is given excessive focus. This is an indication of how the media plays a not insignificant role in constructing and shaping popular perceptions of the phenomenon of 'hooliganism' through its anticipation of violence and the representation of selected incidents. Sensationalist press reporting the dramatic moving audio-visual images of television, can have a powerfully enduring impact.

A degree of reflexivity and circumspection is therefore called for in future representations of England fans. The hooligan element should not be allowed to dominate the media coverage of England supporters in the way they frequently have in the past, so overshadowing the non-violent majority. Great progress has been made during the 2002 World Cup with the championing of the ordinary fans, many patriotic standard-bearers who follow England, at great expense, across the globe, without any inclination towards belligerence, bigotry or bloodshed. This must continue. As and when football-related violence occurs again involving England fans, there should not be a regression back to the one-dimensional portrayal of all supporters cast as villains. The causes and extent of the violence should be considered and placed in their proper context, as should the number of those involved vis-à-vis those not involved. All sections of England's support demand attention, not just the hooligan element who are in the minority, yet whose 'tales of terror' are usually allowed to dominate the front pages and opening television news items.

The next few years will indicate whether or not the 2002 World Cup will mark a further breakthrough in the media coverage of football of England fans abroad. Then, and only then, will the 'Neanderthal fan' butt of Mick Dennis and his ilk be finally filed under 'Stereotype – No Longer Applicable'.

THE ORIENT SELECTION: WHEN EAST MET WEST

With Ingerland in Japan

Mark Perryman and England Fans

The international feast of football culture that's a World Cup hits you the moment you pass through the arrivals lounge bleary eyed at Tokyo's Narita airport. The blue and white stripes of a friendly looking Argie right in front, viking-helmeted Swedes over by tourist information, and everywhere you look, the green of the travelling Oirish.

As for the English–Japanese culture shock, well, we're testing out our *Konichiwa* with a polite bow almost as soon as we're on Japanese soil. Our little taster of the lingo is very much appreciated and helps to pass the time during our quick-fire introduction to the Japanese obsession with queues and form filling. Picking up our Japan Rail pass is an administrative nightmare, topped only by the exhaustive procedure to book our precious seats for trains to Sapporo and Osaka. Never mind, we're on holiday, and what's a few hours between new-found friends, eh?

Everyone who helps us, serves us, guides us, is very much a pal once we pass over our David Beckham goodwill postcards. Strewth, I've never seen such huge grins of appreciation in all my footballing life. The habit here is not to tip, in fact that's thought of as rather rude, but to leave a gift is a massive gesture of respect. Fan ambassadorship has never been so easy, and so much fun.

Next up we negotiate the Japan railways to the suburb of Urawa, home of the J-League side Urawa Reds and part of Tokyo's commuter belt (sort of Watford to central London, and the Reds are similar under-achievers after a half-glorious recent history). We meet up with our hosts for the first few days, Gary Garner and his partner Megumi Araki. See, we don't like doing World Cups the conventional way. Eschewing hotels, we find football fans to stay with and get as close as we can to every possible aspect of the local culture. Gary is working out here for an Internet company; his house is very traditional Japanese with the rather disconcerting sight of West Ham memorabilia covering most spare bits of wall space.

Getting over the jet lag takes a good 24 hours, then it's off to an Irish pub – The Dubliners – in Shinzuku, part of Tokyo's 'Skyscraper District', to watch the opening game. Friday night is one of those weird Planet World Cup moments you never forget. The previous Thursday I'd helped organise a Japanese Language Class for London England Fans travelling out to the World Cup. We'd asked for a willing volunteer up on the stage to practise all the necessary phrases. A week later I shift a huge inflatable 'Hammered by the Irish' hammer which was obscuring my view of the big screen to find that self-same volunteer, QPR supporter Chris Hewitt, sitting behind it. Then Chris told me his particular traveller's tale. He'd come out to Japan via Taiwan in order to hook up with some mates who work in that country. He'd met up with them as arranged at their Taipei local, The Tavern. The landlord could not believe that anybody would travel all this way to support their team. They quizzed Chris. He must be a journalist, a coach, a multi-millionaire? No, he works on the London Underground. The bar erupted with disbelief, amazement and respect. They whipped him off to a photographer's studio and within hours, posters and flyers were printed up 'Come to The Tavern to meet Chris Hewitt – England fan travelled thousands of miles to see his team'. Next up the local radio station ICRT hear the story, and when they meet Chris and discover he's also a football quiz nut a bizarre programme idea unfolds. On the way back from Japan Chris will be stopping off in Taipei again to conduct a phone-in; any caller who can catch him out with a football trivia question he cannot answer wins a crate of beer. With this tale told, it's back to the match. The pub erupts when Senegal score, and the sheer joy on the hundreds of Irish faces all around me made me think they were confusing Senegal with Donegal.

Saturday, and we manage to blag our way into the 'Kick Off Saitama' reception at the England team hotel, Urawa Royal Pines. By now every time we dish out our David Beckham postcards we're being almost mobbed; being English and liked is a new and very pleasurable experience, I can assure you. The reception is full of all the customary dignitaries and niceties. But Paul Donohoe, Villa fan and a student working over here as an English teacher, has a bit of a show to put on for the assembled guests. With a bunch of friends, he'd been asked to teach the Saitama City's World Cup volunteer stewards some handy English phrases, but pretty soon it had become startlingly obvious that what was really needed was to get across the difference between being a loud but friendly passion-filled England fan, and the dangerous psychopaths too many Japanese were convinced all England fans would be. Paul put together a brilliant and easy to understand play, full of chanting, drinking, cheering and waving. They ended up touring it round Japan and the Royal Pines was their final performance. To see a large crowd of Japanese enthusiastically joining in the chant, 'Where we gonna go? The World Cup! What we gonna sing? We're English!' was an amazing sight and sound. The entire room was shouting away full of the bliss of English fan culture. The Swedes followed this with their cultural contribution, a ball juggler. Neat, but not a patch on our lads. 1–0 to the English.

We'd flown out on 29 May, arriving in Japan on the Thursday. England's first match was not until the Sunday, but we were 'Johnny Come Latelies' compared to Steve and Kay Murray, who'd arrived on 15 May with a mission. The first two England fans to arrive in Korea, Steve and his wife Kay are two of the stalwarts who get to the ground early to ensure the best possible position for their flag. More than two weeks before the Sweden match they had taken in England's first Far East friendly against South Korea. 'There were only about 60 of us at that one,' explained Steve, 'and not many more for the friendly against Cameroon in Kobe either.' Steve is hardcore England. His first away trip was Luxembourg in 1983 and since then he's been to the Mexico, Italy and France World Cups, plus almost every qualifier and friendly, home and away. Everywhere he goes, he takes his flag: 'Not Euro '96 mind.' Steve didn't think it was worth it with Wembley wall-to-wall in St George. His flag has 'Bexhill' written across the horizontal bar, with the crossed hammers of his club, West Ham, in the corner. Why Bexhill? 'It's where I live – moved there when I was four years old. It's a way of putting the town on the map. While West Ham, Bobby Moore and Billy Bonds era were my first love, my enduring inspiration.' When Steve first started taking his flag to games there were far fewer than there are today. 'It was flags on poles, we waved them in the early days.' Now the flags are tied up, and when his flag appears on the TV, Steve feels it is saying positive things about his town. 'What else is Bexhill famous for? Old people. Round here, they say the traffic is so severe to the cemetery they need a special set of traffic lights.' Steve's flag being seen is about showing the world a diehard, visible commitment to team and nation, pride in where you're from. 'About being noticed,' is how he puts it, and this means getting the best possible position. He's learnt a few tricks over the years. Most important of all is getting the flag up on the side facing the cameras; anywhere else and you can forget about your flag making it on to the TV. For England's game against Argentina in Sapporo, Steve and Kay carefully studied the Italy versus Ecuador game on the TV. The match took place in the same stadium so they used this research to work out the best place for their flag at what they were sure would be England's most important game of the tournament. The big 30 feet drop between the front row and pitch level meant special preparations. A long length of rope instead of his usual device for hanging the flag, bootlaces, was bought from the bargain Hundred Yen Shop in a Sapporo shopping mall. This was cut into four lengths so Steve and Kay could carefully lower their flag into the best position for the cameras. This was particularly important for what Steve reckons is the worst side of flying the flag for his country. 'No one respects your position, turn your back and somebody will put their flag over yours.' Hardly the all for one and one for all fan philosophy we might expect.

And position really matters to those who will think nothing of queuing up at noon for a game not set to kick off until the evening, rushing past the barriers as soon as they're opened to grab that all-important front row, opposite the camera place. 'Fulham, Feltham, Harlow Town, Brentford, Brentwood, Yeovil Town, Stalybridge, THFC Loughton.' Steve reels off those always first to get their flags up, reserving maximum respect for the Bexley and Hornchurch flags, mainstays not only of England football matches but to be seen at most of England's cricket matches too.

As Steve and Kay rushed past the barriers at Osaka the Japanese stewards smiled knowingly; 'Oh, we know all about you English and your flags.' These were words of respect for what has become part of England's fan culture. This is something that makes Steve proud, though he's generous enough to admit that the biggest flags belong to the Italians and the Argentines, and for mass spectacle he is full of respect for the Koreans' Red Devils. 'But flags with small towns' names on them, places where the fans come from. Nobody else does that like the English, do they?'

Sunday 2 June dawns in the land of the rising sun. Gary and Megumi have fixed up bicycles for all four of us to get to the game. Instead of a packed subway train or a shuttle bus we have a six-mile bike ride along the uncongested cycle path beside the busy motorway. Well, it would be uncongested if the Japanese in their England shirts would just get out of the way. We're pretty soon joining in the Japanised version of 'Ingerland' which translates into 'Ingerland-doh' if you want to sound like an authentic local. The counterfeit kit sellers are everywhere, stitch-perfect right down to imitation hologram seals of authenticity; extraordinary. The ride to the ground and all around Urawa-Minsono station is swarming with Japanese wearing England shirts. This is a surreal experience for the English – our team is liked, loved, adored and so are we? We certainly are. Mutter 'Beckham' and it creates a welcome, hand out a Beckham World Cup 2002 goodwill card and the Japanese fans clamour all around. The atmosphere is completely unthreatening; the English are starting to discover it's much more fun to be liked than feared.

Pre-match snacks in Japan are a tad different. Rice, tuna and mayonnaise wrapped in seaweed knocks spots off hot-dog and fried onions, and doesn't take much getting used to after the first mouthful. The culture clash continues as we make our way to the stadium entrance – a half-mile wander through paddy-fields with the Saitama ground looming larger and larger. Everywhere, the Japanese stewards are desperate to be helpful, the police presence decidedly low-key. Inside the ground the England end is warming to all this hospitality. A fair few have dressed for the occasion, a trio of look-alike Queens; a twin-set of look-alike David Seamans are within rice-chucking distance of me.

Alan Lee is with one of these characters who take a fancy-dress approach to their football. His mate, Gavin Morton-Holmes, is dressed for some inexplicable reason (other than involving a sizeable bet), as Elvis Presley. England versus Sweden, England's opening World Cup match, being there for Alan was a dream come true, though he admits the fantasy had never before included an Elvis Presley impersonator; still it takes all sorts. The Japanese, unsurprisingly fascinated by the sight, and completely unfazed, were holding sensible and well-informed conversations on the case for including Joe Cole in the starting line-up with Graceland's Jailhouse Rocker now revealed as not only alive, but a West Ham partisan to boot.

As kick-off approached the Swedish anthem is listened to in respectful silence, and there's hardly a whisper of all that 'No Surrender' rubbish. Of course the result didn't go quite the right way, and the team couldn't be bothered to come over and give the fans a wave at the end, which was a damn shame, but as we trudged through those paddy-fields once again back to where our bikes were parked, the spirits were still high. Or as Alan Lee put it, 'one down; now we're only six games from lifting the World Cup'.

Next day and there was sightseeing to do. No sign of the monsoon storms we'd been warned about yet; instead, it's baking hot. At the Zenjoji temple we pay our spiritual respects and hope for some good luck by chucking small change into the fountain. Japanese tradition, apparently. Tokyo is a city of huge contrasts, neon lighting almost everywhere, car-filled streets, everybody has a screen to their mobile phone for images as well as texting, then you settle down for dinner and it's back to something more traditional and decidedly eastern. Tonight we're trying out Kushi-age – fried food on sticks – a cut above kebabs and washed down with Japanese beer.

But wandering round Tokyo, seeing the sights, taking in the local delicacies, was nothing to what one group of fans had planned for what Sean McAuliffe describes as the 'in-between days'.

For Sean, this was his fifth World Cup. He's been to Spain in '82, Mexico in '86, Italy in '90 and France in '98. He admits that originally he'd not planned on going to Japan. He'd never accepted a foreigner should manage the national team; Munich had helped him warm to Sven, but the Swede's appointment still went against Sean's principles. Family responsibilities were growing too. After the England friendly in Amsterdam he'd crossed the channel and driven through the night to make it back to Rutland in the Midlands, in time for breakfast, on his daughter's birthday. A few weeks on the other side of the world was a tough call. But when his mate Bob said he was going, Sean couldn't resist the trip. Everything was booked easily enough via the Internet.

Now Sean wanted to find something for his 'in-between days'. Climbing Mount Fuji! That was what he eventually came up with – and when he posted the idea on the *englandfans* website he found 60 or 70 who said they'd join him. Then the bad news; he was informed that Mount Fuji, not exactly a stroll in the park at any time, has a strict walking season which did not begin until July, when the World Cup was over. Sean wasn't having any of this though, he was only going to Japan once and the climb was by now becoming a mild obsession. He managed to persuade the British Embassy to help out and the Japanese authorities co-operated. They must have thought this was the sort of mad Englishman worth giving in to – after all, hooliganism on a mountain slope sounded like a remote possibility. News that ropes and crampons would be required plus a possible wade through a snowfield served to whittle down Sean's volunteers. Never mind, the expedition was really taking off and now had the aim of raising several thousand pounds for the children's charity 'Whizz Kidz'.

Another Sean, Sean Bramton, takes up the story. Sean had been one of those who'd responded to the initial web-posting. He took an afternoon train from Tokyo expecting a pleasant, gentle country walk. Getting off at Shizuoka station he joined the others on a coach journey for a long, steep and winding drive to the fifth station on the Mount Fuji path, which they eventually reached at around 6 p.m. They all kipped down together in the dormitory accommodation – they didn't have much choice, as the lights went out at 9 p.m., swiftly followed by the generator closing down, and they were in the middle of nowhere.

At 4 a.m. the next morning the party were already tucking into their seaweed breakfast and by 5 a.m. they had set off. Sean had to pick his way through rocks that had fallen over an already uneven track, but on reaching the sixth station he was still thinking that it was all 'a bit of a breeze'. However, he only has one word for the next stage – an 'ordeal'. The pace dropped to barely 400 yards an hour, including a wade through a couple of hundred feet of snow. Five hours after setting off the group finally made the summit. Flags and scarves out, photos taken, a huge sense of achievement, doing something precious few other fans will be trying. Then it was back down, including sliding on their backsides across the snowfield until the ever-helpful Japanese guides warned them of the razor-sharp rocks that could lie just below the white fluffy surface. By 1 p.m. they were all back safe and sound at the fifth station and the waiting coach. For Sean McAuliffe, who'd been barking instructions at his climbing party for a little over 24 hours, it was time to relax and get back to the football. £3,500 raised for charity and definitely the only World Cup fans to climb Mount Fuji – so there's one record to take home to England.

Doug Bell and his mate Dave, meanwhile, were on their way to

Sapporo. They'd stopped off to stay in Hakodate on the island of Hokkaido, the northern island of Japan where Sapporo is located. And it was here that the two of them had one of those experiences that show just how global the community of football fans is. Fed up with watching matches on tiny hotel room TVs, they had decided to try to find a big screen in a bar to watch Ireland take on Germany. Making enquiries at their hotel, they were somewhat intrigued when offered a hand-drawn map complete with warning that the owner was a touch weird. But it was their only option, so off they set down some increasingly deserted backstreets as they ventured further and further away from the town centre. Eventually they thought they had found the door of the place they were looking for, but once inside it seemed they had ended up in somebody's front room. 'No, this is the place,' responded the four fellow England fans crowded round one of the tables to Doug and Dave's puzzled enquiry. The owner, the 'weird one' they'd been warned about, was buzzing around and clearly in his element. It turned out that he'd once been to England and taken in a 1970s League Cup final and had never been quite the same since. The match programme was proudly brought out for everybody to study.

Sushi, sake and the hurried filling-in of the DIY World Cup wallchart that had been carefully pinned up on the wall all helped to make this an unforgettable evening, not to mention Robbie Keane's last-minute equaliser. Toasted cheese sarnies, all free, were passed out from the tiny kitchen to keep the session going late into the night. When the final bill came, the party of England fans reckoned it could hardly have come close to even covering the owner's costs. But he didn't seem all that bothered – he'd had some fellow supporters, English ones, in his bar in the back of beyond.

Andy Stonestreet was staying in Aomori with his mates, just south of Hokkaido across the sea on the main Japanese island. Brighton and Hove Albion fans, plus Birmingham City and Scunthorpe United, the eight of them were all seasoned England travellers. They are well organised too. Andy was responsible for booking the internal flights, which he'd snapped up via the Internet at £35 for Tokyo to Aomori, the same for Sapporo to Osaka and Osaka-Tokyo. Scare stories in the British press about hugely inflated Japanese prices had proved to be totally unfounded with just a bit of investigation online. Tragically though, the stories had proved to frighten some off from bothering to bargain-hunt and many flights were scarcely half-full. Some had done their best though to spread the word, generously posting details of the cheap flights on the *englandfans* website, which was where Andy had first read of them.

Having arrived in Aomori and settled in to their hotel, they were looking for somewhere to drink. This was a place with none of the

'English-style Pubs' of Tokyo's westernised Rappongi district. Andy led the way, sticking his head through the curtains that seem to act as front doors, for more traditional homegrown Japanese bars. After a long search they found a place where some fellow English were drinking. As the evening wore on, more and more would stick their heads through the same curtains and much to the delight of the little old lady who owned the place there was eventually a party of 17 in her bar. She rushed out to restock her supply of beer, twice, but that wasn't all. When the football had finished on the TV she insisted on switching on her top of the range Karaoke rig. This was a challenge Andy and his mates couldn't resist. The standard Queen numbers were easy enough to perform but when Scunthorpe fan Darren polished off the Japanese love song on the tape the hosts were overcome with admiration. The next night the fans came back for more, and were joined by an audience of locals only too eager to join in the fun. It turned into a bit of a Karaoke World Cup, first the English up at the mike, then the Japanese. Eventually they'd run through the machine's entire repertoire of songs so the English started up with 'Simple Simon Says'. The huge Sumo wrestler at the bar standing beside Andy looked on in puzzlement; Andy took him by the hand; 'Simple Simon says tap your head,' and soon enough the guy was joining in.

The next morning Andy and his hungover party make it down to the harbour for the ferry that will take them to Sapporo – they travel in style this lot. Imagine their surprise though, to be met on the jetty by the little old lady with a packed lunch made up specially for each of them. Her takings had been quite extraordinary. Apparently, in two nights she'd cleared what she usually took in six months. But more than that, the English had come to her bar and joined in with her culture, shared some of theirs too, and given her a handful of nights she, and her customers, would never forget. At the end of the final evening she'd taken down a poster of one of the local Karaoke stars, turned it over, insisted all the England fans sign it then put it back up in pride of place.

With the Argentina game the plum pick for most England fans a lot flew out for just this one match. Geoff Morphew and Doug Snaith were amongst them, setting off from Fratton station, Portsmouth at 10 a.m. on Tuesday 4 June. By lunchtime they're at Heathrow and already feeling as if they're at the World Cup as they join some Denmark fans to watch South Korea beat Poland 2–0. Having boarded the plane, exchanged a nostalgic chat about Roger Milla with a Cameroon fan in traditional African dress and tucked into the free wine, Geoff and Doug are left comatose somewhere over Siberia. Which leaves them to wake up Wednesday 5 June as the plane taxis to a halt at Narita airport. Another flight to Sapporo and by 5 p.m. they're finally touching down in Sapporo. Trouble is, they can't make head or tail of the train departure board. The fans who travelled out early have had nearly a week to get used to the Japanese way of organising things, but for Geoff and Doug, there's no time to waste. No major panics yet though as they climb on to the express train to Sapporo Central Station. They're a bit fazed though by the quizzical looks from the Japanese; 'Do they think we're about to smash their train up?' the two of them wonder, not aware yet of the wave of friendship that's been rolling over the English since they arrived in Japan.

At the station, the size of Sapporo begins to dawn on them. A city of 1.8 million residents, this is a major metropolis. The address Doug has for their hotel amounts to what seems like a riddle 'R&B Hotel N4 W2'. Geoff works out that Sapporo is laid out US city-style with a grid of roads and they make their way to what they've realised is North 4, West 2 only five minutes from the station. They wander round this block made up of skyscrapers and on the third corner there is the sign they've been looking for; 'R&B Hotel'. Checked in and settled down, by 7 p.m. the hotel room is already feeling like home from home, and within half an hour they're off out to find a bar to watch Ireland versus Germany. They eventually find one, packed full of English, all supporting Ireland.

Game over, jet lagged, the two of them decide it's too early for bed so head off to try some more bars and Japanese food. Not surprisingly, the next day they're not out of bed much before three in the afternoon. They stagger, bleary eyed, out of the hotel and find themselves in Odori Park, the square in the centre of Sapporo where fans are most likely to gather. St George Cross flags are already being tied to every available tree, but nothing rowdy, just curious looks from the locals, and smiles all round. By the evening the two of them are hitting the bars again – after all, they've only got three days at this World Cup and they intend to make the most of it. They end up at a very plush establishment, all businessmen in suits knocking back shots of whisky. There's an all-round look of surprise as Geoff and Doug enter. 'Whoops, wrong sort of place for us,' they think. Then there's a round of applause. Proud to be entertaining the English, within minutes they're having drinks bought for them, which don't even stop when the inevitable Karaoke session begins and they treat the bar to The Sex Pistols' version of 'God Save the Queen'. To bed at 2 a.m., one night's sleep, and it will be match day dawn in the morning.

Nine o'clock the next morning and, like many fans who've made it out to Japan, Geoff and Doug are keen to do as much sightseeing as they can. With only a few days in the country the two of them head off to Sapporo's nearest mountain range for a cable car ride. The trouble is that the view from the summit, while magnificent, takes in the strange sight of the city's Dome where that evening's match will take place. All thoughts of soaking up the scenery are pretty soon gone as every possible result races through their imagination.

So giving in to the inevitable, Geoff and Doug join the fans heading off to the Dome. Amongst them was travel writer Bill Bryson, who summed up what ensued rather neatly in *The Times*: 'Nobody told me – did not even come close to hinting – how unbearably exciting, how joyously nerve-wracking it is, to attend an England match in a World Cup. This is particularly so, when the opponents are Argentina, the score is close and the alternative to victory is probable extinction.'

I don't know if Bill Bryson managed to make it to Odori Park after the match. We did, along with just about every other England fan in Sapporo. The park was actually more like a city centre square, the kind of place I'd normally avoid before and after an England game as the most likely site for any trouble. It was certainly what the locals have been warned to expect. But there's no fear tonight, just joy. And the really weird thing is that it's the Japanese who are dancing, singing and chanting just as much as the England fans. This is so very strange. We're used to being feared at best, fought at worst. But loved? Never before. The Japanese aren't just great hosts, they're England fans too. Everywhere you look around Odori Park young Japanese have their England shirts on. They want not just to share in the moment; they feel the weight of celebration, shrugging off 1998 and 1986 in one almighty night. On the street corners vendors are dishing out a special one sheet edition of one of the local papers. There's one huge headline, easy enough to understand in any language, '1–0!' It's the souvenir the fans who have travelled to the other side of the world wanted more than anything else but hardly dared to dream about. Neatly rolled up, this is something we'll treasure for a long time to come.

On the mobiles, we're ringing home. 'You're at work? Demand the day off! Declare a national holiday!' Then late into the following morning we're supping sushi and knocking back the beer Sapporo is famous for. I'm sitting next to a guy who'd paid £420 for his match ticket – that's a season ticket at plenty of Premiership clubs – but he's not regretting a penny of it. In this world of spin and hype it's so hard to be somewhere and feel you are grabbing hold of, keeping hold of, a moment of history to be a part of. But tonight that is precisely what we fans packed under that roof in Sapporo did, and we're savouring every moment of it. Staggering around this city with a great big grin on our faces and adoring the fact that the Japanese not only smile back, but they understand what this moment means too.

In the subway trains to the stadium the England fans had been singing 'We're the friendliest fans at this World Cup, la-la-la'. The song had a nasty kick to it . . .'But you wouldn't want to meet us if we lose.' After a night like this maybe we won't have to add this health warning that has been our lot for too many tournaments to mention. The Japanese have taken the best of English fandom, given it back to us wrapped in something nice and topped it all with a footballing night we'll never forget. *Sayonara* Sapporo, this is a night we'll remember for a long time to come.

Geoff and Doug were certainly still full of memories as they touched down at Heathrow after their three-day World Cup, while for those staying out it was on to Osaka. Alan Lee is on his way south and still chuckling about the lad who had flown out specially for the Argentina game only to miss Beckham's goal as he was caught short and in the bog. No bad luck for ex-Royal Marine Alan though, who unashamedly hugged mates Ian Potter and Nic Banner when Becks' ball crashed into the back of the net.

Billy 'The Bee' Grant arrived in Osaka on the Sunday before England's final group game with Nigeria. 'The Bee' is for Brentford; Billy's a bit of an atmosphere junkie but he denies this is down to too many dull afternoons at his beloved Griffin Park. Still, with a few days to kill he's soon listening out for an interesting way to fill his time. Watching Japan versus Russia on the big screen at the Osaka Dome, the city's indoor baseball stadium, sounded like it might be worth a look, though Billy wasn't convinced. How can a Jumbotron broadcast come close to matching the excitement of actually being there? Thirty thousand Japan fans clearly thought otherwise as they packed into the Dome a full two hours before kick-off. And the atmosphere was something else. The first thing Billy noticed was that every Japan fan was wearing the team colours; there were just no exceptions. Inside the Dome Billy checked his watch – he was sure there was still a good while to go until kick off. Yet all around him the fans were going mental. *Ni-iii-pon! Ni-iii-pon! Ni-iii-pon! Ai! Ai!* They chanted, jumping around furiously – and what were they cheering? A Nintendo computer-game version of Japan versus Russia played out on the big screen. So this was just a taster of what was to come. By the time the actual game was under way the entire place was whipped up into a wild frenzy the like of which Billy had never experienced before. Huge Japanese flags were passed over supporters' heads up and down the stands. Cheerleaders goaded the crowd into more chanting by blowing horns and various other instruments. The incessant chanting and cheering went on non-stop for the entire first half. Billy was converted, he'd found his second team for the tournament, *Ni-iii-pon! Ni-iii-pon!*

Goalless at half-time and there was all to play for. Then the local boy, Junichi Inamoto, scored. Inamoto was still officially on Gamba Osaka's books – the deal with Arsenal was a loan – so when his shot hit the back of the Russian net it was a very special moment for all those watching in his home town. The chant stayed with Billy the whole of the tournament *Inamoto Sy-ko! Inamoto Sy-ko!*, which roughly translates as 'Inamoto, the best', or words to that effect. All over the stadium they chanted it in perfect unison. Then they did a little dance; in every stand, the fans turned to the left and did a shuffle down the aisle they were standing in – nobody was sitting by now – then they'd turn to the right and shuffle back. And all the time chanting and shouting. The celebrating continued late into the evening, topped by hundreds of fans throwing themselves off the city's Ebisu and Dotunbori bridges into the river below.

Meanwhile, the night in Osaka the day before the Nigeria game was proving to be a bit of a blur for Alan Lee. He woke up in his hotel room the next morning on the day of the match only to find his prized England shirt replaced by a Nigerian top. Confusion reigned until he remembered swapping his shirt with the biggest Nigerian he'd ever seen the previous evening. The shed-load of Japanese beer had removed most memories but after a six pints recovery dose, of water, he was ready for what he regarded as the most important game of the campaign so far.

Osaka is not a huge city but the Japanese habit of a minimum of fifteen exits per subway station could throw the most experienced traveller off the route to the stadium. By the time he's safely in his seat the early afternoon sun is streaming down and Alan's bald head is taking a pasting in the heat and glare. Alan's been involved with the 'Raise the Flag' initiative at England home games since the start, and in his local town, Grantham, he regularly meets up with fellow England fans committed to a positive support of their national team. He's suitably chuffed, therefore, that the Nigerian anthem is listened to in respectful silence. These things matter to fans like Alan.

The game of course ends in a 0–0 draw, enough to send England into the second round. Alan, like thousands of other England fans, finds himself surrounded by very happy-looking Japanese as he makes his way to the exit. Each time a Japan fan smiles and bows Alan finds himself automatically doing the same in return.

Back at the hotel Alan now has a sombre duty to perform. For 20 years he's been very proud of his rather splendid moustache but now his top lip is as bald as his head. His bet on England qualifying for the knock-out stages with mate Gavin Morton-Holmes meant the 'tache had to go. Still, Gavin's side of the bargain was far the riskier; shaving off your pubic hair round your private parts can be a tricky business after a pint or three.

Tara Jewell is basking in the joy of just being there to see England qualify for the second round. Her picture had been plastered all over *The Sun* a couple of weeks before the World Cup opened. Wearing a number seven shirt she was holding up a replica of the World Cup trophy and shouting with all her worth for England. The FA had been keen to get across the message that following England was for everyone, so when *The Sun* came up with the idea of a feature on female England fans they put them in touch with Tara, who is a regular posting all sorts of messages on the FA *englandfans* website. Tara took the call, readily agreed to take part then thought it would be fun to see if there were others who would like to join in too. Both she and *The Sun* were amazed by the response, a complete team of 11 women fans, all travelling out to Japan, with ages ranging from 19 to 63 years. After being holed up in an Islington photographic studio for a day, the resulting three-page photo spread was incredibly positive, if written in the inimitable style of *The Sun* with the banner headlines: 'Spotlight on girls who will do anything to get to Japan. One got a £5,000 loan, others spent life-savings to see World Cup action.' In Japan Tara was part of an Inside Japan tour, 29 blokes, including husband Keith, and herself. She'd always thought the party would be mainly guys but was surprised to find herself the lone woman. But at the games she didn't feel so solitary – there was a definite increase in the number of women travelling to this World Cup and with the lack of trouble and the growing coverage of female England fans, Tara is sure this will grow. She's been following England for a few years now and has a theory why the women fans don't get noticed: 'Men tend to get the attention. I can't see many women throwing chairs across the street.' Radio Five, local paper the *Basildon Echo* and BBC Radio Essex all did pieces about Tara's trip and she's sure that this kind of positive coverage can only help all fans who want to put the trouble behind them. She's a neat way of summing up her World Cup memory too: '29 men, 1 woman and some temples.'

Like many others, Tara, and most of the 29 blokes are heading home after the Nigeria game. For the rest, there are now two days before England's next match, against Denmark – a good opportunity to put in some serious sightseeing. Osaka is in the south, handily placed for a trip to the ancient city of Kyoto or the city that's world famous for a horrific bit of modern history, Hiroshima. Alan Lee is one of many who decide to plump for the latter. A Shinkansen train gets him there in just 90 minutes from Osaka and then it's a very sobering walk through the Peace Garden to the A-bomb Memorial Dome. Alan stops and ponders how it is that these Japanese people who surrounded him and others at the match yesterday have found it so easy to forgive the West for that August day in 1945, which would scar their city for ever? How have they managed to accept what went wrong and move forward?

Alan spends some time in the city museum. It tells the story in graphic detail of the atomic bomb dropped on Hiroshima which killed 140,000 living and working in the city, the overwhelming proportion civilians, not combatants. Alan thinks back to his train journey here from Osaka. The guard, who inspected his ticket, stopped at the end of his carriage, blew a whistle and bowed in thanks to his passengers. The train was spotless and ran on time. Polite and generous, maybe the English could learn something from this faraway culture that only in the recent past has caused so much suffering, and suffered so much in return too. Alan is here for the football, make no mistake of that, but some days there is more to life than football. Today is one of those days.

Friday, and Billy 'The Bee' is back in Tokyo and already converted to Japan's cause, desperate to find somewhere to top his Osaka Dome experience. He hears the Tokyo Olympic Stadium is doing something similar for the Japan versus Tunisia game so gets himself down there. Sold out! 60,000 tickets gone and this is just for a match on a big screen. All around the stadium people are huddled round mini-TV sets to catch the action the best they can. But Billy's having none of that. No ticket, but he cons his way in claiming to be a high-ranking member of the Nigerian Football Federation. Being one of a small but increasing number of England's travelling black fans has its advantages.

Once in the stadium all Billy can see is blue, blue and yet more blue. Nowhere could Billy spot a fellow western face, but not once did he feel intimidated or out of place. On the contrary, every couple of minutes he'd find himself mobbed by Japanese wanting to thank him for coming along to support their team. He'd thought Osaka couldn't be topped, but double the crowd equals double the madness. Horn players, drummers, young lads with megaphones perched high on posts issuing instructions to the fans below on what cheer and chant to bellow out. Lo and behold when the mood turned to a good old football sing-song the crowd favourite turned out to be *The Great Escape*. Orchestration though wasn't just about singing and chanting. One of Billy's abiding memories was 60,000 fans, no not a single person didn't join in, with hands outstretched in front of them and slowly humming while they waited for a crucial free kick to be taken. With the final whistle and a 2–0 Japanese victory securing the much-prized second-round qualification, the whole of Tokyo was set for a party the like of which it had never seen before. Billy was sold on all things oriental, with the possible exception of the dodgy Japanese dance records they insisted on playing to celebrate a win. Never mind, you can't have everything.

For most England fans all thoughts are now on the Niigata game and come Saturday morning that's where they are all heading. Not Dave Lowe and his friend Paul though. Dave's stuck in South Korea and not regretting it for a moment. He's taking in five games, none of them involving England and having a great time along the way. That's not to suggest Dave doesn't like England, far from it. He's been following the team since the mid-'60s. But he's in Pusan for the South Africa versus Paraguay game, then South Korea versus Poland in Pusan again. 'Wild and magnificent' is how he describes being part of the Red Devil experience for their first World Cup victory, ever. Third game and it's France versus Uruguay, once again in Pusan. Then it's off to Daegu, described apparently as the 'Milan of the East', which seems to amount to being incredibly hot in the summer and freezing cold in the winter. No ticket for South Africa versus Slovenia but Dave manages to buy a Category Three, the cheapest ticket, at £45, not bad. Then it's on to Incheon for Dave's final match of the trip, France versus Denmark. Being a Norwich City fan he is used to football's crushing disappointments but he can hardly imagine what it must be like for the World Champions to go home with one point and no goals.

Dave now has no more tickets but he's in Incheon for South Korea versus Portugal as Paul's lucky enough to be going to this, the final group match for the hosts. Victory and qualification for the second round turns the entire city into one gigantic party. Dave is in a bar joining in for all his worth and eventually makes it back to his hotel in the early hours of the morning. Dave and Paul will watch the England versus Denmark game on TV before heading home, via Kuala Lumpur. They didn't catch England themselves this time round; like many hundreds of England fans they just wanted to be at the World Cup for the experience. At every game, whoever was playing, TV viewers would spot a St George Cross, testament to what Dave, Paul and others were getting up to in the cause of their love of football. It's another feature of England fan culture that barely gets a mention. No other country's fans do this, the best of supporters, committed and well informed we like to think. As for Dave, he's off to Scotland in August. Norwich City are going there on pre-season tour and there are a few Scottish grounds he's not visited yet. This football adventure knows no boundaries.

Lynn Smith managed to make it to both Japan and Korea, plus Los Angeles, Australia, New Zealand (for England's cricket tour there), back to Australia to take in some Australian Rules football, followed by South Korea for England's pre-World Cup friendly. Then the opening ceremony and France versus Senegal, followed by Japan to follow England then back to South Korea for the Korean knock-out stage matches. She'd fallen for the fan appeal of the Red Devils. Sitting on a stationary Shinkansen for four hours at a platform near Shizuoka while a typhoon passed over was one of her many memorable moments on this extraordinary five-month, multi-sport trip. She also remembers, rather fondly now, the Buddhist monks who knocked politely on her tent-flap. She'd pitched her tent the night before in the dark on the lawns of their temple, expecting to be able to slip away unnoticed. Sleeping in put paid to that, but with sweetness and smiles the monks welcomed Lynn as their first World Cup guest and showed her around the temple.

Lynn, of course, was amongst those heading for Niigata for the

Denmark second-round match. Only two hours from Japan, travel-wise this game was a bit of a doddle. But we England fans don't like to make things too easy. Jerry Drew and the FA's James Worrall, who've been handling the huge (and we're talking side of your house dimensions here) 'Come on England' flag at all the previous games, have headed home and some kind sod has volunteered yours truly for the task. So on the shoulders of our Tokyo host in downtown Hirai, Trevor Ballance, and my shoulders is a giant laundry bag, and it weighs a ton.

Still we manage to make it, safe, sound and sore to Tokyo Central station and hop on the Shinkansen. Trevor's without a match ticket so he's not going to the game. Not to worry though – we're meeting up with some mates in Niigata. On arrival, the station is heaving. It's one of the delights of the World Cup that you can spend a day or so with the locals, tasting the food, taking in the sights and sampling the culture, then come match day the city you're heading to is like a little bit of England all over again. We meet up with our Urawa host, Gary Garner, and a few of his friends. Two of them have got big floppy St George Cross hats on and are draped in England flags in a sort of sarong style. It's very slow progress through the station, as all the Japanese want their photos taken with these two, kids as well. 'Ingerland' in town has become a very different spectacle to the one we'd become too used to presuming it had to be.

Eventually we find a restaurant. Another huge and delicious Japanese meal, this one's 'Soba', a big pile of cold noodles, savoury sauce and heaps of meat, all washed down with a nice cold bottle of Asahi dry. Then it's downstairs for the first half of the Germany versus Paraguay game. More and more English are piling in, shoes off, cross-legged around tables not more than six inches off the floor. The Japanese and us are all together, willing the Paraguayans to victory. Strangely enough, I've not seen a single Japanese person wearing a German shirt yet – all England – which when you cast your mind back 50 or 60 years is a bit weird really; but very, very nice all the same.

Paul Probyn meanwhile is on the other side of town. He'd been trying to find the 'Black Pig', that strange phenomenon you find in most big cities anywhere in the world, 'The English Pub'. Never quite as popular as 'The Irish Pub' mind you, but just right if you fancy a frothy pint of bitter with a plate of fish and chips. The trouble for Paul was that it seemed several thousand England fans had exactly the same thought – fourteen days of sushi and sake had obviously proved too much for some. Unable to get anywhere near the door, let alone the bar, Paul settled himself down in the nearby shopping arcade, a more eccentric place to put up a giant screen to televise Germany versus Paraguay it would be hard to imagine. Surrounded by busy-looking Saturday afternoon shoppers, Paul sat with fifty or so locals to will

Germany to defeat. It didn't happen, but they were kept well supplied with beers by a local cafe, teased the odd Dane and when three German fans joined them, they had a bit of friendly banter at their expense too. And all the time a constant swarm of shoppers would pick their way through in search of a bargain, oblivious to the fact that this was a crowd of those fans their government, police, chambers of commerce, TV, radio and newspapers warned them for six months or more previously would in all likelihood raze their city to the ground, kidnap their wives and daughters and generally be their worst nightmare since Godzilla was the nation's scariest movie star. Strange things happen.

Three hours to kick-off and we head to the stadium. There are four of us now carrying the weighty flag so it's not too awkward. We're heading for 'entry gate north' on free shuttle buses. The transport, as always, is faultless, and puts a lot of what we don't lay on to get to matches back in the so-called 'home of football' to shame. At the stadium I mangle my latest handy Japanese phrase kindly taught me by Trevor's Japanese wife Kinuko; *England-doh Official Hattar*, which translates as 'England's Official Flag'. By now we've got it out of the bag and have had a half-arsed go at unfurling it and folding it up again, so I look a suitably eccentric sight with the flag covering me in yards and yards of material, head to foot and all around. I'm with my partner Anne who, being a sensible type, will have nothing to do with manhandling this flag into the stadium, while Gary's party are all heading off to sit in other sections of the ground, so this leaves me carrying it on my own. With a very red face, sweat streaming, and grinning politely, I'm a walking flag roly-poly Sumo man saying 'England-doh Official Hattar'. Kinuko's careful tutoring of my phraseology works wonders. I'm let in, though trying to get the flag through the x-ray machine was a bit of a handful. Up on to Level 2 and by kick-off, Alan Lee, Ian Potter, Emma Kirkham and her brother Mark have rallied round to tie the flag to some railings. After a rushed rehearsal the flag is rather expertly unfurled over the fans' heads immediately after the National Anthem. It certainly was gigantic and all part of the carnival that unfolded over the ensuing 90 minutes. All those po-faced observers who reckon the English can't handle the carnivalesque should be force-fed videos of this game. A conga to the chant 'Let's go Oriental' just took off after the third goal went in, and spread all around the stadium – English and Japanese all joining in together. The stewards took ages to get everybody back to their seats. Briefed to handle crowd trouble, they hadn't anything in their manuals on how to control a party. This wasn't like Sapporo, hanging on for victory. This was 45 minutes of unbridled and, let's be honest, unexpected celebration.

But when the final whistle blew there was still the big matter of that blasted flag and how to get it back to Tokyo safe, sound and in one piece. Once again we unfurl it and fold it up as best we can. Then with the chant '*Sayonara Niigata*' somehow we struggle back on to the shuttle bus. The journey to the train station is great. The bus, fifty–fifty Japanese and English are swapping chants of '*Gambare England-doh*' with '*Gambare Nippon*' ('Gambare' means come on). At the station the local council are even giving everybody a goody bag as they leave. The cold tea takes getting used to but the thought is there.

The Shinkansen Express back to Tokyo is a double-decker train, and with football specials (now there's a Far East back to the future blast) running every ten minutes there's a seat for everyone. We sup out of our cold tea sachets, munch our 'calorie-beater' – someone must have told the Niigata Prefecture about an Englishman's propensity for a beer gut – biscuits, and it feels like heaven. The train is fast, the ride smooth and at around 3 a.m. we arrive back in Tokyo. The subway isn't running but there's the longest line of taxis I've ever seen. Within ten minutes or so we're in bed and struggling to make out the distinctions between dream football and the finest World Cup night most of us have ever experienced.

Next morning and it's that blasted flag again. It has become bulkier and heavier, almost impossible to carry. I try unfolding it on the quiet road outside Trevor and Kinuko's flat in Hirai, but I need an eight-lane motorway, not a backstreet – far too narrow. Then I spy what I think is a park, about 100 metres away. Perfect. I struggle up the road to find that what I thought was a park is actually a school playground. They must have a seven-day school week out here as the space is full of kids; a football match, tennis practice and baseball pitching are all in studious progress. So I try the street outside. I'm making a right pig's ear of this unfolding business but pretty soon I'm surrounded by curious youngsters. Quick as a flash, I try '*England-doh official Hatter origami*' and point hopefully at the playground where I notice the tennis court is now empty. The kids pick up the flag – we're in. And as we unfold it to its full magnificent size the school classrooms empty and we've got ourselves a party. *The Great Escape*, conga dancing, '*Gambare England-doh*', and my full crib sheet of faltering Japanese; I do the lot to much incredulous hilarity.

With the flag now neatly folded, much bowing and '*Arrigatoh Gozaimas*', (that's thank you very much) I head back to the flat. Mind you, every ten metres or so I'm stopped by a gaggle of schoolgirls desperate to confess their great affection for David Beckham. Another round of swapping chants, '*Gambare England-doh!*' '*Gambare Nippon*! All this friendly fan stuff can be a tad exhausting when you've got a 3–0 victory to get over and a match against Brazil to look forward to.

Not everyone though could stay out for what was proving to be a much longer campaign than we might have reasonably expected when that fateful group draw was made. Craig Brewin and his wife Philippa were amongst those at this stage homeward bound. If they looked a touch more tired than some it was mostly down to Nancy, their one-year-old, who was making her World Cup debut. Craig freely admits that most of his friends thought they were mad; just looking after the ever-constant needs of a small child can be demanding enough, throw in a World Cup on the other side of the world and the prospect would be a lot too daunting for most parents, never mind the kid. But with nobody to leave Nancy with back in England it was either Nancy went or none of them went. And anyway, Craig reckoned he could earn a lot of PC kudos with his workmates – wasn't the modern way to involve children in all that we do, eh?

Not many children of course join the England Supporters Club on the day they are born, but Nancy did, making her probably the youngest fan to be put through the FA's rigorous cross-referencing against criminal records before an application can be accepted. Offences to be taken into account? Dribbling down my bib, officer.

Craig thought that some hard-bitten fans might resent Nancy's presence – after all, a one-year-old takes up a seat in the stand that some would argue should go to an adult. But none seemed to think she was out of place. Instead, fans would gather round to 'ooh' and 'agh' and mention approvingly 'she'll remember this for the rest of her life'. Though Craig thinks that improbable; even a prodigious memory-bank is unlikely to recall anything at all, no, not even 1–0 against Argentina, from just twelve months of age.

Match day preparations when you've a one-year-old are a tad different. Up early, find the nearest playground. Do your best to entertain child whilst surreptitiously tiring her to point she'll want to fall asleep. Back to hotel, put Nancy to bed, hope she sleeps. Hope this keeps up for most of morning. Prepare to get to game early. Put sleeping Nancy in pushchair. Make way to ground. Find pushchair park; yes, the Japanese have thought of everything. Wake sleeping Nancy up, hand in hand Craig, Philippa and Nancy make way to their seats. Nancy loves all the shouting and cheering, so England scoring is always her high point of the excursion; some things are common then all through our footballing lives. Her favourite part of being a fan though is clapping along to the supporters' band. Her request for them to play 'Twinkle, Twinkle' to date, however, remains unanswered. Quite what the rest of the crowd would think of a terrace rendition of this nursery favourite defies comprehension.

Craig does admit that despite all the excitement, 90 minutes is a long time for Nancy to endure. The Sweden game was therefore a blessing. Like most of the crowd, Nancy could snooze through the last 20 minutes and not worry that she might miss anything worth watching. The Denmark game, well, 3–0 up at half-time, left the second half ear-splittingly loud in celebrations, so Nancy and Craig popped outside for a respite. The Nigeria game was in the full glare of the afternoon Osaka sun so Nancy sensibly wore a hat. Being blonde too, she made quite a picture and duly obliged as one person after another queued up to take a snap. Like the Sweden game, she wasn't missing much on the pitch as England played out a 0–0 draw.

Bang on full time Craig, Philippa and Nancy always make a mad dash for the first shuttle bus. They'd decided between them that injury time, extra time and penalty shoot-outs would be too much. Craig checks his watch and when 90 minutes is up the three of them head for the exit. They pick the pushchair up from the pushchair park and are back in their hotel, carefully chosen for its proximity to the ground, within 30 minutes of leaving the stadium. Craig reckons this World Cup scores pretty highly as child-friendly. Lots of entertainment around the stadium, dancers, drummers, jugglers and the like, while the large number of young Japanese women who clearly thought it perfectly natural to bring their children to the games with them helped too. His fellow England fans impressed Craig too, full of the carnival spirit, not even a hint of trouble, which leaves Craig, Philippa and Nancy hopeful of also being there in Portugal 2004. It's unlikely on the anglicised Algarve though that they'll commit the sort of translation error they made in one Japanese supermarket. Twenty-eight-inch waist incontinence pants didn't go down too well with Nancy as any sort of alternative to her more regular choice of nappy.

As Craig, Philippa and Nancy flew home, Alex Roy and girlfriend Linda Danson prepared to spend the few days before England's quarter-final on a Japanese beach. Alex had managed to persuade Linda that a three-week trip to the Orient would make a dream honeymoon. They never did get round to organising the wedding, but why pass up a holiday like this just because the church hadn't been booked in time?

One condition Linda insisted on was that a three-week trip meant they had to visit a beach at least once. Curiously enough, for an island, Japan is rather short of seaside resorts complete with sand and sea safe and clean enough to swim in. Most of the coastline seems to have been concreted over – it must be something they have against the place that those whales they love to eat come from. Okinawa is the favourite beach destination for the Japanese but far too far away when the furthest south that England would be venturing was to Osaka. So Alex thought he'd been really clever when he spotted Shimoda on the Izu peninsular for a short break before the Shizuoka game. Shimoda proved to be a small, quiet town and when they took their first stroll around the place they hardly noticed any other visitors, still less fellow England fans. By evening though, when they ventured out to a small bar, there were more than 20 other English in the place watching the Korea versus Italy game. 'Lonely Planet or Rough Guide?' the crowd asked Alex. He should have guessed. Armed with one or other of the guide-books, 'off the beaten track' soon loses its anonymous ring. The bar was run by a Japanese guy with a Mohican that would have done Becks proud. No fan himself, the English had persuaded him that for their custom a TV would be a worthwhile investment. He happily obliged, though revealed his true allegiances at any given opportunity by turning down the sound and playing one of his favourite jazz records to the throng. When the game finished, and after much beer all round, he clearly decided his jive wasn't jumping sufficiently so he knocked the TV off its appointed stool on stage and treated everybody to a jazz impro jam that lasted well into the night. The god-awful racket was still ringing in Alex and Linda's ears the next morning when they left Shimoda for Shizuoka – having duly visited the beach.

We didn't make it to the beach but took in Hiroshima and the ancient city of Kyoto for a spot of sightseeing between the Denmark and Brazil games. Before leaving Tokyo though for our trip down south there were a few preparations to be made. Brazil in a World Cup quarter-final; win or lose, this was going to be a bit special. I got on the phone to my mate Hugh Tisdale, design guru behind the England Fans' 'Raise the Flag' initiative at home games – thousands of red and white cards to form the St George Cross. Hugh was holding the fort at *Philosophy Football* with his frighteningly efficient wife, Deborah, sending hundreds of T-shirts out to those hankering after being dressed by the self-styled 'sporting outfitters of intellectual distinction' company Hugh and I formed after one of my brighter blinding flashes of inspiration. 'I've got an idea.' I could almost detect Hugh's heart sinking, he'd heard that one more times than his bank manager would like to remember, but boosted by the Denmark match euphoria he let me continue. 'We've got to do a "Raise the Flag" in Shizuoka, and I think I know how it can be done.' I'd spotted in a Japanese football magazine a picture of their fans at one of the group games. Each one was holding up a big sheet of paper with their flag printed on it, a red circle in the middle of a white rectangle. No layout required, no attaching them to seats; all that was needed was to get them in the ground and pass the cards along the rows of the section where England were sitting. Hugh was convinced, on the case straightaway. He had 24 hours to design, print and dispatch 1,250 St George Cross flag cards out to Tokyo. Trevor agreed to bring them down to Shizuoka for when we would meet up on match day. Plan one executed. Then I had to ask Kinuko for some more linguistic advice. Watching the Japan team go out to Turkey I'd been struck by their lap of thanks for the fans. They'd stripped off their team shirts to reveal vests underneath with the slogan 'Thank You Japan'. Brilliant! After three weeks in this country every single England supporter I'd met shared precisely this sentiment. It would blow away all the negatives in the most positive of fashions if I could rig up a huge banner with these words. But we'd also noticed that what really touched the Japanese was our faltering attempt at a word or two of their language. This was how Kinuko could help, carefully showing me the calligraphy to spell out in perfect Japanese *Arrigatoh Gozaimas Nippon.* With this carefully recorded in my notebook but without any obvious idea of how to make a banner to write it on, Anne and I headed off to see the sights.

In Kyoto, while Anne took in another round of temples on Thursday morning, I visited one shop after another. I needed about ten metres of material, about a metre deep. A sheet was no good, wrong shape; wallpaper would tear too easily and curtain material would cost me an arm and a proverbial. Almost giving up on the stupid idea I finally found the answer. An 'obie' is a very long piece of material worn as part of Japanese women's traditional dress wrapped round and round the waist. Quite what the shopkeeper thought I'd do with it I don't know but for the purpose shortly to be at hand it was near perfect. Getting hold of red paint and brushes was a doddle after that and I now retreated to a quiet side road. The obie was stretched out and carefully I painted, first in English, then diligently following Kinuko's instructions in Japanese. One careless brush stroke and I could be painting – I don't know what – gibberish replacing the words of thanks. The sun was very hot so my efforts dried virtually as I went along. I just hoped I'd got the lettering right.

Friday morning and we catch the train north to Kakegawa, the nearest station to Shizuoka stadium, where I'm due to meet Trevor before getting the customary shuttle bus to the stadium. Trevor is quite possibly the only person working in Japan without a mobile phone but he promises me it's a small station and we'll meet up easily enough. Off the train, I'm as ridiculously early as always, but catch up with a couple of Dagenham and Redbridge fans from the London England Fans travel forums. They're complaining about the FA decision to admit Boston United into the league even though there have been financial irregularities proven against them. It's a small world, football.

Now on to weightier matters. Trevor's arrived, found a call box and is telling me where to meet him. He's looking a bit red in the face. Hugh's cards had turned up on his and Kinuko's doorstep the day before and he'd somehow managed to stuff them into a rucksack and a very big shopping bag. They weighed an awful lot. Just one problem remained. The stadium stewards were very strict on preventing fans bringing bags full of paper into the grounds, they didn't want ticker-tape style effects to clear up after us. So what was to be done? Another blinding flash – stuff them down at the bottom of bag and backpack, and cover them in my dirty washing. Only the most committed official is going to risk going past the pong of my smalls.

So feeling like two extras from *The Great Escape* and with a ten-metre banner stowed away, we board the shuttle bus. All of Japan's stadiums have been pretty amazing, and the Shizuoka one is no exception. The vehicle snakes its way along a motorway empty of all traffic except fellow shuttle buses, all heading in the same direction. The motorway doesn't seem to have any other obvious purpose than to transport fans to the stadium. The drop-off point is in the middle of a forest, the ground surrounded by acre after acre of paddy-fields. We jump off the bus and it's a mile or so pleasant country stroll along a footpath before we reach the ground. We got there early – after all, we had our smuggling operation to complete followed by distributing the cards – but what were all these other thousands doing here four hours before kick-off? As the turnstiles opened, at least a few of them had an excuse, as off they sprinted at a hugely impressive turn of speed up the steps to get their flags tied up in prime position. Leading at the front I spotted Steve Murray. That Bexhill St George Cross would be in the best spot, I had no doubt of that. Meanwhile, Trevor and I shuffled mildly nervously towards the gates. We needn't have worried; one whiff of my pants and socks, a hurried explanation as to how we were carrying a week's supply of reading on our backs and in our bags (to explain the heavy weight), and we were through. Hardly up with Dickie Attenborough doing his Stalag Luft wotsit turn but we felt quite pleased with ourselves nevertheless.

In the England section we were right in the sun, but with no time to top up the tan as we set to work handing out the cards. 'Mobbed' would be the right word for the response. Not by the English, they were cool, calm and collected, most had been a part of something like this at home games, many had seen the postings of what we planned to do on the *englandfans* website. It was the Japanese who were going crazy. Each time we went up and down another aisle to pass the cards out we'd be surrounded – mums, dads, kids, young and old fans, all desperate to have a St George Cross of their own. Who said nationalism is the polar opposite of internationalism? In Shizuoka it certainly isn't. I'm sure all these Japanese the week before had been desperately keen to see their team win, but they had no hang-ups in adopting England as their second favourite side. And the English, to a fan, were deeply affected in return.

At the appointed moment, when 'God Save the Queen' struck up, hundreds of the cards went up in the air. As the poet Rupert Brooke put it, 'some corner of a foreign field that's forever England'. Yes, thank you very much. Being in and amongst the cards though, we couldn't see the effect. That evening as we watched the game again on TV the cameras panned to the England end during the National Anthem. The cards looked magnificent, then they zoomed in on Prince Andrew who was in the VIP box for the match, he grinned at 'Raise the Flag' appreciatively. Not quite the result an arch-republican like myself was looking for, but in the circumstances, nice all the same.

Meanwhile we were settling down to enjoy the game – well, the first 44 minutes at any rate. The less said about the pitiful second half performance the better. Our World Cup was over. It had been good, more than most of us could ever have imagined it would be and a big, a huge part of that was down to how the Japanese had received us as fans. Trevor's lived in Japan for 14 years. And for most of it he's been proud of the appreciative comments when asked where he comes from. The Japanese think of England as the 'land of the gentleman'. It is a genuine deep-seated fondness that rubs off on the expats like Trevor working in their country. But for most of 2002 the comments had changed to 'land of the hooligan' and Trevor isn't ashamed to admit he shared some of that nervous trepidation too. Of course by Shizuoka we all knew everything had gone spectacularly well for the fans, and listening in to others' conversations in the stands Trevor was struck by the reason why. They were chatting about Japan in just the same way he had when he first arrived to work in the country all those years before. A sense of discovery, the thrill of being immersed in a different culture, what Trevor now took for granted had proved to be an adventure that the fans threw themselves enthusiastically and pleasurably into.

The adventure might be coming to a close but we had a banner to unveil. At the exits everybody was looking pretty miserable so I was a bit cautious as I cleared a space. The banner, unlike that huge flag in Niigata, was very light but at ten metres across, it was still very long. Out we stretched it then raised it high as we carried it along. The response was incredible. 'Grand idea mate, well done,' one fan after another commented. And when the Japanese saw it, especially the bit we'd carefully, respectfully, written in their own language – with it turned out not a single letter out of place – well, I've never seen anything like it. They stood, cheered, clapped and waved. One simple little grateful gesture and we get this sort of response, incredible. The walk back to the bus took forever. We were in a long slow-moving queue but I didn't regret a single step. The whole way back, wave after wave of affection and appreciation for The English was shown. '*Arrigatoh Gozaimas Nippon*' we shouted, '*Gambare Nippon! Gambare England-doh!*' until we were hoarse. BBC TV rushed over to film and I later heard from friends back home that the banner, and me, all red-faced and mildly incomprehensible, made it on to the *Ten O'Clock News* as well as a big picture in *The Guardian.* Fan ambassadorship, it makes a difference. So say all of us who shared in the Nippon experience.

Still, the disappointment at England going out remained severe, to say the least. Mark Raven felt this as much as anyone, possibly more because he'd made not one but two trips out to Japan to cheer the team on to World Cup glory. Mark follows England everywhere. He's one of a group of Brighton and Hove Albion fans who will always be there, from Amsterdam to Albania, loyal to the core. The distance and the expense of journeying to Japan wasn't going to put Mark off but how he could fit this around some crucial accountancy exams slap bang in the middle of the tournament, was more of a problem. The group games were OK but if England made it any further Mark reluctantly had to accept he'd have to miss out. So after the Nigeria game he flew back home to face a nervous week in the examination hall, toiling over figures and calculations which he hoped he'd be able to make head and tail of while putting Sven's possible formation against the Danes to the back of his mind. He did manage to keep his concentration focused but the temptation to return was too much. By the morning of the Denmark game he was back at the travel agent, flight booked – with a fall-back option to cancel if England failed to beat Denmark. Optimism, even amongst the most loyal supporters, has its limits. No need to cancel, just three days of exams to look forward to. At 1 p.m. on Wednesday the final paper is completed and he's straight out the hall to a waiting taxi. Seven hours later he was in the air somewhere over Russia on his way back to Japan and arrived in Tokyo the next day, Thursday, with 24 hours to go to the Brazil match. To arrange a ticket Mark had had to set his alarm clock on Tuesday for a 3 a.m. call to Japan. He's a member of the official supporters club and an additional allocation was being made available for this game. Friday morning Mark is in Kakegawa to pick up the ticket; he can hardly believe it. A nervous 30-minute wait and the much prized piece of paper is in his hands. He'll be sitting in the Brazil end, but who cares. Mark travelled 27,000 miles and when England's campaign came to a close he was already planning the next journey, Slovakia in October for a Euro 2004 qualifier – that's after a summer taking in some cricket and a hatful of Brighton games, plus pre-season friendlies. Mad? No, just committed.

By the Monday after the Brazil game most fans are starting to head back to England. Alan Lee has enjoyed the trip immensely, for all the usual reasons, but also because he's had the experience of becoming a minor celebrity on Japanese television. From the outset of their trip Alan, Gavin and Brian Humphries have had a TV Asahi camera crew filming them all along the way. The reports went out on a mid-morning show which they were reliably informed had very high audience ratings. Quite what the audience made of an Englishman who goes to a game dressed as Elvis Presley and shaves off his pubic hair when his team wins, we may never know. The thought does occur, however, if it may be similar to when Chris Tarrant treats viewers back home to those bizarre Japanese game shows that seem to revolve around acts of ever-increasing cruelty being visited on the contestants. Alan is convinced, though, that a film featuring three Englishmen sleeping head-to-toe in a Sapporo bed is destined to do wonders for international relations between Japan and ourselves. He's also, joking apart, right behind the idea that England fans can turn around the negative image we've been lumbered with by getting a positive representation out through the sympathetic and interested parts of the media. He did a daily report for his local paper, the *Lincolnshire Echo,* and from inside the stadiums listeners to BBC Radio Lincolnshire were treated to Alan summing up the matchday atmosphere. Early some mornings too, Alan was up and about for some friendly chat with Edwina Currie over the airwaves for what back home was her late-night Radio 5 show. All in all, a good job well done by Alan and many more like him acting as fan correspondents. On the plane, as I plonked myself down beside him, Alan looked contented though, like the rest of us, still pondering over what might have been.

Not every England fan is leaving Japan before the semis and final. Peter John-Baptiste left France before the last World Cup was over and he'd been regretting it for the past four years. Trouble was he had no more tickets. The semi-final wasn't a problem; he picked up a category three ticket at face value, just £120, and had a great time seated behind the goal in amongst the Brazilian fans at Saitama Stadium as Brazil squeezed past Turkey. But the cheapest ticket going for the final was £400, 'too much' Peter concluded, and then he hatched a plan of quite extraordinary ingenuity and outrageous nerve. A guy in his hotel from Manchester had a ticket for the final, so Peter and a mate asked him if they could photocopy it. All three headed down the local 7-Eleven convenience store where they knew there was a colour photocopier. Simple enough, then they took the half-hologram they had from a used ticket and cut off the holgram they had on the wrapping of the World Cup badge, which had been endorsed in this way to prove it was official. Carefully, they glued the two half-holograms into position to make a whole one on each ticket, then scored them down the middle so they would tear easily just like they would if the ticket was new, and genuine. They then repeated the whole exercise a second time to turn one ticket into three. But would it work? At Yokohama on match day Peter and his friend waited and waited in the hope that a big surge of latecomers towards understaffed turnstiles would reduce security and let them in without much of a check. But the orderly, mainly Japanese crowd were arriving nice and early so even with just 15 minutes to kick-off there was no build-up of bodies to mask their cunning plan. Eventually the two of them decided to risk it. Boldly they made it through each checkpoint and before they knew it they were in. 'Lively and very good', was how Peter described his first World Cup final. He was in the German end and couldn't resist holding up his Wealdstone FC flag for their national anthem. The fans all around him were as nice as anything, full of curiosity as to where Wealdstone was. As for where he got his ticket, Peter felt it sensible not to tell. Well, until now, at any rate.

Dennis O'Connor has a thing about tickets too. Not photocopying them, mind you, just getting hold of them. He's a frequent questioner of FA officials at the fan forums organised by London England Fans. Incredibly well informed, he prides himself on knowing how FIFA works, who gets what size allocations and why there never seem to be enough tickets to go around the fans who want them. Dennis is a chartered accountant who whiles away the odd evening poring over FIFA accounts, tracking down the facts of dodgy deals behind FIFA's motto 'for the good of the game'; and Dennis doesn't like what he finds. A fan like this is probably FIFA President Sepp Blatter's worst nightmare. Articulate and inquisitive and unlikely to take no for an answer. So imagine Sepp's horror when Dennis spots him at Narita airport. Sepp almost avoids Dennis, after all, as FIFA President he gets to use preferential channels, but even he has to stop while his passport is checked. Dennis only has a few seconds, so he collars him – not with the facts of his research, that would take much longer than the few seconds he had – but he manages to get off 'I hope the public prosecutor in Switzerland finds you guilty of corruption', before he's ushered away. 'Thank you, Thank you,' is Sepp's response. Maybe something got lost in the translation?

The good of the game? That's not FIFA fat-cattery; it's down to fans like Robert Didd. Robert broke two records in Japan. He was part of the Mount Fuji climb and the Argentine match was his incredible 150th consecutive England game, home and away. That's an unbroken run stretching back to 1988. He actually started in 1986 but in 1988 he had two disasters, an away game with Switzerland clashed with Chelsea in a play-off, which in those days was how the fourth bottom club in the old first division avoided relegation. As his Chelsea run of four years unbroken attendance outdid his two-year England run he plumped for the Chelsea game, only to see them lose 2–0 to Middlesbrough, get relegated and the fans riot. Not a great day. Then in the same year he had to miss an away game in Saudi Arabia which was switched at very short notice from the original fixture, an away game with Morocco. As he couldn't prove he was working in Saudi, visiting relatives or passing through with a connecting flight, there was no way he would qualify for a visa. Robert is sure that no one, except a few working out in Riyadh, made it to the game, which makes it impossible that anyone else can have a longer run of England games than him. Up Mount Fuji he met Nicky, the perfect girlfriend. Her first England away game was in 1993, Holland away and the ignominy of failing to qualify for USA '94. Not in Robert's ultrafan league of course, and she has missed the occasional game in the intervening nine years, but any accusations of being a new fan are answered with the contempt Nicky feels they deserve. And to top it all she's designed a computer spreadsheet so Robert can track matches attended in neat succession, with venues, teams, results, the lot.

Robert had to miss World Cup '86, his mother insisting he sit his O-level exams. It was only after this that he resolved he'd go to every England game, every World Cup finals appearance he could possibly manage. At times this has forced him to live a double life, vigorously taking no notice of football at work so suspicions won't be aroused when bouts of sickness coincide with England matches. Statutory holiday entitlements only go so far.

He's been all over, but for him Ingerland in Japan is the best so far. The culture shock, 'never seen anything like it'. His England trips have included most of Europe, North Africa, Middle East, Hong Kong, China but this was something else. The Japanese were 'so friendly, couldn't believe it'. He'd read up a bit on the customs, he knew bowing was polite, but when he did his bow in a bar on the first night and was bought a beer by a Japan fan whose only English was 'hooligan' but was desperate to discuss, however faltering, England's prospects. Well, after that you don't look back, do you. And Robert's not looking back, he's got his eye on when his two hundredth game might fall only too pleased by the different way of following England Japan gave him, 'Compare Japan to Marseilles, France '98. Then you had to watch your back all the time, you couldn't relax. No trouble? Definitely better.' Happy and glorious. That's how it was for Robert, and the rest of us too.

* * * * *

Nippon's Blue Heaven

Hiroyuhi Morita

The 2002 World Cup was the first world sporting event hosted by Japan since the 1964 Tokyo Olympics. The Japanese aim for both events was to show off their ability to organise such huge ventures. But in the space of nearly 40 years, the perception of the Japanese gained by the rest of the world via these two events has altered dramatically.

The Tokyo Olympics was a real debut on the world stage for post-war Japan. The country had spent the 1950s reconstructing entire towns and cities. Its transport system and industrial infrastructure had to be rebuilt and in the early 1960s the economic miracle started. The Tokyo Olympics was the event where Japan would show the rest of the world that its recovery was approaching completion.

In contrast, in 2002 the Japanese were looking inward. The country's economic success was already proven. Even though the country had now been in a decade-long recession, many Japanese refused to believe they had anything to learn economically from foreign countries – including the USA, once Japan's political mentor. The purpose of hosting the World Cup was therefore much more limited compared to their reasons for wanting to host the 1964 Olympics. It was being hosted in order to give a boost to football in Japan. The early excitement was limited to existing fans. Most people didn't think this would be an occasion to show anything apart from Nakata, Inamoto, Ono and the rest, to the world.

For Korea, this World Cup was more like the Tokyo Olympics had been for Japan. The Japanese didn't see it this way. Tokyo 1964 had a serious intent, but the 2002 World Cup was something the Japanese simply wanted to enjoy as a sporting contest. 'For one month from now, let's enjoy the world of sport spoken in the common language called soccer,' was how an editorial of *Asahi Shimbun*, a leading daily paper, put it on the day of the opening ceremony.

It even looked as if some Japanese expected a hostile invasion. Shopkeepers in Osaka and Yokohama were taking out riot insurance. Police were undergoing special training to deal with riots, and the TV networks were eagerly broadcasting these sessions. Police invented anti-hooligan gadgets like guns to fire nets over them or a scoop to constrain them. In Sapporo, courts adjusted their schedules so that they could deal with the expected prosecutions resulting from the

England–Argentina game. The city had even hired transport to ship the hundreds of expected hooligans to a detention centre near Tokyo. In Niigata, where a shortage of accommodation had been already seen as a major problem, a group of innkeepers decided to shut up shop for the duration because they didn't want foreigners staying. This hooligan brouhaha reminded Rokusuke Ei, a popular TV personality, of the fuss before the Beatles came to Japan in the 1960s. Then the police took up many different ways to constrain violent Beatles fans, but nobody went wild. At that time Ei wondered if the authorities did this training for another, more sinister purpose. After all, it was the 1960s, decade of the youth revolt from Paris to Washington DC, maybe now via Tokyo. But what about this time? Why these kinds of preparations and stories?

Not all Japanese were so hostile, of course. There were some heart-warming stories too. Among them, a village called Nakatsue drew special interest. This small southern village in the Oita prefecture, whose population is less than 1,400, successfully invited the Cameroon national squad to come and stay there. But the Cameroon team didn't arrive on the day they should have. They were late because they reportedly had disputes over their bonuses for the World Cup. Even after their plane departed Paris, it mysteriously made a detour and stopped a few times for refuelling. But villagers in Nakatsue were patient. Children waited with Cameroon's flag painted on their faces. Local schools served Cameroonian food for lunch. The village authority announced every piece of information about the whereabouts of the squad with a loudspeaker. When the team finally landed at nearby Fukuoka airport, virtually all the men and women in the village knew what time they had arrived. 'It was five minutes past three last night,' an old woman told NHK news. 'They are very late. Five days late. But I am so glad they are here.'

Villagers showed a great hospitality. Patrick Mboma, the Cameroonian striker who had played for Gamba Osaka in the J-League, said he was sorry that the hotel's restaurant didn't serve udon, his favourite Japanese noodle during his Osaka days. Next day, the restaurant started serving special udon for the Cameroonians. The squad even arrived late for a training match with a local J-League second division team. But when they departed the village, the whole Cameroon squad was given honorary citizenship of Nakatsue. 'My husband died in the war. I raised my children by myself,' said an old woman in Nakatsue to *Asahi Shimbun*. 'They go to many places for their work and receive people's hospitality there. So we want to be kind to people who come to our village.' On 1 June, villagers gathered at the town hall with Cameroonian flags to cheer the squad on TV. In the match against Ireland, Mboma scored the first goal of this World Cup in Japan.

As Japan's first game against Belgium approached, the ignominy of three straight defeats at France '98, with only one goal scored, haunted all of Japan. Japanese commentators, as well as most fans, knew that every host country of the World Cup has always advanced to the second round. This was a huge pressure.

But back in December 2001, people knew that Japan had been very lucky in the draw for groups. Group H didn't have any one team that all thought would excel. While the most competitive group, England's Group F, was called the 'Group of Death', Japan's Group H was even ridiculed as the 'Group of the Dead'. But commentators and fans still weren't too optimistic. They knew Russia and Belgium were good teams. They might have thought that Japan could beat Tunisia, but they didn't say that openly. After all, in France '98 Japan even lost to Jamaica, a team most commentators believed Japan could beat. On the evening of the draw for the final groups in December 2001, Takashi Mizunuma, former international and now a commentator on the popular football programme Super Soccer, said: 'It is possible that we can win all of the three group games but it is also possible that we will lose them all.

'I believe that Japan are gaining in ability and should do that,' wrote Yasuhiko Okudera, a former striker who played in West Germany, in *Asahi Shimbun*. He balanced his optimism with some hard-headed realism though: 'But the World Cup is very tough. This is the tournament to decide the world champions. Experienced coaches and players will take every possible measure to win.' The most positive views came from foreigners who know Japanese football. 'For the current Japanese team, one win at the World Cup is nothing spectacular,' said Sebastian Lazaroni, coach of Yokohama F Marinos of the J-League and formerly of the Brazilian national team, to the magazine *Sports Graphic Number*. 'They can do more. They can make history. They ought to think they can.'

Most commentators agreed that making it to the last 16 would be a satisfactory outcome for Japan. The team gained their historic first World Cup finals point in their opening match against Belgium, then won the following two group games. Fans may have well have been ready for their elimination in the second round. *Asahi Shimbun* had a big picture of fans raising a banner saying, 'Thank you for giving us a dream', after the defeat against Turkey. They must have prepared it before the match.

Saburo Kawabuchi, who became chairman of the Japan Football Association (JFA) in July 2002, is already looking forward to the next World Cup with a renewed ambition. 'Our goal for 2006 will be the last 16 or more than that.' On the road to 2006, the most reliable player will still be Hidetoshi Nakata. The 25-year-old star of the side used to be seen as a mystery man, rarely giving interviews. He was also said to be an individualist. When his forwards could not keep up with his fast passing game, he didn't hesitate to shout on the pitch, 'Why not?' But as the World Cup approached, he seemed to be determined to take the leader's role. After Japan won a friendly with Poland 2–0 in March, Japan's coach, Philippe Troussier, told the press, 'I think his experience at the moment in Parma (where Nakata spends much of his time on the bench) is good for him, because when he joined us this Monday he was completely different. Before he came with five managers, two doctors and a helicopter. Now he comes on a bicycle.'

Midfielders Shinji Ono at Feyenoord and Junichi Inamoto, transferred from Arsenal to Fulham after scoring two brilliant goals in the World Cup, are still only 22 years old and expected to continue to be key players for 2006. Another hopeful for the midfield is Shunsuke Nakamura, a 24-year-old who has joined Reggiana of Serie A for the 2002–03 season. Nakamura, who is a great passer of the ball and takes excellent free kicks, was excluded from the 2002 squad. Troussier found other players more useful on the left side of midfield. Some fans now hope new coach Zico will organise the Nakata-Ono-Inamoto-Nakamura midfield just like 'the Golden Quartet' of Brazil in the 1982 World Cup, when Zico himself was in the Brazilian side. 'Geniuses can work together,' was Zico's response when told Troussier had dropped Nakamura from the final squad selection – the clear hint being that he would have kept him in the side.

Another of whom a lot is expected is the forward Naohiro Takahara. Born in 1979, the same year as Ono and Inamoto, Takahara is out of 'the platinum age' of Japanese football. Although the former Boca Juniors player couldn't join the 2002 squad because he was suffering from the mild heart and lung disorder 'economy class syndrome', this is now cured, and he could become the sort of predatory striker that Japan lacked in the 2002 competition.

As for 2002, the Japanese sports press almost all agreed that Troussier's biggest achievement with his squad was that he made an uncompromising generational shift in the team's line-up. Right after he became Japan's coach in 1998, Troussier figured that players he was preparing for the Under-21 team at the Sydney 2000 Olympics had much better technique than most of the players in his senior team. Straightaway he started to drop veteran players from the national squad. A Japanese-born manager couldn't have done that because they tend to be bound with social ties that often work against any radical change. Troussier led the Under-20 team to second place in the 1999 World Youth Championship. Among the players were Ono, Inamoto and the defender Koji Nakata. These 'Troussier Babes' went on to become the core of the 2002 team. The average age of the 2002 Japanese squad was just over 25 years, it was the fifth youngest of the 32 teams. And for most starting line-ups the average would fall to 24 years. Recognising that he was planning for the future – 2006 and beyond – the sports daily *Nikkan Sports* concluded that 'Troussier's grand policy was not mistaken', right after Japan lost to Turkey.

Troussier might have been good at training these young players, but the doubt lies with whether he instilled enough of the winning instinct that drives on the most successful sides. On the sidelines he often looked more like a mad scientist than a football coach, and didn't finalise his best starting line-up until the very final deadline. He even played Atsushi Yanagisawa, a Kashima Antlers striker, completely out of position as a right-sided midfielder on the wing in a friendly match with Slovakia in late April. 'How long will this "test" continue?' wrote Takashi Kumazaki in *Sports Graphic Number*. 'Now players are fighting to survive selection, not for the team to win.' On the day after the match against Turkey, commentators from Zico to Takeshi Okada, Japan's coach at France '98, unanimously questioned Troussier's tactics for the game. 'His tactics were obviously wrong,' Zico told *Nikkan Sports*. 'In Brazil, people say, "Don't change the winning team." Why did he use Nishizawa (a striker who had an appendicitis operation a month before)? He hadn't played in a match for more than one month. Why not Morishima, who did a great job in the game against Tunisia? It was a good idea to use Santos (Alex, a naturalised Brazilian midfielder), but why was he played out of position? And of course it still remains a mystery why he withdrew Inamoto at half-time, when he had previously always scored in the second half. Troussier has the duty to explain to fans why he did all this.'

Right after Gary Lineker came to Japan to play for J-League side Nagoya Grampus Eight, he was surprised to see amongst fans in the stadium so many women. 'It's unimaginable in Britain,' explained Lineker. It was 1993, when the J-League had just started with much fanfare. The first professional football league in Japan successfully drew many fans, male and female. Football had suddenly become fashionable and tickets for J-League games were hard to get hold of. This could be the reason why Japanese football has more women fans than in most other countries. The J-League's history is very short; it has no overbearing masculine-specific tradition shaping its present and future. Before it existed, there simply weren't that many Japanese football fans around.

The same applies for the supporters of the national team. Few of the current fans would have started to follow the national side from before October 1993, when the Japanese squad lost out in the last preliminary qualification game for the 1994 World Cup. In injury time of this match, an Iraq player headed a ball into the far right corner of the Japan goal. This 'Tragedy of Doha', as the Japanese press dubbed it, seemed to kill off forever Japan's long-cherished goal of finally making it to the World Cup finals. But it didn't quite turn out like this. 'This match made the World Cup the real goal for Japanese football,' writes Takeo Goto, a renowned Japanese football writer, in his best-selling book, *The Century of the World Cup*. Before Doha, few fans seriously thought Japan could reach the World Cup finals. For Japanese football fans, the World Cup was the tournament where you could watch good foreign teams and foreign star players, not your own. 'Perhaps, *Nippon Daihyo* (Japan national team) meant the volleyball team some time ago,' wrote author Kotaro Sawaki in *Asahi Shimbun*. Not after Doha in 1993, and certainly not after 2002.

But this is precisely the reason why Japanese fans can still support their own team one day and England, Brazil, Italy or any other popular team the next day. Many Europeans seemed to be surprised to see Japanese fans supporting other countries in this World Cup. 'It was interesting to see a fan with a Turkish flag painted on her left cheek and a Senegal flag on her right,' a British journalist told me. But this has been how the Japanese enjoyed past World Cups. For a long time, they didn't have their own team to support, but 2002 changed that. Still supporting England and others, the Japanese also had their own team to support too.

On 13 July 2002, the first J-League game since the World Cup, Urawa Red Diamonds against Jubilo Iwata at Saitama Stadium, drew 57,902 spectators. It was the third largest attendance in the J-League's history and exceeded the attendance for the Japan against Belgium match held at the same stadium during the World Cup. Masashi Nakayama, Jubilo's 34-year-old international forward, told the press, 'We have a responsibility to show a good game to this large audience.' Nakayama scored two goals in the match.

On this same day, the average attendance of the six games of the J-League first division was 20,421 – a decent-sized crowd for this league. But the only matches that attracted more than 15,000 fans were those at Saitama and Kashima stadiums, both of which were used for the World Cup. The Kobe Universiade stadium, which was not the one used at the World Cup in Kobe, only drew 8,810 fans, which was the lowest total for the stadium in the season.

On the second weekend after the World Cup, 20–21 July, eight J-League first division games drew a total of 204,786 fans, which was the largest aggregate in the history of the league. But more than 52,000 out of this total attended the Yokohama F Marinos game. And most of them went to see the Yokohama midfielder Shunsuke Nakamura, who was to leave for Reggiana of Italy's Serie A the next day. A Marinos' game usually only attracts around 15,000 fans.

Looking back to France '98, the tournament didn't boost the

attendance figures of the J-League. The attendances for the 12 weeks immediately after France '98 were down to 89 per cent on the same period before the tournament. The first weekend after the 2002 World Cup final, the J-League had a whole page advertisement in the major newspapers. It carried a photograph of a small boy saying, 'I want to become a football player.' The copy said, 'Soccer continues into the future.' At present, football is growing in popularity amongst the young generation. Surveys show that few men in their twenties watch professional baseball on TV, it is football that is grabbing the attention instead.

There are now several high schools that are renowned for football. They draw potential players from all over Japan and produce many J-League players. The problem is that most schools lack any good quality grass pitches. The junior teams of J-League clubs are developing a better infrastructure and will be vital to the sport's future. The Asia Cup is contested every two years and is attracting an increasing level of interest, helped by Japan winning it the last time round. However, club competitions between Asian countries are of a poor quality and attract very little TV coverage.

This World Cup was the first in Asia and the first to be co-hosted by two countries – or to be more precise, the first to be co-hosted by a country and its former colony. Japan and Korea have a long history of animosity. And during the tournament, there were anti-Korean sentiments from some of the Japanese supporters.

Many Japanese fans resented the series of bad refereeing decisions that were, mysteriously, all in favour of Korea. Many disliked the Korean fans' habit of loudly booing their opponents, raising banners saying 'Welcome to the Azurri's Tomb' and the nationalistic chanting of 'Republic of Korea'. While most Japanese may simply have envied their neighbour's success in beating some of the top teams – Portugal, Italy and Spain, which saw them advance to the semi-finals – anti-Korean feelings did rise at the same time. Ai Iijima, a popular TV figure, said in a variety television show, 'I will never eat *Kimuchi* (Korean spicy pickles) again in my life!'

Many Koreans and Japanese had never been exactly thrilled to be working together as co-hosts. The hope was that this unusual arrangement would deepen mutual trust and understanding. But that well-meaning aim had been undermined by a series of disputes. Prime among these was the wrangle over the official name of the 2002 World Cup. In 2001 the two countries were briefly at loggerheads after Japan's World Cup organisers placed Japan's name ahead of Korea's on printed tickets for its domestic sale. The Korean side fumed that this was in violation of the original agreement between the two nations and FIFA, under which, in exchange for giving the final match to Japan, Korea had won the right to have its name come first.

It wasn't all rivalry and resentments, certainly not. Thanks to growing personal and cultural exchanges in recent years, many Japanese have developed a new curiosity about Korea. Despite the comments of the aforementioned TV star, more and more people are buying *Kimuchi* at local supermarkets and going to Korean restaurants. During the World Cup, many young Japanese went to see games in Taegu or Ulsan, normally not Japanese tourists' favoured destinations.

'Korea and Japan have a long history of exchanges. But we had few experiences of doing something together,' a former Korean ambassador to Japan, Choi Sang-yong, told *Asahi Shimbun* right after the tournament was over. 'Recently we have been doing some joint cultural events, perhaps once every three days. Many academics are doing joint studies. This World Cup was the climax of those joint events and we completed it successfully. The relationship between us will never step back.' Even if there will be more frictions, it could make for a more 'ordinary' relationship between the two countries than an unpleasant and complex past. 'There will be many more occasions for Japanese and Koreans to meet each other personally and see each other's faces,' a Japanese writer, Koichi Yamazaki, told *Newsweek Japan*. 'Making "productive frictions" will be the key to making a better relationship.' The one month of co-hosting the World Cup is over. But Japan and Korea still have plenty of time to get to know each other.

Recovering the cost of staging the finals in Japan may take a long time too. Among the ten stadiums that Japan used for the World Cup, probably only Kashima stadium in Ibaraki will be used for J-League matches regularly. All of the other World Cup stadiums had to have more than a 40,000 capacity to comply with FIFA rules. At this size, however, the rent is too high for most J-League teams. The local authorities where the ten stadiums are located were very afraid of this outcome when they built them. In some cities and prefectures, there were campaigns against the construction of new stadiums because they were regarded as a waste of taxpayers' money. That is why seven out of ten stadiums were built also for the use of track and field. But there won't be a big track and field event every month either. In Miyagi prefecture, whose stadium held the memorable Japan–Turkey match, there has been a debate over the stadium's future. People who see the stadium as having no future argue it should be dismantled. The yearly cost to maintain the stadium alone is said to be more than 280 million yen. But the expected revenue is only 40 million yen a year.

But what the Japanese will remember this World Cup for isn't the now empty stadiums. It will be remembered more as the first time the country had been awash with *Hinomaru* (the national flag) and

Kimigayo (the national anthem) since the Second World War. The flag and the anthem had been seen as the symbols of our militarist past and were a subject for an intense national debate. Every year, disputes occur in schools over whether they should sing the anthem and raise a flag in their assemblies. During France '98, Hidetashi Nakata didn't sing *Kimigayo* as the players lined up. As a result, there were reports that he was sent threats by right-wing nationalists.

'How will people look back to this June of the World Cup?' asked Tensei Jingo in the editorial column of *Asahi Shimbun* on 1 July. 'Probably it will be as the season of *Hinomaru* and *Kimigayo*. Especially *Hinomaru*. It could be the first time that the country was filled with *Hinomaru* since World War Two, though the meaning is quite different. Young people deal with *Hinomaru* and *Kimigayo* casually, not reverently. This lightness and casualness were very impressive. Next day, they raised the other national flag to support the other country.'

In the stadiums, delirious Japanese fans waved the flags and showed the referee their middle fingers. On the pitch you would hardly have thought the players were even Japanese. Junichi Inamoto smiled after his brilliant goal against Belgium in Japan's first match. His smile was surprising. We knew that Japan now has a football player who can smile after a fantastic goal at the World Cup. Japanese athletes used to be in a more 'samurai' culture, a selfless dedication to the nation. Kokichi Tsuburaya, a Japanese marathon runner who won a bronze medal at the 1964 Tokyo Olympics, later killed himself. He wrote in his will the reason why, 'I can't run anymore.' His life, his role and contribution, were all over.

Japanese players in 2002 were un-Japanese in their appearance too. They painted their hair in their own colours and styles. Jonathan Wingfield, editor of *Numero*, a Paris fashion magazine, told *Asahi Shimbun*, 'Japanese players looked so cool. In the pre-match line-up they were like pop stars or movie actors.' They may have been an image of new Japan to foreigners, but were annoying to some Japanese traditionalists. 'I was going to cheer Japan in the match against Russia, but I was at a loss as to which side I should support,' said Takami Eto, a ruling Liberal Democratic Party member of parliament. 'Boys who have brown hair were Japanese (not Russian). And one even had a crest on the head.' It just goes to prove that even in blue heaven, you can't please all of the people all of the time.

* * * * *

Korea, Red Devils and the Hiddink Factor

Kwon Yong-seok

The Seoul Olympics of 1988 were the platform on which Korea built its contemporary international profile. World Cup 2002, some 14 years later, was widely regarded by the Korean establishment as the vehicle to move this process on. This would involve projecting Korea as a remarkable success – economically and socially – in the face of regional and global adversity.

In January 2002 Korea's President Kim Dae-jung described the tournament in the following way:

> The World Cup is the best opportunity to establish the success of our country. If the event is organised successfully, the image of Korea will be improved and we can expect an enormous economic impact of up to 14 billion dollars and the creation of 300–400,000 new jobs. By showing off the IT industry of Korea we will invite investment and tourists from overseas. Relations with North Korea and Japan will also be improved by the World Cup. And it will contribute to the development of local communities and lead to social harmony.

On New Year's Day 2002, the Korean newspaper the *Dong-a-llbo* described the impending contest in similar ways:

> The success of the World Cup and the Busan Asian Games will be the stepping stone for our national prosperity in the twenty-first century. Especially the successful hosting of the World Cup, which is the first global festival since the terrorist attacks in the US last year, will be a great help to the peace and security of the whole world. Let's make it successful by uniting people's power.

When foreigners look at Korea the image is of a divided country. According to a poll in the *Newsmaker*, 40 per cent of overseas observers have 'division' as their first association with the country. Only 17 per cent cited their memories of the Seoul Olympics. That's why Koreans are in search of a new national identity, and this explains why the official state slogans are 'Welcome the World' and 'Dynamic Korea'.

Co-hosting with Japan had a special meaning, but especially for Koreans. It can be compared to England and India co-hosting the event. One hundred years ago in 1902, the treaty of the Anglo–Japanese Alliance was signed. This was decisive in defining the relationship between Japan and Korea; it signified that for the remainder of the twentieth century, Japan would be the major player on the global stage, not Korea. So Koreans wanted to show the real image of Korea and confirm that the destiny of the Korean twenty-first century, from the start, would be totally different from the twentieth century. In this sense, from right back at the beginning of the World Cup bidding process, Korea's ambitions as host were characterised by a greater drama and enthusiasm for ambitions well beyond football.

As for Korea's footballing ambition, this was threatened at the World Cup tournament draw in Pusan, December 2001. Many Koreans were disappointed at the fate that had befallen their national team. Most commentators and supporters thought that the USA was the only team Korea had a hope of defeating. But even here, the fans knew that the unfancied Americans were improving, having recently snatched 13th place in the FIFA rankings.

The popular monthly magazine *Shin Dong-A* ran a prediction of the Korean team's results as chosen by eleven experienced commentators. Only four predicted that Korea would progress to the second round. Two commentators went so far as to predict that the Korean team would be eliminated following one draw and two defeats.

After the poor performance at the January 2002 Gold Cup in the USA, the Korea Football Association (KFA) suddenly started to consider the naturalisation of K-League player Sandoro, a forward from Suwon Samsung, who originated in Brazil. Meanwhile, the Brazilian J-League player Alex received his Japanese nationality just in time for the World Cup. The spectre of dependence on foreign aid, at least when it came to playing in the national colours, had a deep impact on the Korean people.

The overwhelming fear of the KFA and the Korean people was that Korea might be the first host country not to make it to the second round. This would be an unwanted record. But more significantly, fear of being outdone by Japan became, according to *Newsweek Korea*, a national obsession. In the face of this mounting fear, national manager Guus Hiddink boldly declared that the answer didn't lie with naturalising foreign players. His declaration gave encouragement to his squad of players and helped turn them into a stronger unit.

When Hiddink mentioned as early as March, 'maybe we can surprise the world in June', Korean supporters and commentators didn't really believe him.

Even retired Korean football hero Cha Bum-kun, who had played in the Bundesliga in the 1980s and managed the South Korean team at France '98, would only say 'we have the home advantage; if we do our best, an unexpected result might come up'. Any sort of Korean victory was still regarded as a major upset.

But after the Korean team thrashed Scotland 4–1 in May, people remembered Hiddink's previous optimism. And when the Scotland result was followed by a well-earned draw with England and a desperately close 3–2 defeat by France, these same people recognised that this Korean team was totally different to the ones that had gone down to countless World Cup defeats before. Now there was a growing conviction that a first victory in the finals was a real possibility, and Hiddink's faith was turning into a countrywide conviction.

'Hiddink Makes our Dreams Come True' was a slogan spelt out on thousands of cards held up by the soon-to-be-famous Red Devils fans at Korea's first match against Poland. 'Dreams' meant a first victory in the finals and maybe, just maybe, making it through to the last 16. When Korea beat Poland, TV commentators described it as a historic victory that would be an unforgettable memory for the older generation and a source of hope to the younger one. When Korea beat Italy the Korean mass media dubbed it 'a miracle'. The former national team coach, Cha Bum-kun, commented that, 'You boys have proved that football is not a sport just played by big stars. Nameless players, *you* are the real heroes from now on.' And when Korea defeated Spain to send them home, they called it 'legend of the best'. Every paper was keen to distil the meaning of 'the legend of best'. *Dong-a-llbo* put it all down to three key words – confidence, destruction and adventure.

One outstanding character of Hiddink's Korea is the rise of the fearless young generation. They weren't intimidated by the international reputation of their much-fancied opponents. They were playing against, mainly, European players who had little experience of failure coupled with the confidence of playing in some of the world's best leagues. But the Korean players never let these reputations get the better of them.

A flexibility of strategy and training multifunctional players were the key points of Hiddink's Korea side. The Korean team's extraordinary formation in the second half of the match with Italy surprised the world. Even though Hiddink put six attacking players on the pitch, the total balance was kept and no goals were conceded. This was because almost all the Korean players were able to play decently in two or three different positions. This was a new and exciting style of football.

Dong-a-Ilbo concluded that the Koreans had attracted the world football fan by playing the game in a way that combined both primitiveness and a powerful dynamism. The Koreans showed how an Asian team could beat some of the strongest European sides. They defined their own identity by concentrating on such values as speed, aggression and an incredible physical stamina. As Korea went out to Turkey they kept playing, their determination paying off with the last-minute goal by Song Chong-gug. Deeply moved, Hiddink said, 'Look at this. Have you ever seen a team like this? I am really proud of my boys.'

After the captain Hong Myung-bo led Korea into the quarter-finals, he said, 'I want to kiss the Cup.' The newspaper *Dong-a-llbo* wrote: 'Hong was the first Asian man to recognise that the World Cup does not belong to only selected countries like Brazil, but is a goal which every country could aim for.' This was how Korea, in the future, would approach its footballing ambitions, according to *Dong-a-llbo*. Hiddink had claimed that with four more years of him in charge he could take Korea into FIFA's top ten ranking.

In terms of the next four years and looking forward to Germany 2006, most commentators picked out the 21-year-old Park Ji-sung as a key player. Hiddink used him as a right-sided forward rather than in the position he was used to, in defence. When he scored some spectacular goals in the warm-up friendlies against England and France, he was dubbed 'Europe Killer'. His beautifully taken goal against Portugal destroyed the generally accepted idea that Korean football is just about running around enthusiastically, but to no great effect.

Most impressive was the way Park would celebrate scoring, running towards Hiddink and jumping into his arms like a son or a baby bear. All Korea was moved by this public show of unity and affection, so different to the distance between most players and their managers. Japanese TV showed this scene repeatedly with an obvious question of why there wasn't a similar closeness being shown between their players and manager Phillipe Troussier. The Korean newspaper *Sportschosun* speculated: 'The Korean wonder-boy Park is the player most likely to follow Hiddink to the Netherlands.'

The midfielder Song Chong-gug is another key player. He has been called 'Hiddink's Prince'. He was the only player to play the full duration of all Korea's games at the tournament, and became famous worldwide when he defended against Luis Figo so perfectly. His main position is as a right wing-back, but he can play as a defender, defensive midfielder, or playmaker.

Kim Nam-ll was called a 'vacuum cleaner' by Hiddink. He was the first player in the history of the Korean team to play the important role of defensive midfielder. His obvious physical stength, mellowed by a sense of humour, has helped make him a hugely popular figure amongst the fans. The popularity of Kim and Song, not overshadowed by pin-up boy Ahn Jung-hwan, shows that the supporters are recognising the various contributions players make to a winning team.

Cha Du-ri has already signed for Bayer Leverkusen. His father also played in the Bundesliga, and at 22, the years of preparation in

Germany are expected to make Cha a star of Korea's 2006 side. With all these players in their early to mid-twenties, together with Lee Yong-pyo, Lee Chun-soo and 21- year-old Choi Tae-uk, the core of this side could yet peak in 2006. In looking forwards, Hiddink is confident: 'The spirit that they show by respecting their counterparts but never being afraid of them, will be the future of Korean football.'

Hiddink himself was hugely popular throughout Korea. 'Make Hiddink President' was more than just a throwaway chant of the most fanatical Red Devils. Many Koreans really respected Hiddink for his leadership and charisma, and there has been no one else admired in anything like the same degree in the modern history of Korea.

But Hiddink was not accepted by the Koreans from the beginning. The most severe crisis was after the team's disappointing performance in the Gold Cup, as close to the World Cup as January of 2002. But the President of the KFA and FIFA Vice-President, Chung Mong-joon, along with close ally KFA technical director Lee Yong-su, protected Hiddink from the criticism. This made their personal relationship with him particularly strong. When Hiddink accepted the job offer from the KFA, he demanded total and unwavering support. 'If I ordered the players to climb a tree, would they do it? The answer has to be yes.' They had a deal; Chung would give Hiddink total control. Chung expected Korea's ambition to be to lift the cup. Hiddink liked it that way. He too wanted to aim high. After the tournament, arguments in Korea over Hiddink's impact are endless. Not only on football, but also on politics, economy, education – even the administration of the State. Hiddink's leadership and methods have been noticed by the whole of society. They call it the 'Hiddink Syndrome'.

Arguments that the model of success on the football field should be transferred to the economy are increasing. The *Dong-a-llbo* pointed out that in Korea and Japan the recession is 'due to the lack of competitiveness. Both countries should go for an open-economy in the same way football teams get success by appointing a foreign coach.' Chung Yoon-su in *Newsweek Japan* lauded Hiddink as 'leader of the revolution'. Hiddink's remarks and rhetoric have also led to him being described in *Dong-a-llbo* as a poet. Hiddink awoke in the Koreans a realisation of the importance of word power in sport. After the Portugal game, he said, 'I'm still hungry.' And after the Spain game, he said, 'When you lose, you should pack and go home.'

Professor Herschell L. Grossman pointed out in the *Newsmaker* that the 'Hiddink Syndrome' didn't come about suddenly, nor would it disappear immediately:

> The euphoria of fans whose team wins a major sporting event is ephemeral. But prominent professors at South Korean

universities tell me that the unprecedented success of the South Korean team in the current World Cup competition is causing a turning point in South Korean attitudes toward their own society and economy.

Why? Many South Koreans, especially those who have studied or lived in the West, complain about the 'cronyism' and the resulting importance of 'connections' that they see as pervasive features of Korean society. They assert that cronyism is preventing South Korea from catching up economically with the West.

What do South Korean cronyism and related social conventions have to do with the World Cup? In the past, cronyism apparently has been as pervasive in the selection of South Korean teams for international sports competitions as in other areas of South Korean society. But two years ago, when the South Korean soccer football association hired the Dutchman Guus Hiddink to coach the South Korean national soccer team, Hiddink made it clear that he would select his players on the basis of merit alone. The performance of the South Korean team in the 2002 World Cup competition has demonstrated to every Korean in a way that is easily seen, that meritocracy yields better results than cronyism. It also helps that Hiddink has been able to use his coaching skills to bring out in his team the strengths of the Korean national character: intelligence, discipline, tenacity and perseverance.

Of course, Korean traditionalists reject criticism of what Westernised Koreans call cronyism. Traditionalists argue that criticism of cronyism is really criticism of social solidarity and responsibility, which they see as positive features of South Korean society. Traditionalists also argue that meritocracy implies individualism and that too much individualism and too little social solidarity and responsibility are negative features of Western society. Some traditionalists might even assert that they do not want Koreans to be as rich as Westerners if that would require Koreans to be as individualistic as Westerners.

The Hiddink phenomenon did not emerge suddenly out of nowhere. The accumulation of gradual changes that have already occurred in South Korean society has made it acceptable to import a Westerner to coach the South Korean national soccer team and let him establish a meritocratic regime. But Hiddink has expedited change, and his success has made it look revolutionary. It remains to be seen how fast, in what ways, and with what effects South Korean society will

> continue to change. Koreans are talking about learning the lessons of Hiddink. But the Western model of a meritocratic society is not easy to emulate. A soccer team is a relatively simple organisation. Implementing the lessons of Hiddink throughout South Korean society will present more difficult challenges.
>
> Whatever the outcome, it seems that in the case of the 2002 World Cup the effects of success in a major sporting event will not be ephemeral.

Professor Grossman's 'Hiddink Syndrome' was the result of gradual changes in Korean society. It was these that enabled his success, and created his huge groundswell of popular support. Consequently, Hiddink's impact is so deep that it won't stop now the tournament is over, nor will it be easily reversed.

After the World Cup the K-League started again on 7 July, the *Hangyoreh 21* said, 'Red Devils kept the promise'. They meant that Korea's cup run was something all Korean fans could be proud of, feel part of, want to build upon. The numbers attending the first day of the new season were 123,189 which were the highest since the league began.

The K-League is changing. The *Dong-a-llbo* described these changes:

> It leaves fans, who fill the stands for every game, impressed with teams putting pressure on each other and exciting moves. The professional football of the old days, which the former manager of the Korean national team, Guus Hiddink, bitterly criticised as a 'Walking Game', is gone. The reason why the K-League has changed so drastically is the presence of more than 100,000 fans every match day after the 2002 World Cup.
>
> The manager of the Busan Icons, Kim Ho-gon, explained it thus '. . . the coaches and the players are highly motivated by the thundering cheers of the crowd', and 'the players are affected by the atmosphere, so they play above themselves, and more aggressive and exciting games are the result'. He also explained that there is a consensus between all the players and coaches saying, 'Let's revive Korean football by using this opportunity.' Manager Cho Yun-hwan said that the K-League is finally changing into a European-style league. 'Korean professional football had a renaissance after the World Cup in 1998; this seems different,' is the consensus of the coaches. With the support of the fans, the World Cup stars, old stars, new generation stars and imported players, the quality of competition will rise.

According to statistics in the *Chosun Ilbo* on 7 July, the K-League recorded 123,189 spectators at the four matches played. On the same day, baseball only recorded 9,222 spectators. On 10 July, 108,504 spectators went to see five football games – a record number for a weekday – while 14,184 went to see the four baseball games played.

But the long-term future of the K-League is not so bright. Popular players will leave sooner or later. And veteran national team captain Hong Myung-bo has complained that the clubs have not changed enough since France '98. In the *Daily Sport* he argued that 'they don't pay much attention to management, facilities and the protection of players' health'. He warned that 'if the clubs only think of the money, then football fever will disappear soon'. Some diehard football fans feared that success in the tournament for the national team would simply deflect attention from a long overdue overhaul of the domestic league and grass-roots of the sport.

The major problem in Korean football culture is the lack of investment in an ongoing youth football programme. In *Sports Seoul*, the former national team coach Heo Jong-mu pointed out the importance of this problem, while in the *Newsmaker* it was recognised that 'Korea's Soccer Vision for 2010 depends on creating a second division for the K-League and strengthening the youth football programme'. In *Sports Seoul*, Heo Jong-mu made the case for Korean clubs to compete with other strong clubs across the continent; 'The Asian Champions League starts from this August. This will give Asian club football a new horizon for its development.' KFA President Chung Mong-joon added his voice to this continental perspective when, after the World Cup, he announced that a North-east Asian Championship consisting of four countries (South Korea, North Korea, Japan and China) would be held in the near future. He explained that this championship would include not only the senior team but also women's and youth teams, with the aim of strengthening the development of the sport's infrastructure across the region.

Co-operation to develop football across the region builds on the experience of this, the first World Cup to be co-hosted. But the co-hosting process was not without its problems, after all it is only in the recent past that Japan colonised Korea and the painful aftermath of that experience remains the source of a number of political disputes and cultural mistrust between the two nations. However, a phone survey by Korea's *Chosun Ilbo*, and Japan's *Mainichi Shinbun* showed that 75 per cent of Koreans and 65 per cent of Japanese thought bilateral relations between the two nations had become better as a result of co-hosting the tournament. Only 4 per cent of Japanese said relations had worsened, while not a single South Korean polled felt this. As many as 96 per cent of Koreans and 70 per cent of Japanese also said their respective co-hosts were well organised. With regards to friendship, 42 per cent of Koreans now felt friendlier towards Japan than previously, compared to 77 per cent of the Japanese now feeling more friendly to Korea. The fact that a majority of Koreans still felt no more friendly towards Japan than before the tournament needs to be put in a recent historical context. This same question has been asked by *Chosun llbo* and *Mainchi Shinbun* over the previous decade. The percentage of Koreans feeling friendlier to Japan has been rising consistently; 26 per cent in 1995, 29 per cent in 1997 and 35 per cent in January 2002, so the post-World Cup figure of 42 per cent was a new high. The Japanese people's increased friendliness towards Korea has also risen from 38 per cent in 1995 to 48 per cent in 1997 and 69 per cent in January 2002. Again, the 77 per cent polled after the tournament is a new high.

The treatment of Korea in Japanese society and culture was already changing for the better across a broad range of fronts prior to the World Cup. Korean films like *Shuri* have been hugely popular in Japan with more than a million people flocking to the cinemas to see it. In addition, the top actress Ryoko Hirosue spoke fluent Korean in a TV drama. This was something that was previously unheard of.

During the World Cup, second and third generation Koreans living in Japan felt safe to support Korea. This young generation, whose parents and grandparents had been brought to Japan as imported workers, often in very harsh, exploitative circumstances, were proud to celebrate being Korean in Japan. Clearly the co-hosting arrangement helped this process.

For six years the two countries worked together, at every conceivable level, to organise the World Cup. June 2002 was the culmination of bilateral co-operation on a scale quite unlike anything in the preceding 50 years. The success of this venture is now having a broader impact. The former Korean ambassador to Japan, Choi Sang-ryong, has suggested that both countries should consider a Korea–Japan Free Trade Agreement (FTA) seriously. In *Dong-a-llbo*, Professor Chong Jin-yong urged that now was the perfect opportunity to settle the historic enmity between the two countries.

As for North Korea, the World Cup didn't seem to impact significantly on relations between the North and the South. But there were some signs. At the start of the game against Italy, Korean fans held up cards to form a huge slogan, 'Again 1966', to celebrate their neighbour's own victory over the Italians nearly 40 years previously.

After the World Cup was over the long-term impact on the nation began to be considered. The *Weekly Chosun* wrote, 'now is the time to win economically'. The unexpected success in the tournament of the team has helped offset any immediate popular backlash to the costs of being a host. Instead, the government and private sector have been left to concentrate on how best to utilise the infrastructure they have been left with. On 26 June, the day after Korea's semi-final defeat, the Korean government announced a 'Post-World Cup Policy'. This identified the 'football fever' and improvement of the country's international image as two central World Cup consequences for Korea. In the *Dong-a-llbo* it was reported the government aimed to 'connect the street supporter culture to the national economic interest and social dynamism'. This would include the establishment of six new professional football clubs, increasing investment in youth football, and making good use of the World Cup stadiums. Some would be turned into huge discount shops and others into multi-use leisure complexes.

The same paper also reported that the Korea National Tourism Corporation had a post-World Cup plan for host cities to use their World Cup profile to boost tourism. Nevertheless, the ongoing cost of paying for the infrastructure will remain a heavy burden, especially for a relatively small city like Jeonju.

What Korea will be most remembered for by the rest of the world will be its fans. *Newsweek Japan* got it absolutely right in its World Cup review . . . 'The real champions are the Korean people'.

The number of supporters on the streets of Korea dramatically increased as the tournament went on. According to the *Dong-a-llbo,* there were 500,000 people on the streets for the first game with Poland, 2,800,000 for Portugal, 4,200,000 for Italy, and for Germany, an incredible 7,000,000.

A prominent intellectual, Lee Eo-ryong, has pointed out that the Red Devils are a new popular culture which is both post-traditional – not rejecting Korea's past but building on it – while being open to modern European cultural influences. No longer is there one dominant source shaping this cultural formation – in the past, politics, religion and gender, at different times, would have played that role. The Red Devils are both an individual, and a group experience. In the *Weekly Chungang,* Eo-ryong Lee described this as 'a sign of the new value system of the twenty-first century'.

The Red Devils are of course just a group, a very large group, who support their national football team. But we can also see the wider positive impact of their values and behaviour. When the team lost to Germany, at the end of the match it was the fans who started to clear up all their litter in the stands immediately after the final whistle. And they also clapped the German players with chants of 'See you in Germany 2006'. Hiddink was surprised by the huge support for the team; 'but no trouble, no problems – this, only the Red Devils could do so well'.

The huge banners at matches that read 'Pride of Asia' were a dig at Japan, a nation that was thought of by many Koreans as being more interested in Europe than its own continent. The Red Devils were saying they were proud to be Asian. In *Newsweek Korea* a fan was quoted as saying, 'This is the first time in my life that I feel proud of being born in Korea.' This was typical of the sentiments behind supporting the team. In the past, proud of being Korean amounted to supporting a military government. This was different. The cheer that was ever-constant whenever the team played – *Tae-hanmingukk*, 'Republic of Korea' – was, in the past, about being a nation divided and not being Japanese. But now it was a chant for everyone – that was its real meaning. It transcended social class, generations and gender – areas which had previously divided Korean society. It was a chant that was only possible now because of the democratisation of Korea. It was a chant without a target, it wasn't aimed at an enemy. They shouted it at the sky. When they screamed *Tae-hanmingukk*, of course they were supporting the Korean team, but more importantly they were supporting themselves. It was a celebration of the post-war liberation from Japan but also a liberation from their own recent past. In this sense, World Cup fever really was the second liberation, and the day Korea beat Spain, our second independence day.

Some coverage remained unsure whether *Tae-hanmingukk* really meant so very much. The magazine *Hangyoreh 21* commented:

> The scream of 'Tae-hanmingukk' is not the symbol of nationalism, and the national flag which people hold is not the same flag of 1919 when the people were fighting for independence. This was just people having a good time. The scream of the street was not a message of unity of nations but to claim that space as a playground and finding a means for joy.

The organisation Citizen Solidarity for Cultural Reform took this a stage further. They proposed that the area of Kwanghwamun (around the city hall) should be turned into a cultural square and street. Professor Hong Seong-tae defined that area which includes the government office, American Embassy, Old Palace, major newspaper buildings, city hall and big company headquarters as streets which symbolise ruling power, and he argued in *Hangyoreh 21* that by the fans turning these places into areas where they would celebrate meant that the symbols of rule were being changed into spaces for joy and festival.

The *Newsmaker* described the rise of a new generation who have 'World Cup DNA'. This young generation is non-political yet they are self-confident. They saw the Korean team beat Italy and Spain, and believed that they could beat Germany and even Brazil too. This way of positive thinking could be very important for the future of Korea.

Professor Kang of Seoul City University predicted in the *Dong-a-llbo* that the generation with 'World Cup DNA' would be the most flexibile and creative in Korean history.

The impact of the World Cup on South Korea has only just begun. The 'Hiddink Syndrome' will be with us for years to come. Country and society will change as a result of it, make no mistake.

And yes, the Red Devils are still partying.

REPRESENTATIVE MATCHES: PLAYERS, CELEBRITY AND INTERNATIONALISM

At Our Becks and Cool

Jim White

It was a tar-meltingly hot day in downtown Tokyo and, in search of coolness, much of the population had headed for the one area of green in the place, Yoyogi Park. As the sun ripped down and a group of Irish fans played an intense game of shirts against rapidly reddening skins, I fell into conversation with a local woman. In the shade of a cherry tree, we talked about – what else – the World Cup. She told me that like many a Japanese I had met, she was supporting England. I asked her why. 'Because they are all so good looking,' came back the reply. Ah right, I said, so who's good looking? 'Beckham,' she said. Yup, I replied, he sure is. Anyone else? Martin Keown perhaps. Or Paul Scholes. Maybe Nicky Butt. What about Robbie Fowler? She thought for a moment, creased her brow in concentration and then smiled. 'Beckham,' she nodded. 'Beckham.'

In many ways she had it right; in the World Cup England *were* David Beckham.

Just as Brazil were samba, Italy were grumpy and Cameroon were funny sleeveless shirts, so England were their captain. It was like when Manchester United bought Rio Ferdinand for £30 million and for the same sum they could have purchased the whole of Leeds United on the stock exchange and still had change left to pick up Leicester City; Beckham was a bigger, more substantial property than the rest of them put together. And then some. In Tokyo, his image, looking broody in a pair of Police sunglasses, covered entire fleets of buses. There were posters of him in sports shops, in department stores, his perfect cheekbones appeared on the front of every magazine. On the hoardings featuring other players – even the Japanese – there were little name check captions to let the public know it was Hidetoshi Nakata who was promoting the Sony Minicam, or Zinedine Zidane recommending the seafood pot noodle. But Beckham went uncaptioned. Everyone knew who he was. Like Michael Jordan and Tiger Woods, he had slipped the boundaries of his context and become something more significant: a global brand.

But even knowing that, even being accustomed to his *OK* magazine celebrity back home, nothing prepared you for what happened in close physical proximity to Beckham in Japan. When the England team bus arrived at games, or at training, or just returned to their hotel base, outside on the pavement, you could almost smell the pheromones. Hundreds of girls who had waited for hours for this moment, would fling themselves at the barriers. Television crews would jostle for a sight of him through the coach window. You could sense all round you hearts racing and breathing constricting with the excitement that can only be generated by the impending arrival of a real star. And when he stepped off the bus, always dignified, always controlled, the air would be filled with a mixture I have come to associate with Japan; the pant-wetting screams of adolescent girls and the flash of a thousand Nikons. He would wave, tousle the head of a small boy, attempt an autograph. And then, invariably, he would smile his big, wide, happy grin. It was a smile which said one thing; this is where I belong.

In the 30 years since he self-destructed, Manchester United, their fans and the wider commercial world have been desperate for a new George Best. They thought they had him in Norman Whiteside, but he shared only an accident of birth and a fondness for the sauce with the great man. They almost had him with Ryan Giggs, in the slope of his shoulders when he ran, in the darts and dribbles. But Giggs was too cagey, too canny with his private life to become a public property. When he finally arrived, the new incarnation came in the shape of a player whose game bears no relation to Best's; he is largely one-footed, doesn't dribble, isn't much in the air, his destructive match-winning abilities come from the genius of his crossing and passing rather than his solo runs. But where Beckham has emulated his predecessor is this; he is, after George, the country's second pop star footballer. True, Kevin Keegan cut a single and made an advert for aftershave, sure Gazza was the role model for a certain laddish devilment, but Beckham has that edge, that appeal which crosses all sociological divisions. Grannies want to mother him, girls want to shag him and boys admire him because girls want to shag him. When he plays, he has that look-at-me aura that Best possessed. All eyes are drawn to him. His very presence demands attention. And he loves it. Not in that desperate narcissism of the *Big Brother* contestants. But because he believes it is his destiny, that he has arrived, that this is where he belongs.

If David Beckham was preordained for anything, it was the 2002 World Cup in Japan, the place and time in which style was practically demonstrated to be as important a tool as substance. And that demonstration came in the person of David Beckham. In many ways, Japan in 2002 was the natural consequence of the commercial revolution, which has enveloped our game over the past decade. In Japan, they weren't football fans; they were consumers. This is a nation, which had, until the tournament, absorbed its football entirely through the cathode ray tube. These were followers from the face paint age, their heroes the players they had seen on commercials. Suddenly it had all arrived on their doorstep. Particularly the visiting supporters, who they treated almost like celebrities because they brought with them the sniff of authenticity (which, as humidity levels soared, in the case of some of the Irish was detectable at 40 metres). In the stadiums, the Japanese had to learn how to respond. In the early games, they sat in polite silence, reacting spontaneously only at the moments which could be clipped from the action and reshown in mega slo-mo to a beating rock soundtrack. One of the biggest noises I heard in the tournament's first week was when a Nigerian forward attempted an overhead kick. That he failed to direct his effort anywhere near goal did not matter; this was football as they play it on the adverts.

And who was the man they were most familiar with through the commercial storm which preceded kick-off? David Beckham. Francesco Totti, Ronaldo, Gabriel Batistuta; they knew who all of these were. But Beckham was the image they worshipped. When he took the corner for Sol Campbell to head in England's goal against Sweden, in many ways it was a defining moment in the World Cup. As he addressed the ball, head still in concentration, right leg bending, expensively endorsed right boot swishing, the entire stadium lit up. It was an extraordinary sight, the flashlights popping; night turned to day. It may well have blinded the Swedish back line into statuesque immobility. It happened because every person in the place seemed determined not to watch the action but to record it. To prove to their friends, their family, perhaps to themselves, that they were really there. That they had seen this creature of the commercials in the flesh. Talk about celebrity football.

Importantly, throughout the tournament, Beckham seemed entirely comfortable with his position as the icon of corporatism. He did not kick against it, or rebel, or whinge even once. For every minute, he behaved impeccably, the role model husband, father and leader. Unquestionably he had learned from his previous World Cup experience, when his childish petulance was punished way beyond the boundaries of the crime by a vituperative press campaign. Piers Morgan, editor of *The Daily Mirror*, should be particularly ashamed of the front page vilifying Beckham that he sanctioned after St Etienne. Except, being a tabloid editor, apologies are anathema, hypocrisy a tool of the trade, and *The Daily Mirror* joined in the robust celebration of the man this time round as if it had never called him the spoiled brat who lost us the World Cup. But even given the history, Beckham's conduct was exemplary. In press conferences he was charming, at official functions he was unstintingly polite, on the pitch he was the peacemaker. The first to applaud the fans, the last to stop signing autographs, never once giving the impression that side of things was a chore. He showed the public relations of a master. And with every laudable action, his stock rose. Of course, the cynic might suggest there is a commercial imperative behind all this, that he has signed a contract with the devil of Mammon trading ten years of freedom for a lifetime's wealth. Yet there are many sporting figures – Eric Cantona, John McEnroe, Roy Keane even – whose value only increased with every spiky gesture. Besides, you only have to glance at his contemporaries to admire how he conducts himself.

He comes from a world in which many of his peers have the sense of social responsibility of a crack addict. And that's not just English players; the Italians in this tournament sneered at their hosts by signing 'Mickey Mouse' and 'Donald Duck' in the autograph books of fans who had waited hours for their presence. But Beckham was different, a thoroughly well brought-up young man, he was ambassadorial in the proper sense of the word. And good for England, too. What has been our one enduring export over the past 40 years? Popular culture. The Beatles, minis, dance music, fashion, design, style. Now Beckham. He is cool Britannia without even trying.

The irony in all this – and the unmissable flaw in any campaign to have him deified – is this; the biggest figure there had a very ordinary World Cup. The bravery of his penalty against Argentina aside, he was little more than an also ran. List the telling contributions he made to the cause and they come down to a couple of corners. The long range passes, the lung-busting effort, the tackling back, the cajoling, the never-say-die spirit; all were missing from his game in the Far East. And this is what sets him aside from his predecessors. For Johann Cruyff, for Diego Maradona, for Pelé, the World Cup was the platform on which, by demonstrating the superiority of their skills, they cemented their position as the most famous footballers of their generation. Looking back on the careers of those players, it is not Cruyff's time with Barcelona or Maradona's moments with Napoli that stick in the mind. It is what they achieved in the most testing, the most demanding of footballing circumstances; the World Cup. When the show-reel of this competition is completed to be screened before games in Germany 2006, there will not be a contribution from David Beckham on it. A sudden turn which left his marker dumbfounded, a shot from the halfway line, a glorious mazy run through a leaden-heeled defence? He provided none of those things. In truth, his contribution to history is so far less substantial than that of Archie Gemmill, whose glorious goal against Holland in 1978 was shown on the giant screen in every stadium before every game in 2002.

Of course there were reasons Beckham didn't do it. It didn't help that Gary Neville wasn't there. Neville is not the most popular of England choices, but his authority grew in his absence. He gels so well with Beckham, reads his game, covers for him, knows where he will be, makes runs which distract his markers, that between them they make the righthand side of England world class. And while it would be cruel on Danny Mills to dismiss him as half the player Neville is, even being ten per cent below par makes a difference.

Plus, Beckham wasn't fit. A natural athlete, he recovered with astonishing speed from his broken foot (be honest, before he did his, didn't you think a metatarsal was a species of dinosaur?). But his game is built on dynamism, on stamina, on power. Against Brazil, when England needed all those things, they weren't available. He put his foot on the pedal and found he had run out of petrol.

There was, though, something more. After the Greece game, when he played better than anyone I have ever seen in an England shirt, as he celebrated the goal which took his country to the finals, Beckham thought the script was written for him. When he recovered sufficiently from his injury in time to play in the first game in Japan, when he scored that penalty against the old enemy, when he watched his teammates destroy Denmark, he became convinced. Sure, in his press statements he made the contractual noises about one game at a time and not thinking beyond the Brazilians. But as the draw opened up, as the favourites went home, you could tell by the glow around him that a picture had begun to form in his mind of him holding that cup, lifting it high above his hair, which for the occasion had been fashioned into a cross of St George, providing a photographic image at last to match Bobby Moore clutching the Jules Rimet atop his colleagues' shoulders. Destiny is a hard thing to fight. Especially when you are convinced it is on your side. And that was how England played in the second half against Brazil; as if the script would somehow save them.

Unfortunately, even in the commercialised maelstrom of modern football, the real thing does not turn out like the adverts. Thus England were out and a nation mourned; Japan, that is, obliged to say a premature farewell to the man who had occupied its news bulletins and its wet dreams for three weeks. They turned their affections instead on Ronaldo, who exorcised his demons from France '98 in a far more comprehensive way than Beckham managed. For once, the FA got it right and sneaked the team back home without trumpet or fanfare. There were complaints – from *The Daily Mirror*, naturally. But for the players it would have been too much to be lauded for what they know in their hearts was failure, the failure to take a chance the like of which will not come to many, if not any of them, again.

It is a failure that will have stung Beckham in particular. His last World Cup ended in shame, this one in a whimper. Worse, he must be wondering if he has another one left. By the time Germany comes round in 2006, he will be 31. Supremely athletic he might be, but the next generation of midfield players – Owen Hargreaves, Joe Cole, Steven Gerrard, Jermaine Jenas – are the ones the FA has targeted in its ambitious plan to win the competition 40 years on from England's only victory. Beckham knows he will have to work hard to justify his inclusion ahead of that crowded field of talent once he has climbed over the top of the hill. That's why he needed to be something more than the tournament's pin-up in 2002.

Unlike Maradona, Pelé and Cruyff, Beckham, on the field, was a failure. But they came from a time before Mammon took an interest in football, before to be able to kick a ball was a passport to boardrooms everywhere. Beckham was perhaps the first internationally renowned footballer whose name was not made by what happened in the World Cup, it was made by what now surrounds the competition. And, as the new season began, as optimism freshened the spirit and the new commercials filled the airwaves, as the players were once more workshopped up into the gladiatorial heroes of the modern age, it was quickly forgotten that we weren't very good as a team at the World Cup. What matters more was that, through the person of our captain, in the battle for hearts and minds we were unbeatable. Which is the war they need to win in the boardrooms of Adidas, Police and Pepsi Cola. For them, looking back on it, there was only one winner in the World Cup of 2002. Thank you, David. You are the defining football figure of the commercial age.

*****

Accounting for Football's Feel-good Factor

Wendy Wheeler

No man is an island, entire of itself; every man is a piece of the continent, a part of the main.
– John Donne, English poet, 1573–1631

Human beings are social creatures. In spite of the emphasis on economic individualism, and upon the psychological motivation of the person as an individual – all of which has been so much a part of the history of modern societies in the West for the past 300 years – it remains the case that many, if not most, of our motivations remain social. No human comes to the fullest expression of their selfhood in isolation, but only as a part of a group. And it is our sociality – our evolutionary disposition to co-operate for common ends, to identify 'our own' people, to support 'our' group and its gains in terms of the things necessary to support life – that is the source of both the best and the worst in us. Our capacities for altruistic co-operation run deep; but on the negative side, our group loyalties too easily turn also to the bitter partisanship evident in the extremities of racist nationalism. This has been part of football's history too. If the co-operative group's struggle for the resources to support human survival lies at the evolutionary base of our inclinations to make group identifications, it is clear that, where human societies are concerned, human survival also has equally important cultural dimensions; we need not only to support life itself, but to support ways we live that life. These are the markers of our commonality and our community; they are what we, as a group, share, and what allow us to rub along together in ways that manage each individual's impulses and desires in the context of group imperatives. How is it in football that we glimpse at least the partial realisation of our yearning for community while at the same time we are able to begin to recognise the need for global community in a globalised modern world? What is it about football that provides so many of us with ways to take pleasure in local or national identifications which can coexist with other more, fluid and provisional identifications?

At the heart of any community is language. But flowing out from this core of shared linguistic symbolism is a complex web of other symbolic meanings which find form in belief systems, the rules governing these, appropriate (and inappropriate) forms of behaviour for sacred and secular life, institutions for managing these, and more. Although the history of the modern world has seen local or regional groups incorporated into nation states, and the rationalisation of almost all aspects of social behaviour in the face of scientific, technological and bureaucratic modernisation, our ancient selves still beat within us, and there is hardly any part of our symbolic social and cultural life which is not capable of arousing, sometimes with a devotional intensity, our old inclinations to affiliation. Historically, and today too, managing this without open conflict has proved very difficult. But World Cup 2002, as a part of our symbolic language of territorial conflict and possession, has provided an opportunity for experimentation and play in the matter of passionately held allegiances, along with varied experiences of communal belonging. It represented a moment when people could strive for the goods of community. Such softened explorations give us a clue about what more seriously held collective yet inclusive identifications might also be like.

The slow demise of community has a long history. Religious reform in England in the sixteenth century loosened the intimate relationship between church and state, and this, in turn, made scientific advance and philosophical freedom easier. Relative political stability from the early eighteenth century onwards led to the scientific and intellectual flowering hailed as the Age of Enlightenment.

With the Enlightenment's emphasis on man as a rational creature capable of forging his own destiny via the uses of science and technology, the modern world was born in the furnaces of the Industrial Revolution which followed. Rationalisation and technological innovation in agriculture, and the swarming growth of the new industrial towns in the Midlands and North of England, undermined the old small and traditional communities with their inherited superstitions, beliefs and relationships. The new communities which formed during the nineteenth century were largely based on the affiliations of class in which passion was attached to class interests on both sides. At the beginning of the twentieth century, these class group passions were given political expression in the form of political parties. By the beginning of the twenty-first century, however, the rationalisation and modernisation of politics which took place during the last two decades of the twentieth century, and which included the destruction of much of the industrial base of working-class cohesion, had also destroyed the earlier group passions through which modern politics had been conducted. Alongside the increasing emphasis on selfish individualism, the old human longing for the kinds of passionate allegiance to a group in which individual identity is powerfully affirmed have been left in a political vacuum as older forms of collectivism have been abandoned by their previous champions in mainstream Western politics, Labour and Social Democratic parties. In the home, even the bonds of kinship-belonging appeared weakened in a world which valued self-interested 'life choices' over dogged commitments. At work, casualisation, short-term contracts, and the 'career as portfolio' have all broken down the lifetime group allegiances focused on occupations. The writer Richard Sennett notes in his book *The Corrosion of Character* that the transience of work commitments in late capitalist societies means that: 'such communities are not empty of sociability or neighbourliness, but no one in them becomes a long-term witness to another person's life'. And without such communal witness, life itself becomes immeasurably emptier.

For some, what all these developments produced was the attempt – sometimes patrician and negatively nostalgic, sometimes racist and violent – to return to older forms of the nation as community; but the political expression of these sorts of nationalism have tended to go against the grain of a general Enlightenment progressiveness in which the majority, however troubled, have pretty much gone along with the idea – given particular importance by the deregulation of capital and the recognition of the fact of globalisation – that these older kinds of group identification are no longer either desirable or even realisable.

The best impulses of the eighteenth-century Enlightenment were progressive; rational, increasingly inclusive and increasingly democratic.

Their legacy for us living at the beginning of the twenty-first century has been, and remains, a continuing commitment to peaceful solutions to conflict where possible. Hence the increasing disquiet over the US-led response to the horrific atrocity of 11 September. This legacy also involves the widening of forms of democratisation, affiliation and communication. Much of this has been driven by trade and by the growing recognition, from the eighteenth century onwards at least, that trade and economic growth are facilitated by peaceful relations. Thus the conflict over territory and access to raw materials which fuelled the European colonial and imperial enterprises between the sixteenth and the twentieth centuries gradually gave way to 'spheres of interest', trade treaties and decolonialisation with 'foreign aid packages' attached.

With the demise of the Soviet sphere of influence after 1989, and the global extension of free trade which, unopposed, followed it, the largely 'national' identifications through which human beings had managed their group loyalties came under increasing pressure. The unconstrained power and movement of multinational corporations and electronic capital seemed to erode the economic sovereignty of nation states, and, just as capital was set free to roam the globe in search of the most profitable locations, so humans, too, sought to migrate in search of the same. One response to this crumbling of older sources of group identification was a retreat to earlier – usually religious – forms of group identification and often concomitant territorial and cultural struggle. That these should arise largely in those parts of the world which had benefited least from 'the triumph of capitalism' is unsurprising. Another response was the attempt, by new populist right-wing political parties across Europe, to resurrect and reaffirm a nationalism that sought to exclude migrants and impose a homogeneous moral and social order.

One of the most important arenas in which personal and group identity is formed remains the realm of creative play. This is never a matter of complete freedom; it is always a matter of learning the rules (or 'grammar') of social interactions and, at best, making imaginative use of these in order to make new ways of living and interacting. This is true in art and it is true in sport. It is in these areas of everyday experience that our culture is most alive in our hands.

Football has long been a site of cultural identifications. Like most team games, it is a staging of possession and territory. It is unsurprising that it very easily gives rise to group identifications and to all the accoutrements of symbolic war on and off the pitch. When national teams play, all the national identifications are, of course, on display. However, football's coming home. Its familiarisation, one might say, in the successful attempts to claim it as a family game and to rid it of the worst excesses of racist and xenophobic nationalism, seems to me to have formed a very significant part of a national and international conversation about how we humans are to manage the complex world we now live in whilst acknowledging, in a positive fashion, our old needs for group identifications.

Over the past 20 years, football has traversed the modernisation path of inclusivity and has offered a cultural site where our old and new selves have been able to negotiate via the creative interactions of players, fans, football and media institutions. In Britain, political devolution has been expressed in terms of the much noted appearance of the flag of St George when England are playing, and of course to England's north and west, the Scots' St Andrew's Cross and the Welsh Dragon when our neighbours are playing. As to Northern Ireland the criss-crossing of flags in the North – the Irish Tricolour here, Red Hand of Ulster there – is a powerful indicator of a nation of deeply divided national loyalties. The Union flag – much in evidence during the celebrations of the Queen's Golden Jubilee which coincided with the 2002 World Cup, but a more equivocal symbol associated still with the shame of imperialism – is no longer the flag of choice for the vast majority of England fans. It is clear that the widespread flying of England's St George Cross flag which first appeared at Euro '96 has, even more so in 2002, been the expression of a much-longed for sense of English national community. From the start of the tournament in Japan and Korea, these red and white St George Cross flags were everywhere – hanging out of windows, draped outside shops and pubs, flying from numerous cars.

To call this simply 'the feel-good factor' would be to underestimate its symbolic importance. National governments may have bought the idea that there is no alternative to a selfish and greed-driven global capitalism focused on rewards to individual CEOs and individual shareholders but ordinary people still affirm the importance of group solidarities. Poised between the seemingly irreconcilable drives of human self-interest versus collective interests and, by extension, the seemingly inevitable conflict between same-group self-interest versus the human will and need for co-operative activity, football has helped to produce a creative new model. This is not to say that international football does not have its share of commercialisation and corruption; of course it does. But football as a symbolic practice negotiated between the players and the wider national (and international) community of fans has the potential to transcend this. At its best it achieves this by collecting up national support, and a national desire for communal identifications, in a positive and forward-looking, rather than nostalgic, fashion.

Because to be fully human is to act within a social group, human beings are unlikely ever to lose their inclinations to group identifications. However, in a fluid world, and via the powerful symbolism of co-operation and conflict which football has the potential to offer, we might discover a creative way of exploring the possibilities of more fluid identifications. Doubtless, primary (and primal) identifications – with kinship groups, clans, tribes, nationalities, ethnicities – will continue, but perhaps we have also hit upon a model for more provisional identifications which can be joyful, affirming and international. During World Cup 2002, we affirmed our old national identifications, but we also found some room for a more generous, cross-national, sharing of our affiliations. That these new adventures in world solidarity were profoundly pleasurable, and that we could all enjoy, through football, the experience of fluid group identifications, has been the most important lesson that we have allowed ourselves to learn from this World Cup. No one really needs persuading of this because everyone experienced it. This is the kind of international solidarity which has been sought, and often found, in recent more obviously political formations such as the Anti-Capitalist and Green international movements. It has also been long discovered by people obliged to unearth what fluid and hybrid identifications might feel like as a product of colonialism. As the Indian author Raja Rao wrote:

> . . . we are instinctively bilingual, many of us writing in our own language and English. We cannot write like the English. We should not. We can only write as Indians. We have grown to look at the large world as part of us.

Belatedly, football has allowed more nations to join in the experience of looking at the world as part of us.

The idea that identity is more fluid in the postmodern world is not new. The theorist Fredric Jameson wrote about it in *Postmodernism, or the Cultural Logic of Late Capitalism* 20 years ago. Our fashions and cuisines are increasingly international. On the negative side this means the exploitation of the workforce in garment factories in developing countries and the unhealthy nutrition provided by a McDonald's in every city on the globe. On the positive side, it means the creative mixing of diverse traditions.

The dream of world community is an old one; its expression was first given in terms of the religious revelations and community of Christianity and Islam, then later in the ideas of the national group in the form of the nation state, and then later still in terms of the triumphs of democracy and socialism. Throughout the twentieth century various attempts at international bodies and federations were made, but the sticking point has always revolved around national identity and national group identifications. In the European Community the idea of subsidiarity has been the latest attempt to allow for a possible fluidity of political group identifications within the economic convergence provided by the Euro. But these political machinations have only incited negative and backward-looking passions. Can politics, especially in the West and with the pressures towards supranational or world community, learn anything positive from football after 2002?

Football has proved capable of providing a symbolic forum where, over time and with the goodwill of the majority of interested individuals, we have been able to practise how a global community might take shape – most outstandingly in 2002. Supranational and international politics have signally failed to provide any such similar forum of creative and symbolically rich power. To take the European example, Brussels is, famously, grey and bureaucratic. This is, it should be understood, not an observation that people make; it is an accusation. People understand that our life as a polity should move us. That it no longer does so, that numbers voting in elections drop year on year, that politics has been emptied of fire and belief, and filled instead with the cold ashes of accountancy, targets and calculation, makes people cross. People are not politically disaffected; they are angry. This is not voter apathy; it is voter fury, and the sullen withholding of support from discredited parties, left and right. Both national and international politics suffer because they are without passion and without the spontaneous symbolism which any authentic human endeavour accrues. All has been cast off in favour of a pragmatism that often borders on dishonesty and cynical manipulation. Where, in British politics is the great symbolic idea that would inspire, mobilise and animate the followers of any of our political parties? None of them offer this. Instead, all is calculation. What human being can feel any powerful and positive feelings – for greater justice or more democratic participation through greater transparency – when all that is on offer are merely technical calculations?

A human being is an inseparable mixture of a head and a heart; where the modern thinking born of an Enlightenment emphasis on rationality went wrong was in thinking that these two – a head and a heart, a reasoning mind and a passionate body – were separate things. As I showed in my book, *A New Modernity? Change in Science, Literature and Politics*, we now know from recent developments in neurobiology that good reasoning depends upon effective feeling. Successful politics, like successful football, must engage the whole creature – head and heart. The managerialism, utilitarianism, and dependence on public relations 'spinning' which dominates modern politics cannot inspire passion and the commitments that passion produces. In the past politics did – earlier ideological commitments, being authentic and experiential, were often felt with religious zeal – but still no way was found of managing this energy so that it could be both heartfelt and fluidly adaptable to non-exclusionary and common purposes. Is it possible that football in 2002 found a way of letting us imagine, creatively and against the badness of the modern technological world, the goodness of our yearning for authentic, unalienated, community in ways that are open, inventive and non-exclusionary? Has the beautiful game become a place which produces a model of what it is like to be artists in a fluid world?

The World Cup reminded us that human commitment requires passion, and that human passions invoke identifications, especially group ones; but it has also, and importantly, taught us that passion need not be divisive and lead to conflict. It can have the rational aim of global solidarities. Politics, too, might have this rational end in sight. But it will never get there until it provides the kind of deeply and richly symbolic forums for cultural conversations through which we can discover what these forms might be. During World Cup 2002 fans around the world found a way.

* * * * *

Sven, Long to Reign Over Us?

Philip Cornwall

'Ungrateful fool.' This was my reply to the first England fan I came across calling for Sven-Göran Eriksson's sacking after the end of the 2002 World Cup. And it remains the only sensible response to such calls, if your memory reaches back to October 2000, and indeed beyond, with any degree of reliability.

England's amnesiacs may not remember the circumstances that led to Eriksson's appointment, but it's safe to say that few in October 2000 were foreseeing a run to the quarter-finals in Japan – or even a trip there for whoever the new coach happened to be, other than to scout out the opposition for the next set of European qualifiers.

Eriksson was given a five-and-a-half-year contract when he was appointed in 2000, a signal that England were looking beyond Japan and Korea from the outset. Whether the FA were right or wrong to take such a long view, it would be ludicrous of them to turn round not even halfway through and abandon such a policy, and there was no question of critics at the margins of debate getting their way in the summer of 2002, luckily.

So those who still baulk at the cradle of the modern game having to look abroad for a coach will have to foam away for a while longer, barring a bizarre scandal of the kind that did for Hoddle, or a job offer from elsewhere which is so tempting to the Swede that it's worth throwing away the dubious privilege of making Sainsburys adverts with Jamie Oliver.

But that doesn't mean that Eriksson is guaranteed to see out his full contract to the World Cup in Germany 2006, or to be remembered fondly after that date. What we have had so far was both a bonus after the chaos he took over from, and a surprisingly extended chance to learn about the task now at hand.

How can Sven improve his chances of his supporters' faith being rewarded? Which of his experiments so far have been successful? What lessons can we learn from what he saw in the Far East, from our team and from others? For that matter, what can he learn from the valid criticisms of his team from rivals, fans, and even the odd journalist? What must Sven do to make sure that I, and many more like me, remain a grateful fool?

World Cup qualification is no achievement for a country with England's pedigree. In 2001 it was only achieved with a last-minute goal from a free kick that shouldn't have been awarded. Only two matches were won in the Far East, and elimination came in the quarter-finals, a worse performance than either South Korea and Turkey, not to mention a certain team England had thrashed 5–1 less than a year previously. Up against the ten men of Brazil in the last 40 minutes England barely threatened to find the net, as inexperienced players seemed incapable of implementing anything except the tactics with which they had started. Michael Owen, the man most likely, was taken off, a move reminiscent of Graham Taylor's infamous substitution of Gary Lineker against Sweden at Euro '92.

Overall, in five matches England strung together maybe three decent halves of football, and at times had fans reaching for the snooze button. Overseas observers wondered where England had left their attacking style, and frankly their guts, after the defeat by Brazil. The Brazilian winning goal came when a goalkeeper written off in 2000, who had been highlighted as a weakness going into the tournament by some, was made to look hapless.

Such an analysis is easy to make. It is also worth making, because – stripping away the exaggeration – many of the points it raises can be taken as guides to what Eriksson does next. But it ignores entirely the context, of taking a team that weren't expected to make the 32 finalists through to the top eight in the world, and all but guaranteeing a seeding if they can qualify for 2006, more than anyone could reasonably have asked for.

To return to Eriksson's beginning. After a dismal Euro 2000, defeat by Germany at Wembley in the opening World Cup qualifier led Kevin

Keegan to desert the cause in response to the paralysis that had gripped him on the bench as his badly laid plans fell apart. Howard Wilkinson was plunged into a caretaker role to travel to Helsinki at four days' notice, and escaped with a point from a performance that left the Finns wondering what might have been, and the spectators wondering what the formation was supposed to have been.

Keegan had lasted less than two years at the helm, his predecessor, Glenn Hoddle, just a shade longer, and obvious successors were thin on the ground. Wilkinson, the FA's Technical Director, openly asked whether the right thing to do was to abandon this World Cup and look to the future, and that in part is what the FA did. They sought out a coach who could lead England not to the Far East in 2002, but to Germany in 2006, via Euro 2004 in Portugal.

Back then, I was ridiculed for writing on the website www.football365.com that things weren't so bad if we could pull ourselves together under a new coach. The defeat by the Germans in the old Wembley's last match may have made winning the group almost unthinkable, but I felt England were in with a decent shout of reaching the play-offs after drawing 0–0 away to Finland, our principal rivals for a runners-up slot.

The search for a new coach was nonetheless carried out against a justifiable background of depression about the national game, not helped by this lack of an obvious successor. Keegan had been appointed in the first place more as a result of blind faith in his status as a messiah than on the basis of any obvious qualification for the role, and in the absence of many serious alternatives. The penchant for our leading clubs to appoint managers either from overseas or from elsewhere in these islands meant that Brian Little (League Cup with Aston Villa, 1996), Joe Royle (FA Cup with Everton, 1995) and Wilkinson (League title with Leeds, 1992) were the last Englishmen to land our domestic trophies, and subsequent career developments meant none were serious contenders (to put it mildly in the cases of Royle and Little).

Two men had enjoyed more recent success abroad, but Bobby Robson was in his late 60s by 2000, and the coach who took England to the semi-finals in Italy was too old to do more than mentor a younger man, such as the then Leicester City manager Peter Taylor, a former Under-21 coach. The other contender, Roy Hodgson, had crashed and burned on his one English assignment, at Blackburn Rovers.

This was perhaps unfortunate, because Hodgson would have been an intelligent choice. Yet he was a successful English coach who was not a product of the English system, and in part despised it – especially the kowtowing to the tabloid press, which meant he had few supporters at the mass end of the media. There could never be a Hodgson bandwagon to match the one for Keegan, which had rolled the under-qualified disaster area into the job in 1999. This left one other possibility: Terry Venables.

Few disputed his footballing credentials, just as they hadn't when he was appointed to lead England through to Euro '96, in early 1994. Though the only major trophies of his career were one Spanish Championship and one FA Cup, he was widely acknowledged by players and peers as the best English coach of his generation. And he had – and still has – plenty of supporters in the press and on TV.

However, his off-the-pitch activities were questionable to say the least – he had been barred from holding directorships for seven years by the Department of Trade and Industry in early 1998, admitting 18 offences, most of which related to his time in charge of football clubs. The beginnings of those troubles, at Tottenham, had led to him not having his contract extended prior to Euro '96, as the FA doubted he was fully committed to the job. This in turn meant he opted not to wait and seek a new contract if he was successful, but to announce that he would move on regardless of what happened in the tournament. So the FA had installed Glenn Hoddle as successor weeks before the semi-final defeat by Germany on penalties that ended Venables' reign.

Though he still has his loyal pack of media hounds, there were plenty of dogs at his heels, too: he was brought down in part by journalists who exposed his business dealings. It all made a reappointment of someone who would be a step backwards into England's past too risky for the FA in 2000. Venables was destined only to be an England pundit at the 2002 World Cup.

So to howls of anguish from some, the FA looked abroad, to name the Swedish coach of the Italian champions, Lazio, as the new man. A man who had won domestic trophies at home, in Portugal and in Italy, and at European level too. Strip away the question of nationality, and the only one of the actual or potential England coaches whose qualifications came close to matching Eriksson's was the venerable Bobby Robson.

Was it really any surprise that the FA chose a man who had won trophies regularly for 20 years, more than most of his rivals combined?

It was a gamble by the Scot in charge, Adam Crozier, one he committed to for five years but which paid off in one. Eriksson delivered not only qualification, but Munich. Yes, he rode his luck, but that 5–1 win was an achievement that amazed the world of football, not just the English, and rightly so. Only once before, and then only after they had already won their group, had the Germans lost a World Cup qualifier, home or away. Here they were, demolished. Michael Owen's European Footballer of the Year award, voted for by journalists across the continent, surely hung on that hat-trick in the 5–1 win that allowed England to go from bottom to top of their group a few days later.

After a few nerves in that 2–0 win over Albania, and some agonising moments against Greece, David Beckham spun some free-kick magic after Teddy Sheringham's stumble to earn a decisive draw. A nation rejoiced.

Still, England were written off at least three more times on the way to the quarter-finals. After the draw, which placed Argentina, Sweden, Nigeria and France firmly in their path. After the injuries which afflicted the squad beforehand, depriving the team of two automatic starters. And again after the opening 1–1 draw, against Eriksson's native land. On each occasion, while all about were losing theirs, the Swede kept firm control of his cool. And even the most sceptic of sceptics must have been pretty excited by the time Michael Owen opened the scoring in the quarter-final.

And yet, we failed. For all the celebration that accompanied the win over Argentina, the delirium that greeted the half-time score against Denmark and anticipation of victory over Brazil, it was not to be.

Significantly, though, there is one block to future success that Eriksson did all he could to remove from our path for next time. Because if England qualify for 2006, then unless FIFA fix the seeding system against them, they will be in the top eight, and so able to avoid any of the game's great powers in the early stages of the next tournament, at the very least. In part this is because England did well, but also because others did badly, either now or previously.

The other losing quarter-finalists in 2002 were the United States and Spain, who both failed to get out of their France '98 groups, and Senegal, who had never previously qualified for the finals. Turkey and South Korea, semi-finalists in the Far East, were non-qualifiers for the competition and the second round, respectively, in 1998. The Netherlands and Croatia, that year's semi-finalists, were non-qualifiers for the competition and the second round, respectively, this time.

The system used currently gives single weighting to the tournament 12 years prior, double weighting for the tournament eight years back, and triple weighting for the most recent competition. Which suggests England are fourth, behind Brazil, Germany and France, in spite of England and France both failing to reach USA '94. Spain, quarter-finalists at USA '94, will be close behind, as will the Dutch. But England should be fourth.

Such a high rating is nearly borne out by FIFA official rankings. The monthly charts are a peculiar beast, a statistical camel giving peculiar weightings to different matches and competitions. But the system produced results in July 2002 that had England eighth in the world. Pretty much the minimum for a beaten quarter-finalist, you'd have thought, but of course teams don't drop out of sight for one bad performance, so France and Argentina, who didn't get out of their groups, are amongst the teams ahead of them, as are Germany, humiliated at home nine months before the tournament.

England were held down by the lean spell before Eriksson. Yet in those post-tournament rankings they were within touching distance on points of Mexico and Portugal, and therefore sixth spot. Brazil had such a commanding lead at the top, that England were closer to the teams in joint second, those World Cup failures France and Argentina, than that pair were to the champions.

Since the rankings were launched, in late 1993, only twice have England been ranked above eighth – when the rankings first started, and the Italia '90 semi-final was still counting for a lot and the failure to reach USA '94 hadn't bitten, then between Glenn Hoddle's triumph in the Tournoi de France in the summer of 1997 and exit from the World Cup a year later.

The performance at Italia '90 itself would have been a high point, but the relative failures in the World Cups and European Championships (in finals performances or non-qualification), of 1974, 1976, 1978, 1980, 1984 and 1988 mean that a ranking as high as eighth would probably only have been achieved by Sir Alf Ramsey and Bobby Robson – at the time in 1990 when he was in the process of losing the job.

Looking at it through the prism of dispassionate, if perhaps flawed, mathematics, England are now more of a force in the global game than at any other occasion in my lifetime, or the working lives of most of Eriksson's national press critics. Blimey.

Of course, such statistics will be of little comfort if they represent only a temporary high point, and if the 2006 seeding isn't even realised because of a failure in qualification. We have to reach Euro 2004, too, in spite of being drawn withTurkey, in the only group with more than one team that reached the second round in the World Cup.

What matters is that England go on from here. This is where the honeymoon ends, not in the usual metaphorical sense of an instant falling out of love spiralling inevitably to divorce, but in terms of the marriage settling down, in the hope that, in due course, there will be a happy announcement. What should Eriksson do in order to hasten that day?

There are things to learn from rivals in the Far East, for a start. There were conflicting messages: the team ethos which enabled the United States and the two hosts to turn over opponents on the one hand, versus the individual brilliance and all-round technical ability of the Brazilians which led to ultimate victory. But the balance swings in favour of the former because the champions showed great discipline in conserving their lead with ten men against England, and the latter is to a degree inimitable.

Certainly, England players cannot overnight acquire the confidence on the ball that the Brazilians showed, not only coming forward across the tournament, but also when the dismissal of Ronaldinho convinced them to hang on to their 2–1 lead in the quarter-final, rather than trying to extend it.

England held out against Argentina partly through a series of aggressive counter-attacks, which forced the opposition to keep men back, one of which led to a 17-pass move that came close to producing the goal of the tournament. But as players wearied, a series of heroic stands and challenges were necessary. How much would the pressure have been eased if England could more frequently have just kept possession, once they won it?

Of course Eriksson cannot be held responsible for the technical deficiencies of many English players, though the good news is that things are improving. In one key area, more of the same is the order of the day: pick the youngsters.

With the exception of the goalkeepers, it was a young squad and a young team that travelled to the Far East. In 1990, Paul Gascoigne was the babe of the party. He was 23. Michael Owen was six months short of that landmark when he played his second World Cup, and the Liverpool striker was one of eight original squad members who could have played in the European Under-21 championship team instead of travelling with the seniors. (In case you're bothered by the maths, you have to have been under 21 at the start of a qualifying tournament, in this case in the summer of 2000, to make the junior team.)

It became commonplace to call Eriksson lucky by the end of his first qualifying campaign, but some called him that within days of his appointment. Patrick Barclay of the *Sunday Telegraph* is a perceptive critic on most footballing subjects, but on England he achieves a distance rare amongst his colleagues; he is a Scot whose bread is in part buttered by English achievements selling newspapers. He is a genuine enthusiast for the game he reports on, but is a Scot nonetheless.

Writing when the Swede was appointed, Barclay asked if Eriksson was 'football's luckiest man' because of the emerging generation he would get to coach. Within a few weeks, there was some confirmation of this. Peter Taylor, temporarily in charge of England, named a squad containing many of his former Under-21 squad from when he'd successfully managed that team, and no one at all over 30, for a friendly in Turin against Italy in November. Though they lost to an experimental Italian side, the margin was just 1–0, and the winning goal was the kind of rarely repeatable drive from distance that would beat any keeper.

That team, many of them debutants, restored faith, showing that Englishmen could pass a ball to someone wearing the same coloured shirt and stick to a tactical plan. They carved out chances against a notoriously parsimonious defence, whose victory was never safe. This was managed without two of the most obvious talents of the present and future, Michael Owen and Steven Gerrard. The youngsters in general, those two Taylor absentees especially, went on to play a major part in Eriksson's successful qualifying campaign.

There is one achievement of Eriksson's that is taken for granted, but proved beyond his English predecessors, getting the best out of Owen. Distrusted by Glenn Hoddle, given at most an hour at Euro 2000 by Kevin Keegan, and left to warm the bench in Helsinki by Howard Wilkinson, it has taken a Swede to elevate England's foremost striking talent to the place he deserves (helped by the Frenchman in charge at Anfield).

Gerrard, too, excelled, and was sorely missed in the Far East, another 22-year-old. Rio Ferdinand, 23, moved up to a higher level in the finals, and was rewarded with a £30m transfer straight afterwards.

David Beckham, Paul Scholes and Sol Campbell, at 27, were the senior outfielders in the initial starting line-up in the Far East, with only Trevor Sinclair brought in as their senior – and still Eriksson was criticised in places for not fielding some youngsters often enough.

West Ham's Joe Cole (20) got only one opportunity in the finals to show what he could do. Darius Vassell (22 during the tournament) may struggle to be an Aston Villa regular, and was dropped after the opening game in spite of playing well as an individual against Sweden on the grounds that he didn't form a partnership with Michael Owen. His replacement, pulled forward once more from the left flank, was Owen's Liverpool colleague, Emile Heskey, himself just 24. Matt Jansen, who just missed out on a finals slot to the disappointment of many, is seen as something of a late developer at the same age.

Another to have his opportunities limited was Bayern Munich's Owen Hargreaves (21), sadly crocked by Michael Owen of all people against Argentina, but Ashley Cole (21) of Arsenal and Danny Mills (25) of Leeds shone at full-back, proving the doubters (this writer included) wrong after making mistakes against Sweden.

To some extent, Eriksson paid a price for the lack of experience in the squad, when push came to shove against Brazil. The ageing Teddy Sheringham was seen by the coach as too old for the conditions, while thirtysomethings like Graeme Le Saux and Steve McManaman he'd decided to leave out of the squad altogether.

Southgate and Keown were there, of course, but the defence was doing fine.

The showings of Ashley Cole and Wayne Bridge justified their preference over the chippy but ageing Le Saux (his age was surely only held against him in relation to his inability to learn to control his temper). Robbie Fowler had been usurped in the striking stakes by

Darius Vassell, but it was midfield that was the problem, with everyone recovering from injury, or inexperienced, or both.

McManaman, the former Liverpool player who has enjoyed a successful but chequered three years at Real Madrid, had his supporters before the tournament, in spite of rarely delivering a high level of performance for England. I bow to no one sane in my admiration for the Scouser, but though he had picked up a second Champions League medal just after missing out on Sven's 23, that was as a substitute, like most of his appearances in his third season for the Spanish giants. Was he really fully match-fit to play a full role, in the way that Trevor Sinclair did?

I was horrified when Sinclair was preferred to McManaman as the injury cover for the final squad spot, but Sven's faith in the West Ham man was well rewarded up to the point that Brazil took the lead. It's the kind of decision a coach who has done this much is entitled to make.

Overall, it is too late for regrets about the World Cup; the task is to accentuate the positive. Eriksson must stay open to the still emerging talents, at the same time as cashing in on the fact that those of the young crop that did play have so much more experience. They will all be better players, whether all they had was a glimpse of the world stage or a leading role on it. Though there is one area of the pitch where he does have some real problems with getting a balance across the ages.

David Seaman looks set to play on for country as well as club. Whether a fluke or – as any fair-minded observer must conclude – a moment of brilliance, the critics would surely have been more entitled to carp if he had been beaten from a cross which he could have cut out, had he not been rooted to the line. Before Ronaldinho's coup de grace, Seaman had had a superb tournament and was clearly England's number one number one. Nonetheless, it can't be long before Eriksson will have to face up to the succession. The Arsenal keeper will be 39 on 13 September 2002.There are plenty of candidates – but it's not going to be easy picking the right one.

Nigel Martyn and David James, the two back-ups in the Far East, both have their shortcomings. The 36-year-old Martyn has twice been called upon in crucial competitive matches recently, against Romania at Euro 2000 and Greece at Old Trafford in October 2001. Both are matches he would want to forget. James, the comparative youngster at 32, has never been anything but reliable for his country. But at Liverpool he earned the nickname 'Calamity', and while his subsequent career at Aston Villa and West Ham has been happier, his one mistake in the 2000 FA Cup final did cost the Midlanders the game. All his international experience has been in friendlies, too.

There are some promising youngsters about. Richard Wright was the third choice at Euro 2000, while Paul Robinson and Chris

Kirkland, his successors at Under-21 level, have both earned rave reviews. But none were first choices at their clubs in 2001–02. Wright, whose form anyway had faded since he moved to Arsenal, was stuck behind the evergreen Seaman, and has moved on to Everton where he is promised first-team football. Robinson had fewer chances than in the previous season at Leeds, as Martyn stayed fit. Kirkland, meanwhile, moved to Liverpool from Coventry in August 2001 believing he was about to become first choice, only for Liverpool's move later the same day for Jerzy Dudek, Poland's number one, to succeed as well.

Robinson is likely to edge out Martyn at Leeds. Wright at Everton will have to pick up virtually where he left off all over again when he was sold by Ipswich to Arsenal as a promising youngster a year earlier. Elsewhere on Merseyside, Kirkland's only immediate hope seems to lie with Dudek's poor World Cup show continuing, as the Pole had an exceptional first English season, and was only 29 at its conclusion.

Which leaves Eriksson with a problem that is to some extent out of his hands. If Seaman does retire or long-term injuries catch up with him, he has to find the least bad option. James would be the safe choice from one perspective, as he is more or less guaranteed first-team football if fit and has been playing well. You can't yet say the former about Martyn or Robinson, still competing with each other, or Kirkland, while you can't yet say the latter about Wright.

The idea of James between the sticks does not inspire confidence, nor is he someone thought worth a spot by any of the country's major teams, unlike most of his rivals. Eriksson will hang on to Seaman for as long as he can, in the hope that a solution will present itself. In the long run, he must hope that whoever does emerge as successor goes on to deserve the accolade.

Of course, once Seaman had been beaten by Ronaldinho, the first time England had been behind in the tournament, it turned out it was all over. It cannot be that simple again.

England led Brazil for longer than anyone else managed in the World Cup. They were one decent clearance away from taking that lead into half-time. The longer time went on with Brazil behind, the more chances there would have been to hit them on the break and extend the lead. Even when the game was stood on its head and Brazil were 2–1 up, the eventual champions' commitment to attack could have proved their undoing.

However, once Ronaldinho was harshly sent off and his teammates settled for holding what they had, England's inability to break down their opponents was fully exposed. Whatever the mitigating circumstances on this occasion – the heat, the injury status of Beckham, Owen and Dyer on the pitch and Gerrard away from it, the quality of the opposition, the inexperience of many players – it was a deflating end to the campaign to say the least.

There is nothing fundamentally wrong with playing counter-attacking football, especially if you have the players to do it. Draw them in, hit them hard and fast. But you have to be able to vary your game, or you risk coming unstuck twice over; against lesser opposition who are content with what they start with and give you no space (Albania and Greece in September and October 2001) and better sides, who take a lead.

For Michael Owen, especially, there must have been an unpleasant sense of reliving Liverpool's Champions League defeat by Barcelona in November 2001, when he also gave his team the lead only to have it cancelled out just before the break, and then saw them outclassed after the interval.

It will make perfect sense if England need a point in Istanbul in their final Euro 2004 qualifier, for Eriksson to start the match looking to hold on to what he has, if the defence is performing as well then as it was in 2002. Against Argentina and, indeed, Brazil, in the Far East, Eriksson took a pragmatic decision which paid enormous dividends in the former and threatened to in the latter, and he would be justified to try this again.

A greater tactical range is needed, though. At home and against weaker opponents, certainly, England should look to dominate, something which would stand them in good stead against anyone. In friendlies against quality opposition, when England have nothing to lose, the sights should be set higher. The team cannot again look as toothless as it did when trailing teams of such contrasting abilities as the Greeks and Brazilians. Imagine the Turks, who played well against Brazil twice in the Far East, taking the lead in a vital qualifier.

Of course, the need for some attacking variation feeds into another element which both alleviates criticism and improves morale (though could, in the event of failure, make it all the harder to take). The more entertaining England are, the better. The more convincing a lead is, the less likely it is to get overturned by late mistakes. The greater the margin of victory in competitive matches, the better the position in the group (qualification for Japan was on that basis) and the greater boost to the team's world ranking position (which is factored into some seeding decisions).

In the end, too, the ability to play more attacking football means that even if you have a defensive nightmare, you are still in with a shout. There is something else that would have helped against Brazil, something to consider for 2003 and 2005.

If you have the stomach for it, try and watch a video of England's match with Nigeria, the vital 0–0 draw that almost sent the country crawling back to bed. It was not a pretty sight, not so much a football match as an exercise in the conservation of energy. It prefigured what would happen in the Brazil match, when England would again play in the mid-afternoon sun, albeit not in quite such extreme conditions.

The Far East conditions were difficult for many European teams. Before the tournament many pundits were writing off their chances, citing the statistic that only Brazil had ever won the World Cup outside their own continent. As it happened, these pundits were dead right. Anyone watching Germany's listless win over Paraguay, the first match of the knockout stages, would not have classed them as potential finalists, and there were plenty of other strugglers in the heat.

It is too rarely noted that, in fact, every major tournament, even one held in northern Europe, throws up conditions that English players aren't used to performing in. We do not play our club football in summer. There is the odd match at the start of the season on a boiling August afternoon, but that is very much the exception. Even the 1966 World Cup, played in July, meant that acclimatisation would have been useful. Eriksson's side did not do enough of it for 2002.

Yes, England played two matches in South Korea just before the World Cup, but at a time when players were worried about aches and strains. The match with Cameroon also showed just what would happen when matches were played in that heat for real, but it was too late to learn the lessons.

In 1985, England went to Mexico a year before playing there in the World Cup. In 1997, they won the Tournoi de France in baking hot weather. In 1993, they were humbled in America, prefiguring what would probably have happened a year later had Graham Taylor's side qualified for USA '94. These trips, even the last one, were good ideas. Portugal, Spain, Morocco – England should really be going to that region in the summer of 2003. Mad dogs and Englishmen preparing for major tournaments should go out in the midday sun.

As it is, South Africa seems to be the destination for a friendly. If so, it should be staged in as warm conditions as possible in what will be late autumn or even winter in the summer hemisphere, but in a country where you can find heat if you want it.

It was those 2002 matches in the heat, especially the Brazil game, which cast a shadow over one problem position which some were happy to declare solved; the left of midfield. Trevor Sinclair just scraped into the squad thanks to injuries to Steven Gerrard and Danny Murphy, making trips across the world and back, and then was thrust into the team by Owen Hargreaves' injury. He far exceeded expectations. But he wasn't good enough against the best, nor was the man who replaced him, Kieron Dyer – on that flank, anyway.

Dyer is young, and perhaps can grow into the role, but he's another right-footed player whose international appearances on the left have been unconvincing – he managed to struggle there in the 4–0 friendly win over Paraguay in April, while everyone else was making hay.

The situation is better than it used to be on this flank. Previously two right-footed players, Phil Neville and Steve McManaman, would both be expected to play out of position down the left side. With a promising choice of left full-backs in Ashley Cole and Wayne Bridge, there's a long-term prospect that we can avoid that situation again; it is far less serious to have only one player on the wrong flank.

But the awkward fact remains that the only player to have shown he can get round the back of defenders on the left side is the perpetual square peg that is Emile Heskey, hence his frequent appearances there in qualifying and to start with against Sweden.

Sinclair deserves a vote of thanks for what he did do, but is surely not the answer. Even if he is, at 30 he won't be for long. Joe Cole, perhaps – but is he really best used as a wide player? The problem with Dyer is that he is yet to show that he can do that job at the highest level. His best England showings have come on the right. Perhaps if he is fully fit it will be different.

Some have suggested that the answer is to play both Bridge and Cole, with the Arsenal man playing in midfield. Whatever the solution is going to be, it remains a priority to find one, someone who plays there on merit, not as the least bad option.

Some would say the same about the support striker to play with Michael Owen. The incumbent, for club and country, is Heskey. Is there any more divisive player in English football? His coaches, his teammates, and his beaten opponents praise and respect him, but the rest of the world has barely a good word to say for him. Eriksson must hope that his faith, and that of Gerard Houllier, in Heskey as Owen's number one partner, is rewarded more and more, even if the general public remains sceptical.

A few more goals would come in handy – though his problem is partly exaggerated by the number of times he has only been a sub, and all the appearances he has made on the left wing; few criticise David Beckham for scoring just one goal from open play for his country, from the opposite flank, up to the end of the World Cup. But more than anything, more confident displays and fewer diffident ones will produce a virtuous circle as he thrives on results.

Heskey is a player who, for all his shortcomings, has more winners medals than most in his age group and endures ludicrous levels of criticism without a murmur. A hard-working, uncomplaining regular at one of our top clubs, he has played a full part in the international revival under Eriksson. His critics ignore entirely his successes and accentuate the negative; he has a lot in common with his international coach.

So Sven, don't rest on your laurels; keep playing the youngsters; learn from your opponents; solve the keeper question; acclimatise better; broaden your tactics; go for the jugular when you can; find a left-footed left midfielder to go with the defenders you have promoted; get the best out of Emile Heskey as you have done with Michael Owen.

But football remains a game whose charm is based on its unpredictability.

Sven could do everything I have asked, and anything you may want to add on top, and still there would be no guarantee of success. Teams were eliminated from the 2002 World Cup off the back of a refereeing error, one mistake by a keeper, or a moment of genius or panic in front of goal. Injuries, too, can play an enormous role in what happens, especially in knockout situations. There is no guaranteed route to success; luck will always play its part in football.

It was Napoleon who, when told the tactical merits of a new general, asked, 'But is he lucky?' One of his commanders, Jean Bernadotte, was later made a monarch, like many others in the literal and extended Bonaparte family; but he was the only one whose reign survived the overthrow of the emperor himself, and his descendants today still reign. In Sweden. Let's hope their luck has rubbed off good and proper on their humble subject, Sven-Göran Eriksson.

* * * * *

THE INTERNATIONALISTINGS

Going Oriental covers a range of themes. 'The Internationalistings' provides details of books, websites and other resources for those who would like to take their interest in these topics further.

The starting point of the book is that the World Cup is a celebration of football internationalism. There is now an encouraging range of books for fans who want to read up about football in other countries. Amongst the best are by David Winner *Brilliant Orange: The Neurotic Genius of Dutch Football*, Ulrich Hesse-Lichtenberger *Tor! The Story of German Football*, Phil Ball *Morbo: The Story of Spanish Football*, Charlie Connelly *Stamping Grounds: Liechtenstein's Quest for the World Cup* and Alex Bellos *Futebol: The Brazilian Way of Life*. In one book, *Football Against the Enemy*, Simon Kuper manages to take in football from 22 countries and provide an insight into what football internationalism could mean.

The academics Gary Armstrong and Richard Giulianotti have put together a series of collections that explore football culture in almost every part of the world. Incredibly informative, intelligently written and very accessible, these books are a vital starting point to understanding the global game; *Entering the Field: New Perspectives on World Football* followed by *Football Cultures and Identities* and *Fear and Loathing in World Football*. Whatever the country or countries you're interested in, it's unlikely you won't find a chapter to help your enquiries amongst these three.

Going Oriental puts the case for a football internationalism while celebrating the cause for a positive English patriotism. Mark Perryman's Institute for Public Policy Research report *Ingerland Expects: Football, National Identity and World Cup 2002* offers practical proposals towards a national pride free from prejudice (the report is available from www.philosophyfootball.com).

Most books on Englishness either pay no attention to football's contribution to framing our national identity, or treat it as a wholesale negative. Nevertheless it is at least encouraging that there is a growing literature on what it means to be English. Amongst the best reads are *After Britain: New Labour and the Return of Scotland* and *Pariah: Misfortunes of the British Kingdom*, both by Tom Nairn, *Patriots: National Identity in Britain 1940–2000* by Richard Weight, *Who Do We Think We Are? Imagining the New Britain* by Yasmin Alibhai-Brown and the collection of short stories *England Calling* edited by Julia Bell and Jackie Gay.

There are a huge amount of books on this increasingly popular buzzword 'globalisation'. Joseph Maguire's *Global Sport: Identities, Societies, Civilisations* is an excellent starting-point to understand what this process means for football. *No Logo* by Naomi Klein and *The Silent Takeover* by Noreena Hertz are very readable, and brilliantly researched accounts of the growth and significance of global corporate power. *Empire* by Michael Hardt and Antonio Negri is a powerful vision of a world in motion and one of the few books on the subject that recognises globalisation can both be resisted and its dominant big business purpose transformed to very different ends.

To find out more about Chaos Theory and how it might aid making sense of the failure of a flat back four to cope with one big bloke up front, or indeed France's ignominous exit from World Cup 2002, a basic, and easy-to-understand guide is provided by *Introducing Chaos* by Ziauddin Sardar and Iwona Abrams. The writer, cited in David Winner's chapter on Chaos Theory, who reckons it helped his viewing of the World Cup, Manus J. Donahue III has a really good website www.duke.edu/~mjd/chaos/chaos.html. From the site you can even email Manus direct with your queries, for the intellectually inquisitive well worth a visit.

The role of FIFA in the management, or perhaps the mismanagement, of world football is superbly chronicled in two books by John Sugden and Alan Tomlinson, *FIFA and the Contest for World Football* and their latest *Badfellas: FIFA Family at War*.

To follow the history of the World Cup there are two classic accounts to choose from, *The Story of the World Cup* by Brian Glanville or from Chris Freddi *The Complete Book of the World Cup*. Some of the best books on particular World Cups are Mario Risoloi's *When Pelé Broke our Hearts* on 1958, Dave Hill's *England's Glory* on 1966, *Back Home* by Jeff Dawson on 1970, Mike Wilson's *Don't Cry for me Argentina* on 1978, *All Played Out* by Pete Davies on 1990, Don Watson's *Dancing in the Streets* on 1994, *Back Home: How the World Watched France 98* edited by Andy Lyons and Mike Ticher on 1998. Some of these will be out of print but if you want a really good read through how the World Cup experience has evolved it will be well worth tracking them down via a secondhand book website like www.bibliofind.com.

Two books that will aid an understanding of how football, fans and popular culture mix are *Post-Fandom and the Millennial Blues* by Steve Redhead and *The End of the Terraces* by Anthony King. *Sightlines: A Stadium Odyssey* by Simon Inglis puts the environment in which we watch football, and other sports, into a broader, and fascinating, context. A read through *The Football Business* by David Conn will leave you in no doubt that money rules football.

The monthly football magazine *When Saturday Comes* covers football from West Africa to AFC Wimbledon, and all points otherwise, with an uncanny mixture of the polemical and the humorous. Available from all good newsagents, visit their website www.wsc.co.uk for a taster. Two other sites also worth a visit for their fan focus on the wonderful world of football are www.onetouchfootball.com and www.football culture.net.

To track the impact of the media on our consumption of football read Emma Poulton's chapters in *The Ingerland Factor* and *Hooligan Wars*. The book *Media Sport Stars: Masculinities and Moralities* by Garry Whannel looks particularly at how sports coverage frames gender, while *Football, Europe and the Press* by Liz Crolley and David Hand examines the representation of national identity through newspapers' football reporting in France, England, Germany, Italy and Spain.

There has been surprisingly little written on England fan culture, the majority is almost exclusively of the 'hoolie-lit' variety. Dougie Brimson's *Barmy Army: The Changing Face of Football Violence* is a good effort at getting past the clichés and stereotypes which affect most writing of this type, the author also has his own website www.brimson.net which is a good way to explore further the kind of issues that Dougie raises in his book. *An English Fan Abroad: Euro 2000 and Beyond* by Kevin Miles is a fan activists' view of the conditions that shape what kind of England support we end up with. Mark Perryman's edited collection *The Ingerland Factor: Home Truths from Football* remains one of the most wide-ranging explorations of Englishness as it is represented by the ways we support our team with contributors including Billy Bragg, John Peel, Gary Armstrong and Liz Crolley plus Pete Davies, John Williams and Emma Poulton from *Going Oriental*. Looking specifically at how football affects race *The Changing Face of Football* by Les Back, Tim Crabbe and John Solomos is a fascinating piece of long-term and in-depth research involving supporters from a variety of clubs as well as followers of the national team.

If you would like to follow England abroad it is best to join *englandfans*, the official England supporters club organised by the FA. Visit www.thefa.com/englandfans for a membership application. The club is the best way to access tickets, offers various discounts on home games, has a members-only website that is full of advice and argument from committed England supporters. There is also the beginnings of an independent fan culture around England, committed to fan-led initiatives to maintain and develop the positive England reputation out of World Cup 2002 while finding ways to build a constructive dialogue with the FA and other governing bodies. One example of this is the independent London England Fans group, they run an e-loop which provides news of their monthly fan travel forums. To join send an email to, LondonEnglandFans-subscribe@yahoogroups.com. The Football Supporters Federation (previously FSA) runs fan embassies, mobile supporter advice and help centres, at all England games, information on their activities can be found at www.footballsupportersinternational.com. The website www.kickitout.org is run by the Kick Racism out of Football Campaign and is the best source of news on racism and anti-racism in the game.

A small number of books have now been published on football in Japan and South Korea. *Japanese Rules: Why the Japanese Needed Football and How They Got It* by Sebastian Moffett and *Ultra Nippon: How Japan Reinvented Football* by Jonathan Birchall, both deal specifically with Japanese football, the fans, the J-League and the national team. Edited by John Horne and Wolfram Manzenreiter *Japan, Korea and the 2002 World Cup* covers football in both South Korea and Japan, the impact of co-hosting on relations between the two countries and the impact of football on society and culture in Far East Asia. The websites of the Japan and Korea World Cup Organising Committees provide full details on World Cup 2002, for Japan www.jawoc.or.jp, for Korea www.2002worldcupkorea.org. The Japanese FA website is www.jfa.or.jp and the J-League website www.j-league.or.jp. The Korean FA website is www.kfa.or.kr. A good general website on Korean football, including coverage of both the K-League and the national team is www.korean-football.com. For coverage of football more widely in the region visit www.asian-football.com. To keep up-to-date with the player who is Japan's version of the Beckham phenomenon, and not a bad player either, visit Hideotoshi Nakata's suitably cool and trendy website www.nakata.net. All these sites have English language sections. If you are planning to visit Japan the best source of information is the Japan National Tourist Organisation, www.jnto.co.uk. The Korean National Tourist Organisation likewise provides an excellent source of information, www.tour2korea.com.

The phenomenon that is David Beckham is carefully chronicled and provocatively analysed in *On Beckham* by the journalist Julie Burchill. Ellis Cashmore's *Beckham* goes into considerable depth to examine the cult of celebrity, role of marketing and advertising, and the crossover between football and entertainment that 'Becksmania' represents. Andrew Morton has turned his biographer's eye on David and Victoria in an unauthorised account the gilded couple tried to stop being published, *Posh and Becks* while David's own *My World* provides words, but mainly pictures, on how the man sees himself. Up-to-date information on Beckham's club is contained in the new edition of Jim White and Andy Mitten's *Rough Guide to Manchester United.*

Ziauddin Sardar and Borin Van Loon's *Introducing Cultural Studies* with *Introducing Postmodernism* by Richard Appignanesi and others, plus *Introducing The Enlightenment* by Lloyd Spencer and Andrzej Krauze are three easy-to-read guides. The books help explain some complex ideas that can prove useful if you are interested in trying to put an event like World Cup 2002 in a wider social and cultural context. The author Umberto Eco, best known for the novel *The Name of the Rose,* is one of those deep thinkers who combines theorising with writing on football. *Umberto Eco and Football* by Peter Pericles Trifonas sets out to explain how Eco manages to do both and in turn helps us see football in a different way.

And if this little lot doesn't keep you mighty busy a word about *Philosophy Football.* Self-styled 'sporting outfitters of intellectual distinction', the editor of *Going Oriental,* Mark Perryman and designer Hugh Tisdale are the co-founders of this company which takes words to the wise by philosophers and footballers and turns them into T-shirts; quotes on the front with name and squad number on the reverse. No, it doesn't really make sense when you read the description so visit their website www.philosophyfootball.com to view the entire range from Rupert Brooke to Lev Yashin via Pelé, Cruyff, Nietzsche, Guevara and too many more to mention. The website also carries regular news on *Philosophy Football,* a dictionary of quotations and a discussion forum.

INDEX